D1572631

Across The Northern Frontier

Across the Northern Frontier

Spanish Explorations in Colorado

Phil Carson

Johnson Books
Boulder

Published in the United States by Johnson Books, a division of Johnson Publishing Company, 1880 South 57th Court, Boulder, Colorado 80301. E-mail: books@jpcolorado.com

9 8 7 6 5 4 3 2 1

Cover design: Debra B. Topping
Cover illustrations: Portrait of Don Juan de Oñate courtesy of Marc Simmons and artist Jose Cisneros; historic map of the northern frontier courtesy of New Mexico State Records Center and Archives.
Maps by Jim Roth

Library of Congress Cataloging-in-Publication Data
Carson, Phil
   Across the northern frontier : Spanish explorations in Colorado / Phil Carson.
      p.   cm.
   Includes bibliographical references and index.
   ISBN 1-55566-215-3 (cloth: alk. paper).—ISBN 1-55566-216-1 (pbk.: alk. paper)
      1. Colorado—Discovery and exploration—Spanish.   2. Colorado—History—To 1876.   3. Explorers—Colorado—History.   4. Explorers—Spain—History.   5. Indians of North America—Colorado—First contact with Europeans.   6. Indians, Treatment of—Colorado—History.   7. Southwest, New—Civilization—Spanish influences.
   I. Title.
   F780.C37   1998
   978.8'01—dc21   98-5316
                                                                              CIP

F
780
.C37
1998

Printed in the United States of America
Johnson Printing
1880 South 57th Court
Boulder, Colorado 80301

♻ Printed on recycled paper with soy ink

For the people of Colorado,
toward understanding among us.

And for Genaro,
we shared the immense journey.

Contents

Maps

Acknowledgments

SCHOLARSHIP IS performed by standing on the shoulders of those who have gone before. I thank the following individuals, both living and deceased, whose work and advice must be acknowledged.

Authors who led the way include Herbert Bolton and his student A. B. Thomas, plus Ralph Twitchell, LeRoy Hafen, A. P. Nasatir, George Hammond, J. Manuel Espinosa, C. Gregory Crampton, David Weber, John Kessell, Marc Simmons, and Hugh Thomas.

Professional historians and anthropologists who allowed me to visit, travel along on field trips, or pester them with questions include Arnie Withers, James and Dee Gunnerson, John Kessell, Marc Simmons, Charles Bennett, Curtis Schaafsma, Joseph P. Sanchez, Elizabeth John, Donald Blakeslee, Thomas Witty, Joe Carter, James Hanson, Tom Kavanaugh, Austin Leiby, Ted J. Warner, and Steven K. Madsen. Leon Bright assisted with translations, and J. Richard Salazar often assisted with archival requests during his tenure at the New Mexico State Records and Archives Center.

Fellow authors, aficionados, and travelers on historic trails whose companionship and guidance were invaluable include Ruth Marie Colville, Ron Kessler, Richard and Willard Louden, Lonnie Jackson, Deborah Espinosa, and Don Garate. These friends kept me honest, showed me historic sites, and spurred me on. Thanks go to Bill Kahl for reading an early version of the manuscript. Jose Cisneros and Marc Simmons graciously gave permission to use the reproduction of Cisneros's portrait of Don Juan de Oñate, which was commissioned by Simmons and appears on the cover. Mark Gardner made valued suggestions when he read an early draft and also recommended the project for publication, generosity for which I am indebted. Thanks, too, go to Stephen Topping of Johnson Books for his interest in the topic and his faith in this book, and to Jody Berman who copyedited the work.

A portion of this study benefited from a grant from the Colorado Endowment for the Humanities; thanks to Maggie Coval, Chris Gerboth, and the CEH board in 1994. My parents, Bill and Miriam Carson, faithfully contributed toward the creation of several maps, and for that help and greater contributions I am forever grateful.

Thanks especially to Carol Elaine Kennis for her patience, careful reading of the manuscript, and joyous companionship.

I ... left this place and took the road leading to the land of the Yuttas.
New Mexico governor Don Diego de Vargas
July 7, 1694

Introduction

THE TALE OF Spanish explorations across the land known today as Colorado forms a poignant chapter in the rise and fall of the Spanish empire over four centuries. In the Colorado region, as with other frontiers worldwide, Spanish explorers in the sixteenth century and thereafter traversed unknown lands for conquest, diplomacy, and trade. The early Spaniards who crossed Colorado's plains, mountains, mesas, and canyons clashed and collaborated with diverse native peoples, a familiar pattern in the greater conflict between the Old World and the New. These early Europeans exhibited an innate drive to seek and dominate new peoples and unknown lands that characterized the explosive growth of the Spanish empire a half-millennium ago. Thus the story of Spanish explorations in Colorado is local history on a grand scale.

Traditional rivalries among the New World's native peoples allowed the Spaniard Hernán Cortés to gain a foothold in Mexico by 1521, using an ancient strategy of divide and conquer. Other conquistadors rapidly spread south into the jungles and mountains of Central and South America and north into the interior of North America, today's American Southwest. A number of those northward explorations in the mid- to late 1500s eventually led to the founding of the province of New Mexico in 1598—a new kingdom hundreds of leagues (more than a thousand miles) north of Mexico City, just a century after Christopher Columbus's first landfall in the Caribbean. New Mexico provided a base for further exploration of the continental interior. North of New Mexico, the northernmost province of New Spain, loomed the region's high-

est mountains. East of those mountains stretched seemingly limitless plains covered by moving black hills of buffalo and inhabited
by myriad native peoples. To the west lay a broken land, a bewildering maze of mesas and canyons, also held by a wide variety of
natives.

The grand sweep of country that Spaniards called the "Kingdom
and Province of New Mexico," and its frontiers, included all or
part of the modern-day states of New Mexico, Colorado, Arizona,
Utah, Wyoming, Nebraska, Kansas, Texas, and points beyond. By
historical happenstance, a substantial portion of colonial New
Mexico's northern frontier is today part of the state of Colorado,
thus the focus of this book. At the time of the events described
here, "Colorado," of course, did not exist. Moreover, expeditions
that traversed the Colorado region often reached well beyond it.
Although the phrase "Spanish explorations in Colorado" provides a useful definition for this study, and a focus for modern
readers, the subject must remain elastic. For there are profound
differences between the mysterious northern frontier of colonial
New Mexico as perceived by sixteenth-century Spaniards and our
modern geographic concepts and outlooks.

Colonial New Mexico, sprawling as it did over much of the
American West, was simply one among many New World provinces that made up Nueva España, or "New Spain." New Spain, in
turn, though it encompassed unimaginably vast territories throughout the Americas, was itself but one of the Spanish empire's global
holdings. At the height of the empire's strength in the sixteenth century, its far-flung territories included most of Mexico, Central and
South America, the southern portion of North America, parts of
Italy, northern Africa, the Canary Islands, and the Philippines.

Viewing Colorado and its neighboring states from the perspective of Spanish colonial settlement and exploration reveals much
about early European influences on our region's geography and

culture. Spanish explorers in this region left an indelible imprint on the land and its people. From the Spanish word *colorado,* meaning "reddish," to the peoples and traditions of the southern part of the state, the Spanish empire bestowed a deep and abiding legacy here. Today's vibrant Hispanic culture in this region can still be traced to the Spanish empire's northward reach, which took root long before the British colonies on the eastern seaboard revolted against their king.

An evenhanded examination of the record, however, does not permit glorification or romanticism of the Spanish colonial period here. Spaniards forced their culture, religion, and labors on the interior's many native tribes, which wrought much misery for both Europeans and Native Americans. Life frequently proved bleak and disheartening on the edge of Christendom for Spaniards. Christendom itself oppressed the natives it subjugated. Spaniards, however, despite a few dissenters, rarely agonized over the righteousness of their conquests. They ruled with the proverbial iron fist and devastated or forever altered many of the region's indigenous cultures, including myriad Pueblo peoples, Apaches, Navajos, Utes, Comanches, Kiowas, and their respective divisions. It speaks to the resilience of Native American cultures that descendants of these tribes survive to the present day. In many cases, though, Spaniards cruelly obliterated entire peoples. Sometimes they did so violently, burning native pueblos (and their inhabitants) to the ground, killing or maiming male warriors, raping or enslaving native women, and selling children into slavery. Spaniards also conquered through the equally insidious, naive piousness of cultural imposition, religious oppression, and forced labor. The Spaniards' long isolation in colonial New Mexico over many generations irrevocably changed them as well. There is little room for romance in a story woven from such sobering facts.

In fairness to those early Spaniards, the "Black Legend"—the dogma that Spain's hand in the New World had been uniquely cruel—must be qualified. The English and the French had their own impact on New World natives, sometimes as savage and no less pervasive. It was in England and France's interest to blame their Spanish rivals for transgressions both real and imagined. Much of the Black Legend has been perpetuated by modern ethnocentric, Anglo-American historians. It should also be noted that Europeans in general, and the Spaniards in particular, did not introduce frontier wars, slave trading, and violent conquest to the Americas. These practices already existed as time-honored traditions among natives of the New World.

Despite the disheartening nature of this primal conflict between the Old World and the New, it represents a human drama of a most poignant sort. Spaniards who ventured across the northern frontier of colonial New Mexico passed through regions held by Utes, Apaches, Navajos, and then later by tribes such as the Comanches, Kiowas, Pawnees, Cheyennes, and Arapahos. Few frontier expeditions were routine, for the Spaniards experienced unpredictable encounters with native peoples and exposure to the hazards of the wild. Water and its scarcity loomed over every decision. Great spaces dominated the world of the northern Sonoran Desert, the southern Rocky Mountains, and the sprawling Great Plains.

In traveling across their northern frontier, Spaniards had to find their way, locate water and grass, secure food, and defend themselves. They encountered grizzlies, mountain lions, rattlesnakes, poison ivy, blistering sun, and horrendous storms. Expedition leaders routinely kept journals of their often momentous travels, and those that survive provide rich detail on the mundane aspects of daily travel as well as sharpened perceptions of new lands and strange peoples. These journals provide the earliest written descriptions of this land and its inhabitants in the sixteenth century and the three centuries that followed. Spanish authorities at Santa Fe also kept records of the orders that dispatched these expeditions and of innumerable other matters pertaining to the contemporary period in New Mexico and its northern frontier. The record, though spotty, is voluminous, and it provides a solid basis for the account provided here.

This book is divided into chapters that correspond to distinct eras in the history of colonial New Mexico. Because historical threads by nature interweave, those eras tend to overlap. In order to provide context for expeditions that crossed the northern frontier, the narrative sketches each era's politics, policies, and important events before departing for unknown lands. As historian and author David J. Weber has observed, "Individuals who lived on the frontier occasionally altered the course of empire, but more often than not Spain's imperial claims in North America waxed and waned with decisions made in Madrid and other European capitals."[1] Frontier adventure is exciting stuff, but context is just as important. The Spaniards of colonial New Mexico typically had solid reasons for daring the unknown.

The notes and bibliography should provide scholars and lay students alike with a reliable basis for further inquiry. This book is intended as an introduction to the subject of Colorado's Spanish colonial history, and much work remains to be done. But I urge those who follow along not to spend all their time in archives and libraries. The rural though rapidly changing nature of much of the geography described in this book still allows inquiring minds to see the region's valleys, passes, and prairies through the eyes of colonial Spanish explorers and the natives who once made this region their home. Visiting the sites and traveling the routes mentioned here may have a curious effect upon the reader, for knowledge of past events forever changes one's perception of formerly familiar landscapes. Conversely, traveling through New Mexico and Colorado's astounding geography will enhance an understanding of the events described in these pages. An effort has been made to introduce geographic features by both Spanish and native names, identify them in modern terms, and then use the original names to help the reader to see this land as the first European explorers perceived it.

In pursuit of this story, alone and with like-minded souls, I have spent many joyous days—indeed years—traveling in the footsteps of Spanish explorers and Native Americans. Colorado provides a home to a multitude of history aficionados whose careful work rivals that of tenured professionals, and I have been fortunate to meet many of both and to befriend a few. Together over the years we have learned much, but a path always stretches out ahead, beckoning.

The Northern Lure
1492-1598

CHRISTOPHER COLUMBUS'S LANDFALL in the Caribbean in 1492 sparked the primary conflict of the second millennium—contact between the Old World and the New—and the subsequent European invasion of the Americas. That fateful year also witnessed the success of a unified Spain's effort to expel the last Moors from the Iberian Peninsula after a Muslim occupation that had lasted seven centuries. The *reconquista*, or "reconquest," as the Spaniards' success became known, would echo one day in colonial New Mexico and on its northern frontier. It is emblematic of Spain's ambitions in the fifteenth century that Columbus's accidental discovery propelled Spain's effort to claim the New World as its exclusive domain. That audacious attempt at an instant New World hegemony, and Portugal's vociferous objections, resulted in the so-called Line of Demarcation. Set forth in a series of papal decrees by Pope Alexander VI in 1493, that line divided the New World between Spain and Portugal. Spain sought title to the Americas by divine right, and got half.

This bold move to intimidate rivals and lay claim to a hitherto unknown portion of the world foreshadowed Spanish attitudes toward the native inhabitants of the New World. Contemporary Spanish jurists argued that natives in Spain's new dominions "deserve punishment for their idolatry, their barbarian customs, and their paganism, and that no other nation is more entitled to accomplish this task than the Spaniards because of their superior qualities."[1] The crusading tradition forged in medieval Castile against the Moors found fertile ground in the Americas. A haughty self-confidence kept moral questions at bay. The times called for conquest, rather than questions.

Predictably, the Spaniards' view of the world was not shared by European rivals or New World natives. In a Machiavellian world, papal decrees did little to stop Portugal, France, and England from contesting Spanish claims. Nor did high-flown rhetoric uniformly produce native acquiescence. Early sixteenth-century Spanish conquistadors assembled representatives of a tribe they wished to subjugate and read them a statement called the *requerimiento*, the "requisition," which demanded that New World natives submit to the Spanish Crown and worship the king's god. The alternative would be death or enslavement.[2]

The Spaniards' actual language sounded noble, pious, and legal to themselves, and they evidently felt that they were acting upon the will of their Catholic god. However, the perspectives of the Native Americans receiving this address are more difficult to imagine. Puzzlement, dismay, then hatred must have been widespread. Who were these bearded, mounted, armored strangers? From whence did they come? How could their incessant demands be endured? How could they be defeated and driven out? Competing worldviews clashed, and the conflict that unfolded pitted disciplined European-style armies against a spirited, though splintered native resistance that often relied on guerrilla warfare. In the balance of power Spaniards possessed horses, guns, steel lances and swords, advanced military tactics and—less controllable—the decimating force of introduced disease such as smallpox. Native American warriors, in turn, took a devastating toll on the invaders, for they knew the land and possessed the perennial righteousness of the defender. The bow and arrow in native hands proved to be a fearsome weapon. And disease worked both ways; brazen conquistadors returned home with syphilis. Yet native diversity and autonomy allowed Spaniards to drive a wedge between tribes to divide and conquer. Spaniards and other Europeans often failed to survive this hemisphere's strange and sometimes hostile environments, when they could not or would not adapt to their new surroundings. The Spaniards' grip on the New World proved tenacious nonetheless, and they seized upon every opportunity to expand their reach.

A century of conquest took Spaniards from their first foothold on the island of Hispaniola to the mainland, to Mexico City, and eventually to the founding of New Mexico. In the wake of Hernán Cortés's insanely profitable plunder of the Aztec empire, Spanish conquistadors reached deep into the mountains and great river basins of South America and over the deserts north of Mexico in search of greater riches. As one chronicler of imperial Spain articulated the worldview of the conquistador: "They [had] the capacity for infinite wonder at the strange world unfolding before their eyes, interpreting its mysteries as much from their store of imagination as from their past experience."[3] Not long after Columbus's landfall, rumors propelled Spanish conquistadors north of Mexico into the southern Rocky Mountains. The source of those rumors reflects the fantastic nature of those distant times.

By 1528 Pánfilo de Narváez, former governor of Cuba and former rival to Cortés, had launched his expedition to conquer "Florida." In the contemporary Spanish mind, that province included not only the familiar, modern peninsula, but stretched west along the gulf coast as far as present-day Texas. In April 1528 Narváez left Cuba after hurricanes ominously battered his fleet. He set anchor at the mouth of Tampa Bay on the gulf coast of the Florida peninsula, then made a fatal error. With three hundred men he attempted to march along the coast until he reached a harbor suitable for a Spanish port. Narváez ordered his ships to meet the infantry by sailing west until the ideal harbor could be located. The infantry under Narváez soon faltered in the coastal jungles, beset by quicksand, thickets, and malaria-laden insects. Narváez and his men clashed with natives whose fierce ambushes exacted a terrible price. Of the three hundred men who disembarked at Tampa Bay, only the durable Álvar Núñez Cabeza de Vaca and three others survived. For more than four years Cabeza de Vaca (the honorary name he preferred) spurred his companions toward the setting sun. Eventually they trekked the interior continent from the Texas coast west to northern Mexico, enduring hardship of epic proportions along the way. Cabeza de Vaca's gripping narrative of his experiences, recorded years later, is one of the great adventure stories of all time.

Eight interminable years after Narváez's folly at Tampa Bay, Cabeza de Vaca and his companions—Andrés Dorantes, Alfonso de Castillo, and Dorantes' Moorish slave, Esteban—encountered a Spanish slaving party north of Culiacán, Mexico, and their wilderness ordeal came to an end. Cabeza de Vaca later told Viceroy Antonio de Mendoza that as he traveled the continental interior (he was the first European to do so), he and his companions had seen "undeniable" evidence of gold, silver, emeralds, and other precious metals and stones. "The people gave us ... fine turquoises from the north," Cabeza de Vaca wrote later in reference to an encounter with natives, probably the Pimas of southern Arizona. "I asked where they [came] from. They said from lofty mountains to the north, where there are towns of great population and great houses."[4]

Though he possessed no physical evidence to back his assertions, Cabeza de Vaca's testimony, sober and even reluctant, ignited Spanish interest in the land north of Mexico. It appears that the Pimas had described Pueblo peoples on the upper Rio Grande in present-day New Mexico. The Pueblo Indians indeed worked nearby turquoise mines in that period, possibly including mines in present-day southern Colorado. And they lived in houses, great houses. The story kindled memories of the fabulously wealthy Aztecs of Mexico.

In 1539 Viceroy Antonio de Mendoza sent the Moor, Esteban, and a missionary-adventurer named Fray Marcos de Niza north from Mexico City to investigate Cabeza de Vaca's story. In a heady mood of self-importance, Esteban marched ahead of Fray Marcos and his companions and reached Zuni pueblos near the present-day border between Arizona and New Mexico. His pompous demands on the natives cost him his life. Whether or not Fray Marcos actually reached the Zunis afterward and viewed the multistoried pueblos for himself remains in question. But the friar fled south with word that he had seen one of the Seven Cities of Cíbola perched on a hill.

Cíbola, a native term Fray Marcos learned on his travels, now supplanted Antilia in a long-running Spanish legend. That legend told of the Seven Cities of Antilia founded by Portuguese bishops who, fleeing the Muslim invasion of Iberia, had sailed west across the Ocean Sea. Just as the legend of El Dorado—a native chief who coated himself with gold dust before diving into an Andean lake to propitiate the gods—had driven Spaniards deep into South America at horrendous cost, so the Seven Cities of Cíbola now sparked Spanish interest in the lands north of Mexico.

Fray Marcos's report, fabricated or at least exaggerated, instigated an expedition by Don Francisco Vásquez de Coronado the following year.[5] Coronado's *entrada* from Mexico to the upper Rio Grande and his encounters with numerous, disparate tribes there followed the pattern set by his predecessors: he read the *requerimiento* (requisition), then attacked those who resisted. Nearly all native groups chose to fight the bearded strangers who had arrived, unbidden, from the south.

Coronado's expedition of three hundred soldiers, nearly a thousand horses, and a host of eight hundred Indians represented a vestige of the medieval world thrust into the Stone Age continental interior. The conquistador and his well-to-do followers wore suits of armor (corsolets), including breast plates, chain mail shirts, and morions (helmets). They wielded swords, pikes, crossbows, even primitive muskets known as *escopetas*. Many in the ranks were out-of-work opportunists who sought status and material reward through New World conquests, and they made do with what they could afford. As with other Spanish expeditions before and after, Coronado's included a smattering of European exiles of many nationalities.

After discovering that Fray Marcos's Seven Cities of Cíbola were nothing but clifftop dwellings of earth and rock rather than palaces of gold and gems, Coronado sent the friar south toward home. But the conquistador and his army plunged deeper into the interior, lured by the promise of their fertile imaginations. Coronado attacked the pueblos of Zunis and Hopis, which resisted. Then he turned eastward, and reached accommodation with Acoma Pueblo before making a peaceful tour of the many pueblos he found clustered along a great river that flowed down from the north. By the onset of his first winter in this new and seemingly barren country, Coronado forcibly evicted inhabitants of Tiwa-speaking pueblos at a site the Spaniards dubbed Tiguex, near present-day Albuquerque. In the process of seizing what he needed to survive a long winter, the desperate conquistador torched pueblos and burned native defenders at the stake. The following spring he made an abrasive foray through the pueblos north to Taos. For some reason—perhaps daunting terrain, the fierce resistance of Taoseños, or a lack of time or interest—Coronado did not explore further north to the source of the great river. During 1540–1542, Coronado explored east to the plains of central Kansas while

López de Cárdenas explored west to the Grand Canyon. The chimera of the Seven Cities now gave way to native tales of Gran Quivira, purportedly located out on the high plains northeast of the humble Rio Grande pueblos. Coronado and his men pointedly questioned native informants on whether Quivira possessed gold and other valuables and, either out of a penchant for providing the desired answer, or in an attempt to send the rapacious Spaniards on into another tribe's territory (a propensity captured by the Spanish term *más allá*, or "further on"), two native informants led Coronado on a fruitless expedition over the plains of present-day central Kansas.

Coronado crossed a land utterly unknown to Europeans. The Great Plains of four centuries ago possessed true wildness and formed a wholly different world than the land we know now. In 1541 the plains east of the Rockies existed in a primeval, dynamic state, overrun by millions of thundering buffalo, grazed by vast herds of elk, deer, and bighorn sheep, stalked by grizzlies, black bears, and mountain lions. Native peoples on the plains hunted, planted, fought, sang, loved, and pondered a Stone Age world governed by endless cycles of days, moons, and seasons. Coronado's entrada in 1541 marked the interruption and subsequent transformation of that world. For their part Coronado's men witnessed buffalo herds that stretched their perceptions beyond familiar boundaries. "Another remarkable thing," wrote Pedro de Castañeda, chronicler of the Coronado expedition, "was that the bulls roam . . . in such large herds that there was no one who could count them."[6]

Colorado historians have often succumbed to the temptation to declare Coronado the first European to enter the state during his foray to Quivira in central Kansas in 1541. That link depends on the possibility that Coronado followed the Cimarron River from northeastern New Mexico across the very southeastern tip of present-day Colorado. Modern scholarship suggests instead that he passed well south and east of Colorado's current boundaries.[7] The controversy over this matter, however, simply underscores an axiom for the story that unfolds here: the reconstruction of explorers' routes from journals or other primary documents is art, not science. Only archaeological sites definitively linked to an expedition (a rarity indeed) can confirm a route deciphered from documentary sources. Although reasonable extrapolations from the record are possible, definitive statements on the routes of early Spanish expeditions should by nature remain suspect.

In practical terms Coronado's failure to find native civilizations worthy of plunder dampened official Spanish interest in the mysterious lands that sprawled north of New Spain. New Spain's frontier settlements continued to inch northward in the wake of silver discoveries. As for conquest, though, times were changing on the frontier. In response to the rapaciousness of early sixteenth-century conquistadors and to hobble rivals to the Crown, Spain's King Philip II issued the Comprehensive Orders of 1573. No new discoveries or military expeditions could set forth without his express approval. Subsequent discoveries would be made only for the purpose of introducing Christianity to native peoples. In this regard the viceroy could still authorize missionaries, with a detachment of soldiers for protection, to search out new mission fields. In New Spain the order of St. Francis performed missionary work on the east side of the Sierra Madre while Jesuits controlled the Pacific Coast until their expulsion from New Spain two centuries later.

After Coronado's expedition, decades passed before events in New Spain once again turned Spanish eyes to the north. In winter 1580–1581 an Indian arrived in Santa Bárbara, Nueva Vizcaya, in northern New Spain, who described lands to the north where the inhabitants lived in houses, planted crops, and wove fabrics. Spaniards at first did not connect this tale with the lands described by Coronado four decades earlier. Nonetheless, Fray Agustín Rodríguez and two fellow priests traveled north to investigate. In keeping with the Orders of 1573 the priests were accompanied by a dozen soldiers led by Hernando Gallegos and Francisco Sánchez Chamuscado and a score of Mexican Indians.

The group traveled up the Rio del Norte in June 1581 to pueblos on the upper river, recording their observations in a journal. The Spaniards were briefly tolerated by local Pueblo Indians, though one priest who sought to return alone to Mexico was waylaid and killed. In early 1582 the group retraced its steps south, leaving Agustín and his remaining priest to entreat inhabitants of the various pueblos to accept Christ. Instead, the natives made martyrs of Agustín and his companion. Although Spanish officials only dimly recalled Coronado's expedition, two generations of Pueblo peoples had not forgotten lessons they had learned in Coronado's time.

Upon returning to New Spain the soldier Hernando Gallegos rode on to Mexico City. (His companion, Chamuscado, had fallen ill and died.) Gallegos's description of the upper Rio del Norte caused the viceroy, count of Coruña, to recommend to King Philip II that the region be explored and settled. In 1585 the king agreed and instructed the viceroy to choose a suitable leader for the task. The selection process ground on for a decade, a victim of a ponderous Spanish bureaucracy acknowledged by Spaniards themselves in the phrase *cosas de España*, "a Spanish matter." Meanwhile, in 1582–1583, frontier rancher Antonio de Espejo traveled north to the upper Rio del Norte with priests seeking word of their brethren's fate. A dozen or so soldiers and servants accompanied the group, with a long pack train of one hundred animals. Upon reaching the upper river the group learned of Father Agustín's death. Espejo took advantage of the opportunity, however, to reconnoiter the eastern plains in Coronado's footsteps and ride west to Hopi pueblos. But upon his return to the upper Rio del Norte, he met a hostile reception, turned south, and attempted to blaze a new trail back to San Bartolomé in northern Chihuahua via the Rio Pecos. Once in Mexico, Espejo vied for the right to colonize New Mexico, but was rebuffed. His journal of this entrada, kept by amanuensis Diego Pérez de Luján, is the first document to mention by name El Rio Grande del Norte, "The Great River of the North"—today's Rio Grande of New Mexico—that dominates our story. Henceforth colonial Spaniards would refer to it simply as the Rio del Norte.

Gaspar Castaño de Sosa, lieutenant governor of New Spain's frontier province of Nuevo León, grew impatient at official delays in selecting a colonizer for Nuevo Mexico. In 1590, without authorization, he led one hundred seventy men, women, and children from his village of Monclova to the upper Rio del Norte to settle the region. The group crossed the Rio del Norte and struggled up the Rio Pecos to Pecos Pueblo, a regional trading center between the pueblos to the west and the Apaches of the eastern plains. Castaño hoped his aggressive move would be forgiven by Spanish officials in light of a spectacular success, but a soldier named Juan Morlete rode north and turned him back. Castaño's *carretas*, two-wheeled carts, left tracks in the dry soil that remained visible for a decade.

In 1593, after chastising rebellious Tobosos and Gabilanes Indians on the northern frontier of Nueva Vizcaya, a force led by Captain Francisco Levya de Bonilla made yet another unauthorized, northern entrada. This expedition spawned one of the more durable legends regarding Spaniards in the Colorado region. Captain Levya and his second in command, Antonio Gutiérrez de Humaña, led a modest party of men north from Nueva Vizcaya, possibly by the Rio Conchos–Rio del Norte route used by Fray

Agustín. Levya and Gutiérrez spent a year among the pueblos of the upper Rio del Norte, making their base at the Tewa town of Bové, later known as San Ildefonso. At some point they sought Quivira in Coronado's footsteps and met their deaths.

The expedition's sole survivor, Jusepe, a Mexican Indian, later testified on its demise: Levya and Gutiérrez left Pecos and spent a month traveling east and north. They crossed many streams, and encountered buffalo herds of unimaginable size. Turning north for fifteen days, by short marches, they reached two large rivers with extensive Indian rancherias, or settlements. Three days' travel further on, the men were "startled and amazed" by a herd of buffalo that blackened the earth to the horizon.[8] Soon after, following an argument in which Captain Levya threatened Gutiérrez, the latter called his superior officer to his tent. Gutiérrez twice thrust a butcher knife deeply into Levya, delivering fatal wounds, then took command of the expedition, which was subsequently attacked and destroyed by an unidentified tribe on the high plains. The attackers burned the battlefield, though a handful of Indians who had accompanied the Spaniards fled the scene. Jusepe and a companion eventually reached an unidentified Apache rancheria, where they were enslaved for a year. Jusepe himself finally escaped to a pueblo near Pecos, where he heard that Spaniards had reappeared on the upper Rio del Norte.

The scant evidence on Levya and Gutiérrez's route to their demise on the high plains includes the subsequent discovery of several campsites by later expeditions. This information suggests that they approximated Coronado's route to Quivira by heading east from Pecos across the Texas Panhandle and north into central Kansas.[9] Sometime later, in the belief that Levya and Gutiérrez had perished on what is now the Purgatory River of southeast Colorado, persons unknown—perhaps a Spanish or Mexican priest—dubbed that river El Rio de las Animas Perdidas en Purgatorío—

"The River of Lost Souls in Purgatory." Levya, Gutiérrez, and their men had died without benefit of the holy sacraments. Though lore holds that they may have traversed Colorado, or actually died on the river bastardized today as the "Picketwire," the scant evidence is inconclusive, though it suggests otherwise.

Don Juan de Oñate, scion of a silver-mining family in the northern frontier settlement of Zacatecas, won the right to settle New Mexico in 1595. Due to intrigue and bureaucratic sluggishness (*cosas de España!*) he did not set out until 1598. Disheartening delays nearly eclipsed his effort before he could leave for the frontier. Oñate's royal contract allowed him to peacefully establish a Spanish colony on the upper Rio del Norte, Christianize the natives, and prosper. The king of Spain would take his "royal fifth" of the colony's productions. Viceroy Luis de Velasco's instructions to Oñate explicitly mentioned the need to find the Strait of Anián, a mythical waterway long believed by Spaniards to connect the Atlantic and Pacific oceans. The Strait would be of critical, strategic importance in Spain's attempt to control the continent.

Oñate led several hundred soldiers, settlers, and their families to the adobe pueblos on the upper river terrorized by Coronado two generations earlier. As he drew near to his goal, with more than eighty wagons and carts of his own, Oñate encountered the tracks cut by Castaño de Sosa's procession seven years earlier. The Spaniards established their capital at a Tewa pueblo of several hundred rooms on the west bank of the Rio del Norte, near present-day San Juan Pueblo. Across the great river, tangled in mosquito-infested reeds and willows, lay the mouth of a substantial tributary that came down from the country to the northwest. That river would become known as the Rio Chama. The pueblo's native name was Yunque-Yungue, but, in a pattern that eventually gave almost all native pueblos Spanish names, Oñate called his new cap-

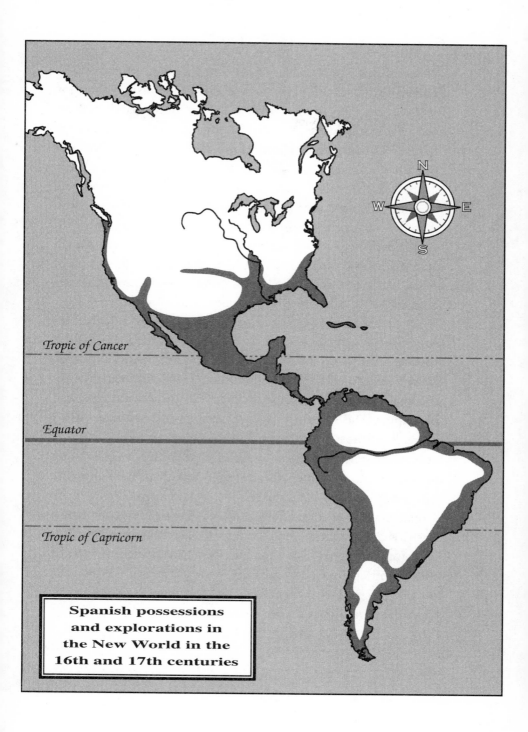

Tropic of Cancer

Equator

Tropic of Capricorn

Spanish possessions and explorations in the New World in the 16th and 17th centuries

ital San Gabriel.[10] His initial settlers were augmented in 1600 by dozens of soldiers and nine friars. Oñate brought suits of armor, the usual complement of swords, lances, crossbows, and muskets, even a piece of field artillery. Spanish firearms in this era remained "uncertain of operation" and were "fearfully inaccurate," according to one historian.[11] Still, they provided a psychological edge in battles with the region's natives. Oñate's men brought armor and weapons according to their wealth. The poorest depended upon layered leather jackets and leather shields, lances and bows. To found a province so far from civilization, the group also brought tools, plants, and creatures for settlement, including thousands of horses, cattle and swine, seeds, blacksmithing equipment, horseshoes, nails, and other essential supplies.

Governor Oñate and his settlers' high hopes were quickly tempered by the realities of their tenuous position on this distant frontier, so far from their countrymen in New Spain. This land, where deserts met mountains, proved to be arid and daunting in its climatic extremes. One major river fed the parched land, and that required the Spaniards to crowd their Pueblo neighbors along the banks of the Rio del Norte. The Spaniards' imposition of foreign laws, labor, and religion on the varied Pueblo peoples along the Rio del Norte created deep resentments. Yet Oñate's humble settlement on the northern rim of Christendom provided the Spaniards with a foothold deep in North America's interior. Frontiers stretched away in all directions. Due to Coronado's and Espejo's travels, Spaniards knew a little of the lands west and east of Oñate's settlement. In contrast, El Norte, "The North," and the source of its great river remained elusive, untrammeled, unknown. Therefore it beckoned.

New Mexico in Disarray
1598-1680

ESPITE ITS HIGH-FLOWN name, Governor Don Juan de Oñate's "Kingdom and Province of New Mexico" consisted solely of San Gabriel, a lonesome outpost at the end of a long vulnerable thread. En route across the arid northern frontier of New Spain, the governor's wagons had cut traces in the hard soil, extending the Camino Real, or King's Highway, to this humble settlement. Of course, that route's royal status did nothing to alleviate its disheartingly long reach deep into the continental interior. So Oñate's settlers clung tenaciously to their new homeland out of sheer necessity, much as cottonwood trees along the Rio del Norte grabbed the river's shifting banks. They set about building *plazas,* ranchos, and missions, tilling the soil, and herding sheep. Their lives depended upon success.

Success for the Spaniards meant misery for the region's natives. For the panoply of Pueblo peoples on the upper Rio del Norte, the Spaniards' road and the struggling community at its northern tip represented a dagger thrust to the abdomen. The Spaniards' demands on the region's natives for labor, food, and abandonment of ancient spiritual beliefs wrought hardship and sorrow up and down the great river. Under Oñate's rule, exacerbated by San Gabriel's isolation, divisions developed within the Spanish community itself that only added to the fundamental tensions between Europeans and natives. In decades to come those conflicts and tensions—plus the simple demands of survival on the frontier—

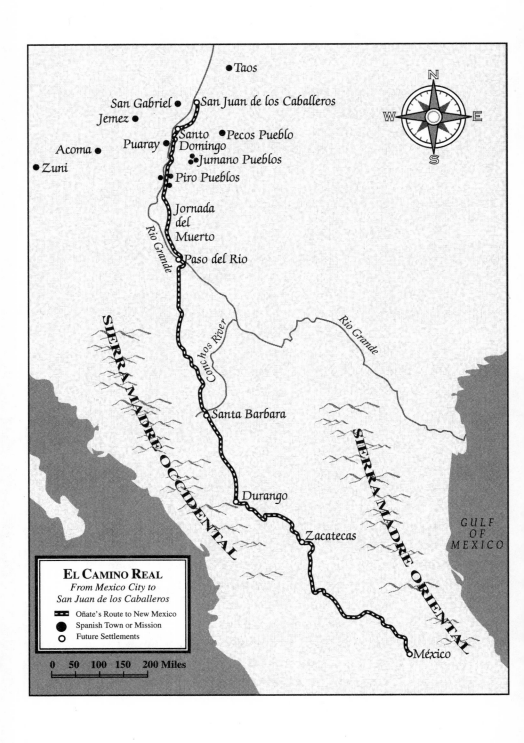

EL CAMINO REAL

From Mexico City to San Juan de los Caballeros

▧▧▧ Oñate's Route to New Mexico
● Spanish Town or Mission
○ Future Settlements

0 50 100 150 200 Miles

would send Spaniards across New Mexico's northern frontier for
diplomacy, war, and trade. During Oñate's brief tenure, however,
the evidence for northward journeys is scant. New Mexico's
founding governor explored far and wide beyond San Gabriel to
points east and west in Coronado and Antonio de Espejo's footsteps, but not north beyond Taos. Perhaps Oñate's men indeed
searched for the great river's source in the northern mountains;
but if so, a record of such a journey has not been discovered. Perhaps the fierce reputation of the natives who held that northern
region or fear of ambush by Taoseños kept Oñate from sending
men upriver.

Finding the source of the great river that flowed through the
province of New Mexico posed a geographic question, a challenge, that could not be ignored. Yet it seems that Oñate's zeal to
find another El Dorado led him in other directions, mainly east
to Quivira and west to the "South Sea," the Pacific Ocean. Those
fervid searches and his high-handed ways have earned him a sobriquet as the "last conquistador" from biographer Marc Simmons.[1] Oñate's quest stemmed from solid precedent. Less than a
century had passed since the Spanish conquests of the Aztec and
Inca empires. Oñate had good reasons to dream, and he had
reached New Mexico flying pennants that displayed a traditional
motto of New World explorers: "Plus ultra" (More beyond).

But the age of conquest was over, whether Oñate and his con-
temporaries yet knew it. The New World held no other native
civilizations laden with gold. Though golden treasures from the
Aztec and Incan empires had fueled the Spanish empire's expansion to the height of its powers in the latter part of the sixteenth
century under Hapsburg kings, they also undermined Spain's
economy. Political and military reversals, symbolized by the defeat
of the Spanish Armada in 1588, slowed the Spanish juggernaut.
Henceforth English corsairs aggressively challenged Spain's ships

on both sides of the Atlantic. By the time Governor Oñate established San Gabriel, in the final year of King Philip II's long, successful reign, the Spanish empire's momentum had crested, though
Spain's primacy and strategic position in the New World maintained its considerable influence there for another two centuries.
Spanish officials both in Madrid and Mexico City probably shared
Oñate's enthusiasm for finding native riches. But in practical terms
they viewed New Mexico as a buffer between the silver mines of
northern New Spain and the reach of Frenchmen and Englishmen
pushing west from the distant St. Lawrence River.

In contrast to the lofty ideals that New Mexico's founder held
for his colony, Oñate's zealous pursuit of treasure consumed his
governorship and led to his downfall. In 1601, as his colony struggled for mere survival, Oñate retraced Coronado's, Espejo's, and
Captain Francisco Levya de Bonilla's footsteps to Quivira on the
high plains, only to meet with the same disappointing results.[2]
During his long absence a number of soldiers, settlers, and clergy
deserted the province, thereby weakening it. Upon his return to
San Gabriel, Oñate entertained a delegation of native Quivirans
who told him that if he sought gold, he should travel north
"through Taos and through the lands of the great Captain Quima."
Though Oñate chose a dozen soldiers to follow this lead, he apparently never sent them, as a contemporary writer later lamented
that "here was lost a very great opportunity and … it will be long
before the lost chance will be recovered."[3]

In autumn 1604, ignoring signs of domestic trouble, Oñate led
an expedition west to the South Sea, a region then rumored to produce a dazzling abundance of pearls. As with Coronado before
him he found nothing to justify his efforts. En route to the Colorado River's denouement at the gulf, however, native informants
told Oñate of a populous land of many nations and languages they
called the Laguna de Copala (Lake of Copala). Chimeras still

beckoned. Over the next century the Lake of Copala would float somewhere beyond New Mexico's northern frontier, forever just out of reach.[4] On his return ride from the South Sea to San Gabriel, less than a week's ride shy of the Rio del Norte, Oñate passed the dramatic, buff-colored sandstone promontory later dubbed El Morro (The Headland). Oñate carved his name and the date on its soft surface. "There passed this way (*paso por aqui*) the Adelantado Don Juan de Oñate, from the discovery of the South Sea, on the 16th of April, 1605"—an inscription that remains legible today.[5]

Governor Oñate's prolonged absences plunged his colony into disarray. Numerous charges against him finally pushed Spanish officials to remove him from office for neglect of duty and abuses of power. In spite of the prohibitions established by the Orders of 1573, Oñate had violently squelched a rebellion at Acoma Pueblo and mutilated survivors. He had attacked Taos, an act that might have made explorations north to the Rio del Norte's source too dangerous, and murdered one of his own officers, convinced the man had betrayed him. He also had ordered the murder of a colonist who requested permission to leave the colony. Oñate submitted his resignation in August 1607. His son, Cristóbal, administered the colony until a successor reached New Mexico.

Oñate's replacement, Don Pedro de Peralta, would find a province rooted in astounding geography, inhabited by a bewildering array of native peoples. Along the Rio del Norte lived the diverse pueblo dwellers known to Coronado and Oñate, whose continued resistance posed a constant challenge to Spanish rule. Beyond San Gabriel, however, the frontier stretched away on all sides in a seemingly limitless profusion of mountains, mesas, plains, and passes.

On the east flank of the Rio del Norte rose a mountain range that the Spaniards subsequently named the Sangre de Cristo (blood of Christ) Mountains, allegedly for their rosy alpenglow. These mountains stretched north and south and reached skyward, clothed in pine and topped by snowy peaks. Passes through those mountains led to the plains, held by various Apache peoples. One pass, today known as La Glorieta, led east to Pecos Pueblo, hub of a thriving, regional Pueblo-Apache trade. West of the Rio del Norte, Spaniards found a maze of river canyons, mesas, and plateaus inhabited by Navajo Indians (called the "Apaches de Navajo" by the Spaniards), who called their homeland Dinetah, "among the people."

The land due north beyond San Gabriel daunted the Spaniards, as gentle riverbanks soon gave way to abrupt canyon walls. But ancient Indian trails led north through the foothills on either side of the river and afforded access to the southern end of an immense, sprawling valley. By Taos the south-flowing river carved a deep, dark gorge, cutting the great valley in two. Taos Pueblo and its inhabitants dominated the southeast edge of that valley. In time the Spaniards would learn that a people they dubbed Yutas, the Utes, claimed the west side of the river and its upper valley, the great river's source, and its mountains. How and when New Mexico's Spaniards first pushed beyond their northern frontier to reach the Rio del Norte's source, however, has thus far escaped the documentary record. Such a journey might have been delayed for generations after Oñate's arrival, as survival in the new land demanded most of the settlers' energies. Building a rapport with the Utes, who claimed the river's headwaters, took time. Yet the great river that flowed south through San Gabriel and on to the gulf posed a geographic question—where did it begin?—that demanded an answer.

The life-giving Rio del Norte made farming possible on the upper river for Spanish settlers, who learned from the Pueblos the local art of irrigation. The foothills, canyons, and mountains on either side of the river provided timber and game, and refuge to natives fleeing the Spanish occupation. The peaks of the Sangre de Cristos captured snows that melted into torrents, and settlers founded ranchos on those musical tributaries that ran to the Rio del Norte. The mountain parks and plains supported buffalo, elk, deer, and mountain sheep, which in turn sustained natives and Spaniards alike.

The Pueblo peoples on the upper river lived in scores of adobe villages from Taos on the north to Isleta on the south, east to Pecos and west as far as Zuni—a layout that mimicked the holy cross, a mere coincidence that Spaniards believed possessed divine significance. The Spaniards' name for the region's natives—*indios de pueblos*—reflected the latter's habit of dwelling in established villages, in contrast to their nomadic neighbors in the hinterland known as the *indios barbaros.*[6] The indios de pueblos, or Pueblos, were a dignified people who used irrigation to grow corn, beans, squash, and cotton, and raised turkeys, wove cotton into blankets and garments, fired pottery, and hunted seasonally. They had well-developed religious lives that included sacred rites and dances, poetry, music, and crafts. Kachina dances, for instance, brought life-sustaining rains. Each pueblo had one or more kivas, which served as underground ceremonial chambers for spiritual matters and male camaraderie. All this would change with the colonization of New Mexico by Spaniards, who equated native religion with idolatry and devil worship and, therefore, banned its practice. In the wake of European colonization, native religion on the upper Rio Grande became cloaked in secrecy. But overt similarities among the Pueblo peoples belied basic differences. The pueblos along the Rio del Norte possessed a half-dozen languages, innumerable dialects, disparate cultures, varied physiques, and political independence. Each pueblo reflected the will of its own inhabitants and maintained staunch autonomy, as alliances and warfare between pueblos had a long tradition. Once bearded strangers arrived on the upper river, however, the pueblos' independence proved costly. Even with modest numbers, Spaniards in New Mexico could divide and conquer to great advantage. The region's natives "conquered themselves," one writer has observed. Their "lack of solidarity ... was fatal."[7] In time various Pueblo groups would augment Spanish troops on forays against rival Pueblo groups or across the frontier into the hinterland of the indios barbaros. Several pueblos are worthy of note, as they make repeated appearances in the narrative of coming centuries.

A common language often bound Pueblo groups living in close proximity. Southeast of San Gabriel, for instance, Tewa-speaking peoples inhabited Tesuque, Nambé, Pojoaque, and San Juan pueblos. Tewas from San Juan Pueblo traditionally traveled north to the central San Luis Valley to gather ceremonial water fowl feathers from the valley's wetlands and turquoise from its hills. The geographic knowledge they gained on those journeys made them valuable guides on later Spanish expeditions across that northern frontier. West across the Rio del Norte, Tewas also lived in the pueblos of San Ildefonso and Santa Clara, whose residents would be recruited for forays against the nearby Navajos. (Spanish names for native groups and pueblos often superseded native names after 1598, at least in Spanish records.)

Farther north of those pueblos, nestled among the piñon and juniper-studded hills, rose Tiwa-speaking Picurís Pueblo. And beyond the Picurís at the western edge of the Sangre de Cristos was the northernmost native settlement, the imposing, populous, and fiercely independent Taos Pueblo, also inhabited by Tiwa speakers. Taos had suffered, yet withstood, Coronado's desperate forays for supplies, and it had resisted Oñate's harsh hand. At Taos memories were long. Both Picurís and Taos pueblos would be among the last to accept Spaniards on the Rio del Norte.

East of the Rio del Norte, at a natural gateway to the plains, Towa-speaking Pecos Pueblo took advantage of trade between the

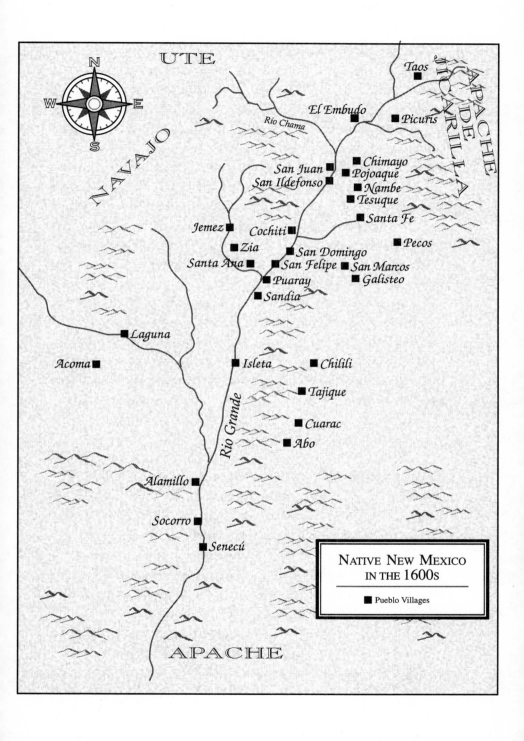

UTE

NAVAJO

Taos

APACHE DE JICARILLA

El Embudo

Picuris

Rio Chama

Chimayo

San Juan
San Ildefonso

Pojoaque

Nambe

Tesuque

Santa Fe

Jemez

Cochiti

Zia

Pecos

Santa Ana

San Domingo

San Felipe

San Marcos

Puaray

Galisteo

Sandia

Laguna

Acoma

Isleta

Chilili

Tajique

Rio Grande

Cuarac

Abo

Alamillo

Socorro

Senecú

APACHE

NATIVE NEW MEXICO
IN THE 1600s

■ Pueblo Villages

Pueblo world and the plains Apaches. Towa cousins lived at Jemez Pueblo on the Rio Puerco, west of the great river, on the margins of Dinetah. Southwest of San Gabriel lived Keres speakers at Cochiti, Santo Domingo, San Felipe, Zía, and Santa Anna pueblos, which also would play a role in Spanish-Navajo relations. Further downstream, southern Tiwas lived at Puaray, Chilili, and Isleta pueblos. Due south lived Tano speakers at San Cristóbal and San Lazaro pueblos. To the southeast lived Tompiro speakers at Quarai, Abo, and other villages. Farthest south, at Senecu on the west bank of the Rio del Norte, Piro speakers had endured repeated Spanish visits in the two decades since Fray Rodriguez's visit in 1581.

Far to the west of this cluster on the upper Rio del Norte, Keres speakers also inhabited the mesa tops at Acoma Pueblo, which had rebelled at Oñate's arrival in 1598. Zuni-speaking Indians farther west still held their mesa-top pueblo, in the wake of Coronado's devastating attack in 1540. Far distant to the west, near the present-day New Mexico–Arizona state line, Hopi speakers perched atop their own mesas.

The Spaniards of New Mexico represented a small, isolated, but dominant society situated among, and greatly outnumbered by, reluctant Pueblo peoples. In like fashion, the Pueblo peoples formed an island in a vast hinterland inhabited by an array of predominantly nomadic peoples. Spaniards first learned of these outlying tribes through Pueblo intermediaries. Then, after expeditions crossed the frontier, the indios barbaros became familiar through firsthand contact.

The Utes held the valleys and mountains to the north and spoke Shoshonean dialects. Their distance from Spanish New Mexico to a degree shielded them and their sacred rites from interference by the Christian Spaniards. Just as the term "Pueblo" tended to

mask an array of cultures, so the terms "Ute" and "Apache" encompassed innumerable bands of those tribes that each possessed
distinct dialects, cultural traits, and political independence.
Apache tribes spoke dialects of an Athabascan language stock, and
included the Navajos west and northwest of settled New Mexico
and the Faraones east of the Sangre de Cristos. On New Mexico's
northern frontier, bands of Acho Apaches lived north of Taos.
Sierra Blancas and Jicarilla Apaches lived east of the Sangre de
Cristos around the Raton Mesa area, and El Cuartelejo Apaches
inhabited a region far out on the northeastern plains. Prior to
Spanish settlement in New Mexico, symbiotic trade relations and
traditional enmities existed between certain Pueblo groups and
outlying Ute and Apache bands. Those links, both friendly and
antagonistic, would affect Spanish expeditions across New Mexico's frontier.

In bountiful times Pueblo peoples had surplus foodstuffs, cotton fabrics, pottery, and turquoise for trade to their nomadic
neighbors. Plains Apaches and mountain Utes had better access to
the region's buffalo herds, and in turn possessed meat, furs, and
hides. Friendly trade relations existed between Pecos Pueblo and
its neighbors, the Faraone Apaches of the eastern plains. Taos
Pueblo traded with the Jicarilla Apaches to the east of the Sangre
de Cristo Mountains. Picurís Pueblo traded back and forth with
El Cuartelejo Apaches on the northeastern plains, just as Jemez
Pueblo traded with its northern neighbors, the Navajos.[8] As with
the traditional enmities between Pueblo peoples and outlying
Ute and Apache bands, Utes considered their enemies to be
Navajo and Taos Indians.

Spanish colonization of New Mexico disrupted the pre-existing
balance among the Pueblo peoples and their neighbors, creating
new relations. In the game of divide and conquer, Spaniards pitted
one pueblo against another or against the Apaches, Navajos, or
Utes. After Spanish settlement, pueblos that cooperated with their

European overlords in order to survive were regarded as traitors by those who clung, at high cost, to independence. Conversely, pueblos that endured reprisals and created hostilities to maintain their independence came to be seen as recalcitrant, the enemies of those acquiescent in a Spanish-dominated world. From Oñate's time onward, moral agonies split the Pueblo world. Spanish occupation of Pueblo lands and homes, and the newcomers' demands on the natives for grain and other commodities also created shortages of food, clothing, and shelter for many pueblos.

Despite their tenuous foothold in this region, Spaniards considered the Kingdom and Province of New Mexico to stretch for hundreds of leagues (perhaps a thousand miles) in every direction. As historian France V. Scholes once described the Spaniards' view of their province: "New Mexico in the seventeenth century was the vast northland. ... No attempt was made to define its limits, for there was no need; and Spain was willing that the area comprised under the phrase 'the Kingdom and Province of New Mexico,' should remain as indefinite as possible, for any delimitation of boundaries would have implied a limit on her claim to the entire trans-Mississippi country. ... Thus New Mexico may be thought of as Spain's *claim* to the north country—an empire in itself, stretching for hundreds of miles in all directions."[9] Southwestern scholar David J. Weber has observed that New Mexico could be described only by "sweeps of the hand across the map."[10]

Sweeps of the hand notwithstanding, less than one thousand settlers clung to plazas or ranchos on the upper river early in the seventeenth century. Only by living in clusters of protected plazas—rectangular arrangements of houses with common walls, a gate, and a courtyard—could the Spaniards defend themselves and maintain their tenuous grasp on the region. Oñate and subsequent governors in this era granted thirty or so *encomiendas* to important settlers, each of which comprised a parcel of land and the productions of its native inhabitants. Franciscan missionaries, however, competed for the best lands, water rights, and Indian labor, which aggravated divisions within the Spanish community. Periodic desertions weakened the province, though the ranks of settlers and clergy were bolstered occasionally by fresh recruits from the south.

Despite the Spaniards' precarious perch on a far-flung frontier amid often hostile tribes, early New Mexico had no formal presidios, the traditional bastion of defense on Spanish frontiers, nor professional soldiers. A mere thirty-five *encomenderos* formed the province's core defense. These well-armed individuals were bolstered by a draft on settlers and Pueblo Indians. The latter were reluctant, poorly armed conscripts who received little if any recompense. Perhaps as many as two hundred armed Spaniards could be mustered throughout New Mexico early in the seventeenth century.[11]

Although the Pueblo Indians suffered the outrageous excesses of both Spanish governors and clergy, in theory they had rights under the Spaniards' system. New World Indians had had Spanish defenders since Christopher Columbus's day. The Dominican Fray Bartolemé de Las Casas arrived in the Caribbean in 1502, received an encomienda in Cuba in 1512, and soon after descried the abuse of native labor inherent in that system. Las Casas's crusade to reform Spanish colonial practices ultimately bore fruit after his death, about the time of Oñate's settlement of New Mexico. The office of *protector de indios* was created to provide, upon request, a representative at court for natives seeking legal redress.

It is not known when the first protector appeared in New Mexico (one enters the record in 1659), but his work on the frontier fell short of its ideal. On paper New Mexico's natives enjoyed a measure of protection; in practice, they fell victim to the Spaniards' material demands and the province's destructive factionalism. In contrast nothing shielded the indios barbaros from rapacious Spaniards, whose law allowed the unmitigated subjugation of heathens.[12]

In 1609 Don Pedro de Peralta assumed the governorship of this volatile region, and the following year he moved the provincial capital from Oñate's San Gabriel to a more favorable spot on the Rio Santa Fe. Documentary evidence uncovered in the 1990s suggests that that spot may have been occupied by Spanish ranchos as early as 1607, when English colonists at distant Jamestown struggled to survive as well. Peralta named the new capital La Villa Real de Santa Fé de San Francisco, "The Royal City of the Holy Faith of Saint Francis." This humble adobe village became known simply as Santa Fe.

Governor Peralta inherited a province beset by two simmering conflicts. One pitted Europeans against natives, the other divided the Spanish colonists themselves. From Peralta's time forward the Spanish Crown changed New Mexico's status from a nearly autonomous fiefdom to a mission outpost with the loftier aim of saving heathen souls from eternal damnation. Once again, however, in practice on the distant rim of Christendom, lofty aims withered under difficult circumstances. In theory civil authorities administered the colony's material and security needs, while resident priests cared for settlers' spiritual needs and performed missionary work. The Spanish governor received his authority from the king and the viceroy. In contrast, New Mexico's prelate, the Catholic Church's highest official in the province, claimed that his authority derived from the pope and, ultimately, an even higher source. From Peralta's time onward these dual lines of authority in New Mexico clashed for supremacy. In a province so distant from Spanish courts and perennially in need of material goods, this conflict colored every aspect of daily life. Support from the south in the form of settlers and supplies arrived once every three years, when a long caravan of wooden-wheeled *carretas* left Mexico City for the interminably long journey north to New Mexico. Civil and religious factions fought over the caravan's material goods and vied for the loyalty of fresh immigrants.

An incident in 1613–1614 brought the church-state rivalry to the fore when Governor Peralta and Friar Isidro Ordóñez fought over the collection of native tribute at Taos. Peralta, Ordóñez, and their subsequent counterparts soon struggled over more important matters, including the allocation of scarce material goods, the appointment of officeholders, the meting of justice, and the ownership of New Mexico's precious arable lands and water rights.[13] This confrontation between church and state led Friar Ordóñez to excommunicate Peralta (who served 1610–1614) as well as New Mexico's third and fourth governors, Don Bernardino de Ceballos (1614–1618) and Don Juan de Eulate (1618–1625). By 1626 the Inquisition reached New Mexico and the province's prelate also held the office of commissary, or representative of the Inquisition. The prelate's expanded powers added another volatile element to internecine strife. In New Mexico's church-state rift, the protector de indios almost always sided with the province's civil governors, a choice that resulted in the Franciscans' use of the Inquisition against two of three known seventeenth-century protectors.

Civil order became fragile. In rare moments free from strife, both Spaniards and Pueblos may have enjoyed a rural lifestyle and the region's natural bounty. Many Pueblos continued their traditional ways in secrecy. Perhaps some Spanish settlers managed to live unaffected by the church-state rift. For the most part, however, the seventeenth century brought painful, brutish changes, hardship, and unease to this stark land and its hard-pressed inhabitants. Those raging forces and the demands of survival propelled several documented Spanish expeditions across the province's northern frontier.

From Governor Peralta's time to the 1640s, only inconclusive documentary clues hint at possible Spanish expeditions beyond the province's northern frontier. In the 1620s, for instance, Fray Gerónimo de Zarate Salmerón wrote of Quazula, land of the Qusutas, probably the earliest surviving reference to the Yutas, or Utes, who inhabited the northern frontier.[14] Whether Zarate Salmerón knew of the Utes because the latter had visited settled New Mexico, or because Spaniards visited Ute country, he did not say. By that time Ute traders may have been regular visitors to the Spanish settlements, as they had traditionally been visitors to the pueblos along the Rio del Norte. Spanish frontiersmen may have plied the trails north of Taos after Franciscans established a mission there in 1617.

Spaniards had to have strong motives for traversing a frontier so fraught with danger. Practical matters like trade and hunting initiated many frontier expeditions, which often left the province without official permission. Efforts at diplomacy sent forth expeditions as well. The siren call of legendary realms still beckoned. Spaniards continued to seek word of rich native civilizations, the strategic (but mythical) Strait of Anían, and mines of precious minerals and metals. The Lake of Copala still hovered north of New Mexico. But as one historian has wryly observed, "With each advance of the frontier, these kingdoms tended to disappear over the horizon."[15]

Official Spanish journeys across the northern frontier often served diplomatic purposes. Fray Alonso de Benavides arrived in New Mexico in 1625 and soon traveled to the Navajos to tend a wounded native named Captain Quinia. (Whether this person is the "Captain Quima" recommended to Oñate has not been established.) How this Navajo received his wound is not stated, but the Navajos were one of the Spaniards' early and consistent nemeses. Apparently Captain Quinia traveled to the Spanish settlements in 1627 and, according to Fray Alonso, sought baptism. In 1629 the

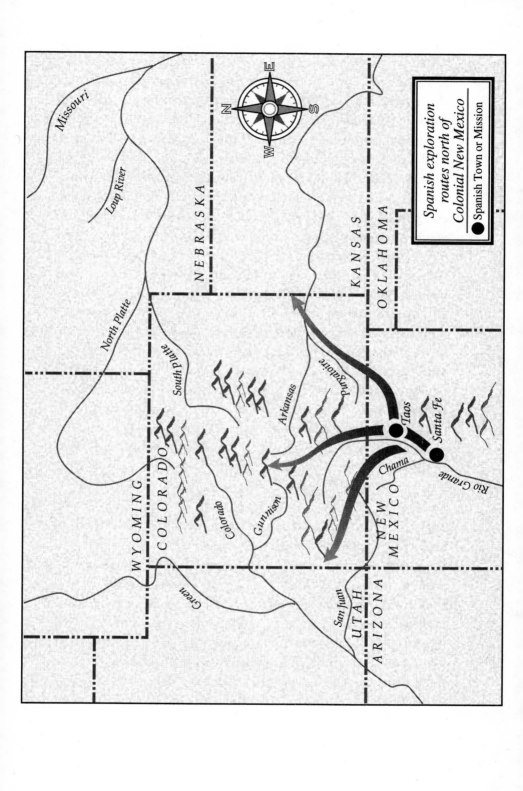

Spanish exploration routes north of Colonial New Mexico

● Spanish Town or Mission

Spaniards even sent an expedition to the Navajos to establish a short-lived mission. Fray Estevan de Perea wrote in the early 1630s of that expedition: "To the nation of the [Navajo] Apaches of Quinia and Manases went the Father Fray Bartolomé Romero, reader of theology, and Fray Francisco Muñoz, preacher. And since it was the first expedition to that bellicose nation of warriors, Don Francisco de Sylva, governor of these provinces, went along, escorting them with twenty soldiers. Although this precaution was not necessary, because on their part [the Navajo Apaches'] opposition was lacking and with exceeding pleasure they besought the Holy Baptism."[16] Whether the Navajo truly sought baptism "with exceeding pleasure," or simply sought peace to facilitate trade and maintain their independence is open to question. After all, Navajos had a well-developed culture and spiritual life that empowered shamans to cure and ensure survival through sand paintings and chants. As Spanish missionaries and soldiers penetrated their land, the Navajos, too, were forced to practice their sacred rites in secrecy. Yet Fray Estevan's anecdotes do indicate that at least as early as the late 1620s Spaniards were familiar with an ancient route that led up the Rio Chama into the province of the Navajos.

Spaniards had joined the region's pre-existing slave trade soon after their arrival in the region. Documented slaving forays sent them east, west, and south—perhaps they traveled north as well. At first, Spanish New Mexicans took advantage of slave raids led by Pueblo Indians and merely awaited their return. Later, Spaniards led expeditions largely staffed by native warriors across the frontier to capture members of neighboring tribes. New Mexico's governors often profited from this traffic; however, scant documentation on this trade has survived, perhaps due to its illicit nature.

Governor don Luís de Rosas (who served 1637–1641) apparently sent at least one expedition east to Quivira to enslave friendly Apaches. Rosas also instigated a treacherous attack on the Utes, but it remains unclear whether this attack—in which many Utes reportedly were killed and eighty were taken as slaves—occurred close to home during a trade fair or on the frontier.[17] Spanish demands on the Pueblo peoples for material tribute and labor increased, as did pressure to abandon native spiritual practices. As the 1600s wore on, violence erupted. In January 1640 members of Taos Pueblo killed their mission priest, Fray Pedro de Miranda. The Taoseños fled east over the mountains to the Apache settlement roughly one hundred leagues distant that the Spaniards dubbed El Cuartelejo, "The Far Quarter," for its distance from Santa Fe. (One Spanish league is roughly equivalent to 2.6 to 3 miles.) At El Cuartelejo, Indians built a modest adobe pueblo among their Apache hosts and lived in exile. The remains of an adobe pueblo discovered in the late nineteenth century in western Kansas have yielded artifacts that establish contact between the pueblos on the Rio del Norte on the west and Quivira to the east. (This site is now encompassed by Scott County State Park.) But whether this archaeological site is the location to which Taos Indians fled in the 1640s remains uncertain. El Cuartelejo may have referred to a region, rather than a fixed location, that encompassed eastern Colorado and western Kansas, north of the Arkansas River.[18] After a season or two the Spaniards may have learned of the Taoseños's whereabouts, for Spanish soldiers were dispatched to retrieve the apostates. This expedition may have crossed southeastern Colorado en route to and from its destination.

The Taos rebellion erupted in the midst of sordid developments. To gain advantage in the ongoing church-state rift, Governor Rosas removed priests from missions at Nambé, San Ildefonso, and Santa Clara. At Santa Fe he removed the resident priest and installed one pliant to his wishes. In early 1640, in a show of solidarity and possibly for safety, Franciscans abandoned their outlying missions to gather at their ecclesiastical capital of Santo Domingo, a few leagues southwest of Santa Fe. The province's approximately one hundred twenty soldiers then split into two factions according to their loyalties to civil or religious leaders. More than half sided with the Franciscans. Rosas's successor, Don Juan Flores de Sierra y Valdés, arrived in New Mexico in 1641 and investigated the latest events rending the colony, but he died soon after. Before a successor could be named, Rosas was jailed by a pro-Franciscan faction, then murdered in his cell. With the province approaching anarchy, both secular and religious factions preyed upon the pueblos for subsistence.

Governor Flores's successor, Captain Don Alonso Pacheco de Heredia (who served 1642–1644), at first feigned compassion for the Franciscans' situation and past actions. But prior to pronouncing judgment, Governor Pacheco kept Franciscan-leaning captains busy on expeditions against outlying tribes. That included sending Captain Juan de Archuleta to retrieve the rebellious Taos Indians from their exile among the El Cuartelejo Apaches. (During a 1636 expedition west of the Rio del Norte, Archuleta, as had Oñate, carved his name and the date into the inviting bluffs at El Morro.) Captain Archuleta's expedition to El Cuartelejo may be the first documented Spanish journey across the state of Colorado, but this remains speculative. Archuleta's campaign diary has not been recovered, and his route to El Cuartelejo remains unknown—though it would be difficult to travel from Santa Fe to El Cuartelejo without crossing lands that lie within present-day Colorado. In fact, little about Archuleta or his journey is known with certainty. His precise orders and the timing, route, composition, and tone of his expedition remain a mystery.

Archuleta journeyed to El Cuartelejo probably sometime before the start of Governor Alonso Pacheco's tenure in 1642. According to Fray Silvestre Vélez de Escalante, writing more than a century later, Archuleta was accompanied by twenty soldiers and an unspecified number of allied Pueblo Indians (probably scores of them). In 1778 Father Escalante wrote of Archuleta's time at El Cuartelejo: "He found in the possession of these rebellious Taos Indians some casques and other pieces of copper and tin, and when he asked them whence they had gotten these they replied 'from the Quivira pueblos,' to which they had journeyed from the Cuartelejo."[19] The father speculated that the copper and tin reached the Quivirans from Frenchmen trading with the Pawnees to the north. Archuleta apparently returned to New Mexico with all or part of the rebellious Taos Indians.

Captain Archuleta's arduous journey across the plains earned him no respite from New Mexico's domestic troubles. On the contrary. In July 1643 Governor Pacheco launched a surprise offensive against his fellow New Mexicans. He rounded up eight captains, including Juan de Archuleta, and charged them with treason. Essentially these men were deemed guilty of excesses in the name of the Franciscan order, and on July 21 Governor Pacheco had them beheaded.[20] The internecine conflict in seventeenth-century New Mexico turned deadly.

Governor Pacheco stoked native resentments when he demanded increases in the annual tribute in corn and cotton. He forbade open travel between pueblos, which challenged Spanish control and might have resulted in a general uprising. In 1640 a Franciscan wrote that the Indians would flee their pueblos "at the slightest annoyance," possibly fearing for their lives.[21] Archuleta's journey to El Cuartelejo may represent only one of many missions to that and other Apache regions to retrieve rebellious Pueblo groups. In 1644 and again in 1647 Jemez Pueblo revolted and its inhabitants fled to the nearby Navajos. The Jemez killed only one Spaniard in these revolts, yet Governor Don Fernando de Argüello

Carvajál (who served 1644–1647) hung twenty-nine natives in retaliation as "traitors, and confederates of the [Navajo] Apaches."[22] Though this governor is credited with bringing some stability to the church-state rivalry, clearly his harsh reprisals against the Pueblo Indians only increased hostility between Europeans and natives on the Rio del Norte.

Spanish reprisals were not always possible, for the province lacked fundamental supplies such as an adequate amount of iron for horseshoes. Though iron always was scarce on the frontier, New Mexico's clergy hoarded what was available for use in the missions. In fact, material privations often governed Spanish actions toward New Mexico's Pueblo Indians and outlying tribes. Shortages of food might propel the Spaniards to attack a pueblo or rancheria. In contrast, just a shortage of iron might hamper offensive forays, for horses would be in short supply. New Mexico's Spaniards must have zealously concealed the ebb and flow of their martial strength, lest that knowledge aid their beleaguered neighbors. Nonetheless, the Pueblo Indians would have difficulty capitalizing on Spanish weaknesses, for they were a battered people. Spanish oppression, violence, disease, and consolidation of some pueblos to facilitate missionary work reduced the number of pueblos in New Mexico from more than one hundred in 1598 to forty-three in the 1640s. As one writer has observed, "the deadly nature of Spanish exploitation was chiefly to blame."[23]

Governor Don Luís de Guzmán y Figueroa's term (1647–1649) included forays against the Navajos in the "Rio Grande," or San Juan River region, near the modern Colorado border. In the late 1640s news of revolts among Apache groups on the southern frontier of New Mexico may have inspired the oppressed pueblos on the upper Rio del Norte to rebel. In 1650 Spanish officials discovered and squelched a plot by Tiwas, Keres, and Apaches to overthrow them. In response to similar threats, real or imagined, Governor Don Hernando de Ugarte y la Concha (1649–1653) hanged nine leaders from Isleta, Alameda, San Felipe, Cochiti, and Jemez pueblos.

The latter half of the seventeenth century in New Mexico witnessed repeated Spanish forays against the Navajos, treachery against formerly friendly Apache bands, and even tighter repression of Pueblo peoples. Life for everyone on the Rio del Norte grew harsh, marked by hostility and shortages of food and material goods. Apparently only the Utes remained peaceful trading partners, despite earlier Spanish transgressions. Tumultuous relations between New Mexico's Spaniards and their native neighbors sent Spanish expeditions northwest to the Navajos just south of the San Juan River, north into the San Luis Valley to meet Ute traders, and northeast across the plains to the El Cuartelejo Apaches, among others. But gaps in the record are profound. Aside from the loss or destruction of records, there can be little doubt that the wretched excesses of seventeenth-century governors remained unrecorded because they did not want their treachery chronicled.

A succession of New Mexico's governors from the late 1640s to the 1670s repeatedly appointed Captain Juan Domínguez de Mendoza to lead expeditions against the Navajos. A number of those expeditions reached clear to the San Juan River near today's New Mexico–Colorado border, "where severe punishment was ... meted out to the [Navajo] Apache enemies, many of whom were captured and killed."[24] On those forays Spanish soldiers could look north to the snowcapped mountains known to them as the Sierra de las Grullas, "Mountains of the Cranes," and referred to today as Colorado's San Juan Mountains. By the 1670s Captain Domínguez had earned a reputation as a competent and experienced soldier, who had served his province for four decades.[25] In keeping with the tenor of the times, however, Domínguez was not universally popular. In his varied duties as soldier and administrator over the decades, he had repeated run-ins with various priests, some of whom were accused of misconduct by their native charges—accusations that fell to Domínguez to record. In early 1666 Domínguez himself became the focus of accusations, including a "long-standing hostility toward the clergy." But the busy Inquisition in Mexico City dismissed the case and advised its New Mexico representative to avoid forwarding frivolous matters.[26] Grossly biased testimony against Captain Domínguez and his solid reputation as a leading soldier cleared his name.

In this volatile period, the plains Apaches brought Quiviran slaves to Pecos to exchange for horses, a worthwhile trade for Spanish New Mexicans that for a time kept the peace between Spaniards and Apaches. This peace would not last due to aggression on both sides.[27] By the 1660s and 1670s Apaches no longer dared bring their wares into New Mexico proper, for by then desperate Spaniards resorted to treachery. During his tenure, for instance, Governor Don Bernardo López de Mendizábal (1659–1661) invited Apaches to Jemez Pueblo for trade, then killed many males and enslaved their families. By this time, through illicit trade and periodic rebellions by the Pueblos, Spanish horses and equestrian skills were making their way into the hands of the tribes surrounding New Mexico. This process eroded the Spaniards' military advantage, and they henceforth suffered increasingly bold raids by mounted natives.

In 1661 Taos Indians again destroyed the Franciscans' mission church, and another native contingent fled to El Cuartelejo. Sometime thereafter, another Spanish expedition may have journeyed to that Apache homeland on the high plains. Two successive governors claimed credit for journeys to El Cuartelejo in this period, but documentation is scant. Governor López in 1661 claimed to have "brought the Taos Indians back from El Cuartelejo."[28] López's successor, Governor don Diego de Peñalosa (1661–1664), claimed that in 1662 he, too, punished Taos Pueblo, and "caused El Cuartelejo to be laid waste for more than 200 leagues beyond New Mexico."[29] To do so Peñalosa would have had to scour the plains for five hundred miles!

Governor Peñalosa forbade direct trade between Pueblos and Apaches in 1664, perhaps to increase Spanish fortunes as middlemen, but also to stymie Pueblo-Apache plots. This prohibition, however, served only to depress trade, worsen material privations, and fuel tension in the province. In the early 1660s Governor Peñalosa attempted but did not complete a journey west to Hopi and a mythical locale known as the Sierra Azul, a mountain rumored to contain gold and mercury, an element critical to the refining process. Governor Peñalosa also heard of a land north of his province referred to as Gran Teguayo from a Jemez Indian who had been held captive there. After the Inquisition stripped Peñalosa of office in New Mexico, he petitioned the viceroy to grant him leadership of an expedition to Gran Teguayo but was denied. He subsequently tried, without success, to sell the idea to Spain's rivals at London and Paris. Peñalosa's stories of Teguayo and Quivira nonetheless eventually reached the French explorer, René-Robert Cavelier, sieur de La Salle, as the latter attempted to establish a French outpost on the Gulf Coast.

Peñalosa's treachery triggered Spain's Council of the Indies to request a report on the two "kingdoms" of Sierra Azul and Gran Teguayo. Fray Alonso de Posada's report of 1686 placed Teguayo with the Lake of Copala, "far to the northwest, beyond the land of the Utahs," and a substantial distance west from relatively well-known Quivira.[30] Posada's conjecture would have located Teguayo in present-day Colorado, and the Lake of Copala in an area synonymous with Great Salt Lake.[31] However, no records have surfaced that reflect seventeenth-century Spanish expeditions in the direction of those mythical realms.

In a series of cases in the 1660s New Mexico's priests exceeded their authority in pursuing charges against secular officials and private individuals, as they had with Captain Juan Mendoza de

Domínguez. In response, officials of the Inquisition in Mexico City advised New Mexico's Franciscans to avoid intervening in secular affairs altogether. In 1668 a non-Franciscan, secular priest was appointed commissary, or representative of the Inquisition. Henceforth, Franciscans focused on missionary work and left civil administration to provincial governors, a move that reduced tensions in the church-state rivalry. From about 1670 until 1680 church and state factions enjoyed a measure of peace, if not harmony. Outside factors pushed both sides to sustain the truce. Increased Spanish treachery against New Mexico's Apache neighbors had wrought perpetual war. In the years between 1667 and 1677, pueblos at Las Salinas, Senecu, Cuarac, and Chilili were abandoned after punishing Apache raids. Now the Apaches, mounted and angry, fought to annihilate the Spaniards altogether.

Prolonged drought and famine brought misery to all who lived in the region. Relentless Spanish pressure on the valley's Pueblo peoples included a crackdown on a return to native religions, which deepened the rift between Spaniard and native. Hundreds of Pueblos died of starvation and disease. Forced labor, religious persecution, and famine all pressed the disparate Pueblo peoples to finally unite as one to expel their overlords. The royal caravan from Mexico that periodically brought the isolated province a new governor and material support no longer traveled safely along the Camino Real north of El Paso del Norte. Apache attacks increased to a devastating pitch. The Camino Real's tenuous link between New Mexico and New Spain could be severed at any time, which contributed to unease among New Mexico's settlers.

The majority of Ute bands, however, remained friendly to New Mexico's Spaniards in the closing years of the 1670s. A Spanish-Ute treaty ensured safe passage for Spanish traders who traveled, undocumented, across the northern frontier to Colorado's San Luis Valley. Closer to home, in 1675, Tewas sparked a movement back to native religion and they killed a half-dozen Spanish priests and three or four settlers, drawing Spanish reprisals. Governor Juan Francisco Treviño, who served in 1675–1677, rounded up native leaders, hanged three (one committed suicide rather than endure the Spaniards' punishment), and two score were lashed, imprisoned, and sentenced to slavery. In response, a large force of Tewa warriors descended on Santa Fe and crowded into the Governor's Palace to demand the release of their imprisoned comrades. Governor Treviño relented, perhaps for mere survival's sake; his limited number of soldiers and militia could not defend him or the *villa* of Santa Fe. Among the prisoners he released was a Taos Indian known as Popé, who returned home with a consuming hatred of all things Spanish, and perhaps a better sense of the Spaniards' ultimate vulnerability. For five long years Popé worked in secret to foster agreement among all pueblos to unite.

Throughout the late 1670s Captain Domínguez led forays against the Navajos, often relying upon Pueblo auxillaries from Zía Pueblo, numerous *genízaros* (Christianized Indians who'd lost their tribal affiliation), and Ute guides. In light of these attacks it is perhaps surprising that the Navajos did not join a general native revolt then about to explode. For in the closing years of the decade Popé and Taqu, both of San Juan Pueblo, men known as Xaca and Chato of Taos Pueblo, and Francisco of San Ildefonso Pueblo worked on the valley's formerly autonomous pueblos to unite against the hated Spaniards.

In a snapshot comparison of the relative strengths of the Spaniards and Pueblos at this juncture, one historian has noted that in May 1679 New Mexico probably contained seventeen thousand Pueblo Indians, including six thousand warriors. Spanish-speaking peoples numbered about twenty-five hundred, with only one hundred seventy capable of bearing arms.[32] Popé understood the significance of this disparity. Unity could deliver freedom.

Governor Treviño's decision to free Popé proved to be a practical though costly act of capitulation. By the summer of 1680 a majority of pueblos secretly agreed to rise and destroy the Spaniards. Native runners left Taos for the outlying pueblos bearing lengths of *palmilla,* rope woven from yucca fibers. The ropes were knotted, one knot to be untied each day until the last, the day of the uprising. Popé even killed his son-in-law just before the appointed day for fear the latter would warn the Spaniards. When Spanish officials uncovered the plot before the agreed date of August 13, the Pueblos revolted immediately. On August 10, 1680, nearly all native pueblos killed their resident Spanish priests and settlers, and drove fifteen hundred survivors behind the walls of Santa Fe. Only two Spaniards escaped from the valley of Taos Pueblo. Pockets of horrified settlers, unaware of their comrades' fates, began an exodus down the river to Isleta as the air filled with smoke from burning ranchos and churches. From Thursday, August 15, until Tuesday, August 20, Governor Don Antonio de Otermín and his countrymen held their capital, aided by firearms and a native reluctance to storm the walls. The triumphant Pueblos fired off muskets, cut off the Spaniards' water supply, and sang victory songs. Elsewhere, according to an aggrieved eyewitness who later reached El Paso del Norte, "The said Indians, taking up arms, carried away with anger, killed friars, priests, Spaniards and women, not saving even innocent babes in arms, and voracious, demon-blinded, they set fire to the temples and images, making mockery in their dances, and with their trophies of the sacerdotal vestments and other church paraphernalia, carrying their barbarous hatred to such extremes of rapacity that in the pueblo of Zandía sculptured images were desecrated with human excrement."[33]

The desperate Spaniards holding Santa Fe became determined to die fighting. At daybreak on August 20, ten days after the carnage began, a small force of mounted men charged out of the walls, trampling enemies underfoot. Two skirmishes followed; the Spaniards, with firearms and surprise on their side, won a moment of opportunity. The natives withdrew long enough for more than a thousand Spanish men, women, and children to make a sorrowful trek south from whence they'd come. Many lay dead at Santa Fe, and hundreds more had fallen amid the burning ruins of ranchos, churches, and fields that had taken a century to build. Among the survivors rode Captain Roque Madrid, with "three lean horses, two lean and tired mules, all his personal arms, his wife, and four small children."[34] Few were as fortunate. The refugees regrouped near Isleta Pueblo, a three-day journey south of Santa Fe, then reached El Paso del Norte, more than one hundred leagues away, where they founded a community-in-exile. In a revealing bit of testimony governor-in-exile Antonio de Otermín reported to the viceroy that one soldier who escaped the carnage north of Santa Fe had just returned from a journey to Ute country.[35]

The Pueblos' unified revolt proved to be the most decisive native rebellion in American history, and the event is still celebrated by New Mexico's surviving pueblos. With the exception of horses, weapons, and other immediately useful items, the Pueblos destroyed all vestiges of the Spanish occupation, including many provincial records. Accounts of Spanish frontier expeditions in preceding years, perhaps including Captain Archuleta's journal, probably perished at this time. According to an eyewitness questioned later by Spanish officials at the new settlement of El Paso del Norte, many rebels afterward bathed in the Rio del Norte, as if to wash away any taint of Spanish influence. Having driven out the hated Spaniards and reclaimed their lands, the disparate Pueblo peoples of the upper Rio del Norte attempted to piece together the remnants of a shattered world.

Respite and Reconquest
1680-1706

THE PUEBLO INDIANS' united success against the nearly century-long Spanish occupation brought both triumph and peril to a native world irrevocably changed by contact with Europeans. After their collaborative victory in August 1680 the Pueblos could practice traditional rites openly and in peace and reap the rewards of their own farming, hunting, and trade. Each pueblo could regain its cherished political autonomy. But with this autonomy came the factionalism that reigned prior to the Pueblos' contact with Europeans. In regional terms, the Pueblos' acquisition of horses and weapons in the uprising altered the balance of power between the Pueblo world and outlying tribes.

Popé had inspired the united rebellion by calling for all Pueblo peoples to return to traditional ways, "as when they emerged from the Laguna de Copala."[1] Having tasted greatness and power, though, Popé instead set himself up as governor at Santa Fe and demanded material tribute from each pueblo. He forbade the practice of Christianity, Spanish language or customs, and oversaw the division of property and possessions abandoned by the retreating Spaniards. Inevitably, many Pueblo Indians came to understand that they had ousted one overlord only to be saddled by another. Popé's assumption of power violated the purpose of the revolt and it darkened the hearts of those who had fought it.

The absence of a common enemy soon rekindled traditional rivalries. The Keres, Taos, and Pecos pueblos fought the Tewas and

Tanos. When the latter groups triumphed, they deposed Popé, electing as their leader a Picurís Indian named Don Luis Tupatú. Don Luis governed the Tewas and Tanos until 1688, when Popé again led various factions in a successful coalition. When Popé died, Don Luis resumed power and other pueblos split off to live independently of these rivalries.[2] Free from Spanish interference, Apache groups resumed trade with their traditional Pueblo partners, and attacked other Pueblo groups. In the Spaniards' absence, Apaches no longer played the role of the region's principal aggressors. In the new configuration various Pueblo groups sallied forth, mounted and armed with steel weapons, to assert their power on the frontier.[3] Northern pueblos such as Taos, Picurís, San Juan, and Jemez made mounted forays up the Rio del Norte into Colorado's San Luis Valley and Ute country. There, mounted and dressed partly in Spanish garb, the Pueblos hunted buffalo and skirmished with the Utes. The Utes in turn raided northern pueblos.

The Spaniards' presence somewhere to the south no doubt weighed on Pueblo minds. Europeans had introduced steel, horses, and firearms, and imposed a language, a religion, and myriad customs. By 1680 many Pueblo peoples had become enculturated into Spanish society, speaking the language, observing Catholic rites. Some lived an uneasy combination of native and Spanish ways. Such fundamental changes in the Pueblo world over the course of a century made it impossible for native peoples to simply resume customs practiced prior to Coronado's visit. And there always remained the possibility that Spaniards might return.

The Pueblo revolt irrevocably changed the frontier calculus for the Spaniards as well, whether or not they returned. Their hasty retreat had transferred numerous horses into Pueblo and Apache hands, which helped disseminate one of the Spaniards' primary military advantages. Knowledge of horse handling and breeding gained by the Pueblos through close contact with Spaniards in

New Mexico's and Texas's seventeenth-century missions gradually passed to outlying tribes. In possession of horses, hunting peoples could travel greater distances in pursuit of buffalo. Nomadic peoples given to raiding and war could henceforth mount effective surprise attacks on distant enemies, then withdraw. Iron-working skills and raw materials had reached native hands as well, along with guns, swords, and lances. By this time Frenchmen hovered to the northeast and were willing to trade guns, lead, and powder, the tools of war, to the Comanche and Kiowa Indians on New Mexico's northeastern frontier in a beneficial exchange for furs. These major shifts in the balance of power on the upper Rio del Norte and beyond could only vex exiled Spaniards.

Governor Don Antonio de Otermín at first refused to believe that his policies or his countrymen's conduct had alienated all the pueblos. The governor suggested to his superiors in Mexico City that many pueblos would welcome his return, as Apache and Ute attacks surely had increased during the Spaniards' absence. For the moment, simply maintaining the Spanish hold on El Paso del Norte proved difficult enough. Yet reasserting Spanish control over New Mexico would be crucial to controlling New Spain's entire northern frontier. So in November 1681 Otermín led more than one hundred Spanish soldiers and another hundred faithful Pueblo Indian warriors across the Camino Real's dreaded desert stretch dubbed the Jornada del Muerto (Journey of Death) and up the Rio del Norte. His soldiers had a stake in the success of their mission: four out of five had been born in New Mexico. (More than half could not sign their names.) Upon reaching the Sandia Mountains at the southern end of the Pueblo world the Spanish army successfully attacked Isleta Pueblo, killed many male warriors, and captured nearly four hundred women and children. A string of pueblos fell in succession. These victories, however heartening, did not represent the open arms Otermín had predicted.

In fact, the Pueblos often defended their homes to the death, or retreated to nearby canyons and hills to wage guerrilla warfare.[4] The Indians' spirited reception soon stymied Otermín's attempt to reoccupy the province; by January 1682 winter and native resistance forced him back to El Paso del Norte. Captain Don Domingo Jironza Pétriz de Cruzate assumed New Mexico's governorship from Otermín, but unrest in El Paso del Norte demanded his immediate attention, precluding another attempt at reconquest. In 1686 Don Pedro Reneros Posada won appointment to the three-year governorship. In the second year of his term he launched a bid to retake New Mexico, but a determined resistance, this time at Zía Pueblo, stopped him as well. Captain Don Domingo Jironza Pétriz resumed the governorship in 1689 and in September of that year he marched upriver. Zía Pueblo's defenders chose to be burned alive in their homes rather than surrender, a measure of the resistance that again forced the Spaniards to retreat. Local rebellions at El Paso del Norte precluded another try the following year.

A growing conviction among Spanish officials that only the reconquest of New Mexico would bring peace to New Spain's northern frontier now dovetailed with the ambitions of a Madrid-born nobleman. His full name was as expansive as seventeenth-century Spanish ambitions: Don Diego Joseph de Vargas Zapata y Luján Ponce de León y Contreras. By 1688, when the forty-five-year-old Vargas was appointed governor of New Mexico, he had spent a dozen years as a civil administrator in Mexico's mining districts. He had come to the New World in 1673 to seek fame and fortune, leaving behind his wife, children, and heavy debts. He believed the New World would be his salvation, both materially and spiritually. If Juan de Oñate could be called the "last conquistador," perhaps Vargas's complexities and contradictions cast him closer to Don Quixote. Vargas had long, straight black hair, a broad face, medium build, and a lisp.[5] As a youth he danced and

earned a fine education. Once in the New World he wrote long
melancholy letters to his family, professing homesickness, worry
over debts, and articulating his drive for honor and glory, but reflecting no immediate plans to return to Spain. In Mexico, after
learning of his wife's death in 1674, he sired another family. His
antecedents had won honor and wealth after distinguished service against the Moors. With that heritage at his back Vargas sought
the reconquest of New Mexico. He also hoped to finesse debts
and win acceptance into the Order of the Knights of Santiago, a
still-revered and exclusive title. Vargas took office at El Paso del
Norte in February 1691. The challenge of his lifetime loomed to
the north.

Vargas actively sought official support and the necessary resources for a reconquest. He argued that the reconquest of New
Mexico would effectively reassert Spanish control over the natives
on New Spain's vast northern frontier and return them to the
Catholic faith. An occupied New Mexico would protect New
Spain's silver mines from European rivals, particularly Frenchmen
pushing west from the Mississippi Valley, he said. Vargas pledged
to search for the Strait of Anián, key to holding the entire continent, and to seek the legendary Sierra Azul, another chimera that
still lured frontier-bound Spaniards.[6] The reconquest of New
Mexico would echo, at least in Vargas's mind, the great reconquest
of the Iberian Peninsula two hundred years earlier in which his
ancestors had earned distinction, and membership in the Order of
the Knights of Santiago.

In August 1692 Vargas himself financed a modest foray upriver from El Paso in which the southernmost pueblos seemed to
acquiesce in a renewed Spanish presence. He entered Santa Fe
without meeting resistance and parlayed with representatives of
the various factions that had formed since 1680. He even reached
the Hopis more than a hundred leagues (nearly three hundred

miles) to the west, pausing to carve his name into the bluffs at El Morro, as had Oñate and Captain Juan de Archuleta before him. Many pueblos either feigned peace to avoid hostilities, or took to the hills. Vargas returned to El Paso del Norte in December, convinced that peaceful resettlement could follow.

Native unity had long since crumbled and the time-honored strategy of divide and conquer again served Spanish interests. In October 1693 Governor Vargas led an enormous procession north from El Paso del Norte. One hundred soldiers, seventy settlers, their families, and priests formed a sinuous line in the desert. Vargas rode in the vanguard with those who had been driven out of New Mexico thirteen years earlier. The immense caravan included two thousand horses, a thousand mules, and nearly a thousand cattle and swine. As Vargas slowly ascended the Rio del Norte, Pecos and some Keres pueblos acquiesced in his presence, but most pueblos openly resisted. Vargas patiently applied both diplomacy and force to retake the province.[7]

Vargas claimed Santa Fe in early December, barely managing to save his winter-ravaged settlers. Once ensconced within the adobe walls of Santa Fe's buildings, however, patience and compassion were no longer necessary. The Spaniards set about punishing pueblos that resisted. In battle Vargas killed all male rebels, unless the entire pueblo surrendered.[8] (Because the Pueblo Indians had once "accepted" Spanish rule, those who resisted the reoccupation could be treated as "rebels.") Pueblos and Apaches countered with ambushes and raids; for a time, neither side won clear-cut victory. In February and March 1694 Vargas attacked Tewas and Tanos holding the mesatop at San Ildefonso northwest of Santa Fe, but couldn't mount a successful siege. In April he defeated the Keres of Cieneguilla Pueblo. Vargas prepared for a campaign against Jemez Pueblo, but in June the Rio del Norte ran high and he decided instead to secure corn for his hungry settlers from the rebellious northern pueblos.[9] He had responsibility for the lives of hundreds of Spanish settlers huddled at Santa Fe who could not safely plant or tend fields.

On the last day of June 1694 Vargas and the Pecos leader, Don Juan, led fifty Spanish soldiers and fifty militia, scores of Pueblo allies, and a long *mulada* (mule train) north from Santa Fe. In preparations for the reconquest Vargas had made certain that his men, mostly cavalry, were well equipped with morions, some body armor, layered leather jackets, and a lance, shield, sword, and musket.[10] In Europe, heavy armor had fallen out of style as speed and maneuverability assumed importance, but styles lingered on the remote frontier due to the sheer scarcity of equipment and the deadly nature of native arrows. Thus, the Spanish procession that ambled north owed more to medieval times than to contemporary European trends.

Vargas reached Taos Pueblo over well-known trails that snaked through the wooded hills north of Santa Fe, only to find the pueblo recently abandoned. On each home hung a cross, a blatant appeal to the Spaniards' piety in hopes of preventing pillage. The Pecos leader, Don Juan, voluntarily walked into a rebel redoubt in a nearby canyon to open talks. He did not re-emerge. The next day Vargas directed his men to take as much grain as their mulada of eighty animals could carry—perhaps as much as ten tons.[11] That night, however, signal fires in the hills south of the Taos Valley raised the specter of an impending native ambush and fear of "total annihilation," Vargas noted to his secretary of war, Alfonso Rael de Aguilar, who actually penned Vargas's journal. Rather than risk ambush, "older natives of the land" on the expedition suggested to Vargas that he detour north up the valley through Ute country, cross the Rio del Norte there, then return to Santa Fe via the Rio Chama. Clearly these men had traveled that route sometime prior to the Pueblo revolt, undoubtedly for the Ute trade. "And so it was decided that the departure should be by way of the land of the Yuttas, a nation which is very friendly toward the Spaniards, and who felt their loss and withdrawal at the time of the uprising in this kingdom," Vargas wrote in his journal. The Spaniards left Taos after sunset. The date was July 7, 1694. "I ... left this place and took the road leading to the land of the Yuttas, taking Mathías Luxán as interpreter ... and captain Lazaro de Misquía, for he was the one who proposed the route," Vargas wrote.[12] Luxán and Lazaro knew their trail so well they could guide the heavily laden expedition through the hills at night. As the Spaniards trundled north with their precious cargo, Captain Juan Olguin led forty soldiers in the vanguard with the mulada in tow. Vargas rode with the main force. A rear guard of thirty soldiers followed.

Six leagues north of Arroyo Hondo eighty Taoseños attacked the Spanish pack train. Vargas repelled them, killing five and capturing two. The two were questioned, absolved of their "sins," and shot. Vargas kept to the edge of the wooded hills for cover, and camped on Rio Colorado, today's Red River, halfway between Taos and the present-day Colorado state line. North of the Rio Colorado they'd be free of danger from Taos ambushes, as well as threats by Acho Apaches. "In order that the Yuttas, whom we are seeking, may know of our arrival in the kingdom of New Mexico and the villa of Santa Fe," Vargas wrote, "I ordered that large smoke signals be raised, and I marched on with the camp to the Rio Culebra ... all country of extended valleys and many arroyos with groves of trees. It is evident, from the dung which was found, that the buffalo pastures here."[13]

Vargas traveled over open ground to the Rio Culebra (Snake River), a stream still so named near where San Acacio, Colorado, would stand more than a century later. His casual use of the familiar name Culebra reflects that the region was well traveled by Spaniards before 1680. The next day the expedition descended the

Culebra to the banks of the Rio del Norte in the midst of the
broad San Luis Valley. Of the Spaniards' lengthy procession, author Ruth Marie Colville has observed: "Vargas's expedition
would have formed a very small string of creatures in a very spacious land."[14] The river proved too swift to cross without rafts,
but a Tewa Indian from San Juan Pueblo stepped forward and said
he knew of a ford. "The [Spanish] interpreters were not familiar
with this route, which led far into the interior of the lands of the
Yutta nation," Vargas noted in his journal. "It was an act of Divine
Providence that on this occasion this Indian of much intelligence
knew well the said road. And so from this place onward he served
as guide."[15] Two leagues downriver the Tewa located a traditional
ford where, today, ancient pictographs on a bluff overlooking that
site imply regular prehistoric use.[16] As Vargas described the spot:
"Here [the river] was very wide, and due to the emptying of the
two branches the current of the river was slowed up, and so even
though it was deep it was passable."[17] The governor supervised the
crossing of the soldiers, their *cavallada* (horse train), and the mulada. The bags of corn were transported in *tercios*, pack bags
perched on the mules' backs, and brush bundles were laid in the
mud at riverside to assist passage by hoofed animals. The animals
were swum across.

The expedition traveled down the Rio del Norte, and turned
west between hills the Spaniards called the Serranía de San Antonio, today known as the San Luis or Piñon Hills. Vargas and his
men encamped in a meadow created by the Rio San Antonio's
meanders, which they called *culebreada*, "snakelike." Soldiers
sighted a nearby herd of hundreds of buffalo and gave chase,
killing more than a dozen. Vargas's frontier camp that night would
have appeared quite exotic to modern eyes. The governor and his
officers pitched tents in one spot, with their soldiers nearby, possibly forming a defensive perimeter. Settlers who had been pressed

into service claimed their own area apart from the professional soldiers. Pueblo warriors tended the horse herd, picketed a sensible distance from the campfires. Men gathered wood and hauled water. Some butchered buffalo meat and roasted long strips over the fires, while others stirred pots of *atole,* a nutritious corn gruel. Someone prepared tortillas on a heated, flat rock brought expressly for that purpose. The crisp evening air in that high valley filled with pungent wood smoke and the thick smell of roasting meat. Whinnying horses and rapid exchanges in Spanish and Pueblo languages created a babel of tongues. After supper men checked their weapons and made certain that powder and flint were dry after crossing the Rio del Norte. Perhaps someone played a fiddle, sang or recited folktales. Long after dark, scouts reached camp, causing a stir, but brought no news of the Utes. Lookouts kept a vigil over the horse herd. The Milky Way pulsated overhead in the same sky that vaulted over the nearby Utes.

The next day Vargas joined his men in a second hunt and they brought in eight more buffalo and two deer. The buffalo were a curiosity to many men who were new to the country, and the chases thrilled them. The Spaniards again attempted, unsuccessfully, to signal the Utes with smoke from fires lit atop nearby hills. After the day's long hunt and feast the men slept soundly. The next morning before dawn, just as Captain Eusebio de Vargas gathered the horse herd and readied the mulada for an early start, native attackers swept through the camp on foot, wielding clubs and discharging their bows. Six Spaniards were wounded before they offered a response, which they did with restraint, uncertain of their foe's identity. Eight attackers were killed before the Indians regrouped across the Rio San Antonio. They numbered some three hundred, including women and children, and signaled peace by waving a buckskin, calling *anche, pauiche,* "brother, friend."

Vargas's interpreters recognized their assailants by their language, build, facial features, and dress. They were Utes, short of

build and dark complected.[18] The Utes signed that their attack had
been a mistake. Their Pueblo Indian enemies, dressed in Spanish
garb, had been coming to the valley to hunt and fight since the
Pueblo revolt fourteen summers earlier. The Utes mistook Vargas's expedition for Pueblo adventurers. The Spaniards accepted
the Utes' explanations, and the two sides mingled amicably, com-
municating by signs alone. Vargas dispensed corn, meat, a wool
poncho, knives, and a horse, partly in reparation for the eight dead
Utes. The Utes urged the Spaniards to return for trade in *ropa de
la tierra* (buckskins), and Vargas invited the Utes to Santa Fe to
trade, as in the days before August 1680.

With his diplomatic business concluded, Vargas ascended the
Rio San Antonio west of San Antonio Mountain and headed south
to camp at a perennial spring west of present-day Tres Piedras,
New Mexico. In mid-July the expedition descended the Rio Ojo
Caliente to the Rio Chama, and crossed the Rio del Norte at a ford
near San Juan Pueblo. Vargas sent most of his men and their valuable cargo on to Santa Fe while he reconnoitered the rebels who remained atop the mesa at San Ildefonso.[19] Vargas' precious corn and
buffalo meat quieted his countrymen's grumbling stomachs and
bolstered their spirits. His northern *entrada* would prove pivotal
in the reconquest.

So determined were the Pueblo Indians to retain their homeland
that Vargas fought native resistance until 1696. But the frequency
of modest land grants to settlers in that period reflects a time of
rebuilding, even expansion. Spaniards reconstructed many of the
plazas, ranchos, pueblos, and missions destroyed in 1680, and
established new ones. When settlers petitioned Vargas for lands
that encroached upon faithful San Felipe Pueblo, however, they
were denied. Vargas sought to establish a standard of fairness in
Spanish-Pueblo relations and, as a result, the province briefly enjoyed peace. Picurís and Taos pueblos remained the only nearby
holdouts. Far to the west, outside the sphere of direct Spanish

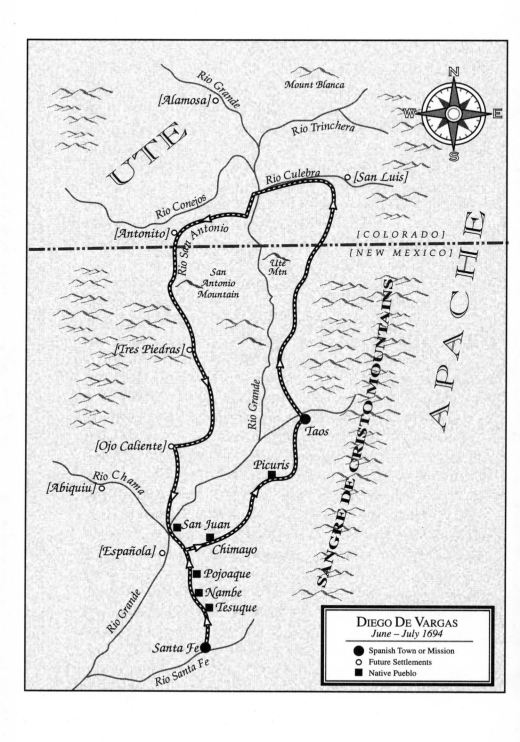

UTE

Rio Grande

[Alamosa]

Mount Blanca

Rio Trinchera

Rio Culebra

[San Luis]

Rio Conejos

[Antonito]

Rio San Antonio

[COLORADO]

[NEW MEXICO]

San Antonio Mountain

Ute Mtn

[Tres Piedras]

Rio Grande

APACHE

Taos

[Ojo Caliente]

Picuris

SANGRE DE CRISTO MOUNTAINS

Rio Chama

[Abiquiu]

San Juan

[Española]

Chimayo

Pojoaque

Nambe

Tesuque

Rio Grande

Santa Fe

Rio Santa Fe

DIEGO DE VARGAS
June – July 1694

● Spanish Town or Mission
○ Future Settlements
■ Native Pueblo

influence or coercion, Acoma, Zuni, and Hopi pueblos also main-tained their independence. Spanish New Mexicans toiled at their labors and soon achieved a measure of stability. Unlike the 1600s, civil order among elements of Spanish society now reigned, though contemporary records reveal that New Mexico still suffered the universal human transgressions of murder, rape, theft, desertion, adultery, gambling, and witchcraft. Miscreants were jailed or fined, even banished.

In an effort to avoid past mistakes, the reconquest of New Mex-ico brought many changes to Spanish administration of the prov-ince. These included the abolition of *encomiendas*, to be replaced by smaller grants worked by owners or paid labor. From the native perspective, however, the new regime still imposed its foreign Catholic religion, and once again drove traditional spiritual prac-tices underground. Gradually, the Spaniards gained allies as each pueblo made its own peace with the new arrangement. Some men from Pecos and San Juan pueblos served as trusted guides on expeditions across the frontier. Vargas actively sought to curtail the church-state rivalry that had crippled New Mexico in the previ-ous century. Now the province served more as a bastion of defense, rather than as a missionary outpost. A presidio was established and a sense of security led to the establishment of new villas. In 1695 sixty-six families arrived from Mexico to join Captain Roque Madrid and José Naranjo in settling La Villa Nueva de Santa Cruz de la Cañada (later known simply as Santa Cruz) just north of Santa Fe. Settlers founded Bernalillo south of Santa Fe that year and spread out along the river. Settlers in this period were known as *vecinos*, meaning "neighbor," "friend." The term implied a head of household, a taxpayer. Despite Vargas's success, he wrote in one of his melancholy notes to his family in Spain that the King-dom and Province of New Mexico existed "at the ends of the earth and remote beyond compare."[20]

Missionaries had returned to the outlying pueblos, but by December 1695 priests throughout the province sensed from the Indians' simmering hostility that another revolt was imminent. They requested soldiers to guard them, but Vargas could not spread his one hundred presidials any thinner. The governor grew impatient with clerical demands, while the friars' resentment grew over not being taken seriously—an angry echo of the church-state rivalry Vargas had sought to avoid. The governor sent four soldiers each to missions at San Juan, San Ildefonso, Taos, Picurís, and two Jemez pueblos. In early June 1696 revolts swept all but five pueblos in the province. Only Pecos, Tesuque, San Felipe, Santa Ana, and Zía remained allied with the Spaniards. A handful of missionaries and a score of settlers fell in battle. Vargas gathered his settlers and missionaries into defensible locations and struck back. Cochiti, Acoma, Zuni, and Hopi pueblos sought peace. Vargas repeated his pleas to the viceroy for more soldiers, colonists, and supplies at this critical juncture.

In September 1696 Vargas led a campaign against Picurís and Taos. At Taos he persuaded the Indians to leave the hills and reoccupy their pueblo. But the Picurís fled their homes. Vargas and Captain Juan de Ulibarrí gave chase and captured some on the western flank of the Sangre de Cristos. Many Picurís, including leader Don Lorenzo and Don Luis Tupatú, son of a principal in the 1680 uprising, escaped over the mountains and plains to reach the distant El Cuartelejo Apaches—just as their brethren had done nearly a century earlier. Vargas pursued rebel leaders throughout the province—though the Taos and Picurís at El Cuartelejo eluded him—and by the time his term drew to a close, he had effectively ended the revolt. The Taos and Picurís rebels remained in exile.

Don Pedro Rodríguez Cubero took office in July 1697 and immediately had Vargas arrested for a variety of alleged transgressions. Spanish officials leaving office underwent a review of their

service known as the *residencia,* which provided their enemies
with an opportunity to level justifiable complaints and, often, spu-
rious charges. The residencia was routinely abused to cripple even
New Mexico's most effective governors, including Don Diego de
Vargas. Vargas languished in jail for three agonizing years.

In 1700 Vargas returned to Mexico City, cleared his name, and
regained the governorship. When he resumed office in winter 1703
Governor Cubero fled.[21] Vargas spent his remaining years embit-
tered over his incarceration, worried over debts, and concerned for
his families in both Mexico and Spain. He died in April 1704 while
campaigning against Faraone Apaches in the Sandia Mountains
near Bernalillo, felled by a recurring illness. Vargas was buried
under the altar of an early church on Santa Fe's plaza. For reasons
he could not fathom, he had never gained membership in the es-
teemed Order of the Knights of Santiago. In that respect Vargas
had been tilting at windmills throughout his illustrious years in
New Mexico.[22]

Upon the accession of Don Francisco Cuervo y Valdés to the
governorship in 1705 the Spaniards began a concerted attempt to
end the Apache threat to their province. That included dealing
with the Navajos on New Mexico's northwest flank, who consis-
tently raided nearby pueblos at Jemez, Santa Ana, Cochiti, Santa
Clara, and San Juan for horses and human captives. Thrice in the
first nine months of 1705 Governor Cuervo sent veteran Captain
Roque de Madrid, age sixty-one, against the Navajos. Madrid
had been one of the forlorn though fortunate settlers to flee New
Mexico in the Pueblo revolt of 1680, and he had played a key role
in Governor Vargas's reconquest. Madrid's expedition against the
Navajo in August 1705 reached clear to the southern flanks of
the Sierra de las Grullas, today's San Juan Mountains of southwestern Colorado. Madrid engaged the Navajos several times on
this campaign though he fought no decisive battles. But his

meticulous journal provides the earliest Spanish descriptions of the Navajos' Dinetah and the Sierra de las Grullas on New Mexico's northwestern frontier.

After mustering his men at San Juan Pueblo on the Rio del Norte, Captain Madrid rode north, then northwest, crossing the great river at a difficult ford northwest of Picurís Pueblo. Madrid intended "to make war by fire and sword on the Apache Navajo enemy nation" in a land "where Spanish arms had not been for thirty years," according to his journal.[23] His army numbered four hundred, including a few score soldiers and settlers and hundreds of allied Pueblo warriors.

Madrid reached a spot he dubbed Piedra del Carnero, today's Tres Piedras, New Mexico, and continued northwest across the upper Rio Chama to the headwaters of the Rio Grande, where he skirted the New Mexico–Colorado border. On the head of the Rio Tusas, tributary to the Chama, Madrid and his men could look north and "see the Sierra de las Grullas and hear the cranes' call."[24] Clearly the Spaniards were already familiar with that range, as it had a name, probably from prior to the Pueblo revolt.

As Madrid reached the southern flanks of the Sierra de las Grullas he remarked on his surroundings: "In these woods and mountains are many creeks with clear waters. I arrived at the eminence of the loftiest peak of Las Grullas and its river. There I took a fall down the mountain with the horse I was riding. Only by a miracle from La Conquistadora did I escape with my life. The Rio de las Grullas runs west to east, splitting two eminent peaks with gentle, cool waters containing many trout." Reaching the very headwaters of the Chama on the New Mexico–Colorado border, Madrid noted the river's "spacious, pleasant valley with many cottonwoods and good pasture."[25] (Thus the earliest description on record of southwestern Colorado.) Madrid and his expedition subsequently torched many native *milpas,* or cornfields, and battled with the Navajos in the tablelands above the many tributaries to the San Juan River. In one case Navajo defenders flung themselves to their deaths from a mesatop rather than face capture by Spaniards. Madrid and his men returned to Santa Fe via the Jemez River on the southern margin of Dinetah.

The following month Madrid led another expedition "by way of the mountain which they call Las Grullas, thirty leagues to the northwest" of Santa Fe, according to the recollection of a participant, Antonio Tafoya. Madrid may have repeated his earlier route. Upon his approach the Navajo again took to the mountaintops. "Consequently," recalled Tafoya, "the whole expedition returned to this villa by way of ... Pedernal Mountain."[26] Pedernal Mountain, still so named, rises above the Rio Chama, on the south side of modern Abiquiu Reservoir.

A shaky truce between Spaniards and Navajos held for three years until Navajo attacks on outlying pueblos in 1708 brought Spanish reprisals. Madrid repeatedly took to the field that winter and in the following year to chastise the Navajos. He was even called upon to lead in 1714 at age seventy after sporadic Navajo raids reignited hostilities. Captain Cristóbal de la Serna also led punitive campaigns against the Navajos in 1713–1716, but the extent of these forays is unknown. By 1720 the two sides arranged a peace that would last a half-century.

In the following decades Christianized Indians known as *genízaros* moved up the Chama to found their own community at Abiquiu, which pushed back New Mexico's northwestern frontier. This village lived under constant threat of attack by *indios barbaros*. Early in the eighteenth century those attacks might have been initiated by the Utes, who had allied themselves with dangerous newcomers known as los Comanches.

Utes brought Comanches to the annual Taos trading fair in 1705, marking the latter's first recorded appearance in New Mexico. The Spaniards at first thought the Comanches might hail from the land of Teguayo, reviving an old chimera that hovered somewhere north of New Mexico.[27] (In fact, the Comanches' origins remain mysterious.) In the first half of the eighteenth century they assumed control of New Mexico's northeastern frontier—Colorado's high plains—by sweeping it clear of Apaches, an act that would have profound repercussions for the Spanish province.

In spring 1706 Governor Francisco Cuervo y Valdés received a messenger sent by the long-exiled Picurís Indians and their Tanos and Tewa companions at El Cuartelejo on the margin of that northeastern frontier. The exiles asked forgiveness for revolting against the Spanish in 1696; they also asked for an escort home. Extricating themselves from the Apaches would prove difficult enough. But now mounted Comanches ruled the plains, which could be safely crossed only by a large, well-armed force. Governor Cuervo agreed to send an armed escort to retrieve the Picurís and other apostates, and he appointed Sergeant Major Juan de Ulibarrí to lead the expedition. (Ironically, Ulibarrí had fired the Spaniards' parting shots at these Picurís in 1696.) Ulibarrí, as Oñate, Archuleta, and Vargas before him, had carved his name into El Morro's sandstone bluffs, during a foray in 1701. (He would autograph El Morro again in 1709.) Because Ulibarrí, as required, kept a detailed journal of his mission to El Cuartelejo in 1706—and his account has survived—his route may be reconstructed with a degree of confidence.[28] Ulibarrí's account also describes a Spanish-Apache encounter, and rich detail on New Mexico's contemporary northeastern frontier and its tribes, flora and fauna, and climate.

Juan de Ulibarrí, a native of San Luís Potosí, Mexico, and his brother, Antonio, had reached New Mexico with Vargas's reconquest. Juan established his valor in campaigns against the Navajos. By 1704 Juan de Ulibarrí had earned the second highest post at the Santa Fe presidio and had helped to establish the new *villa* of Albuquerque. He seems to have married twice. By 1706 Juan was thirty-six years old and a seasoned soldier.[29] Governor Cuervo's cover letter to Ulibarrí's campaign journal noted that the expedition was sent "to the unknown land of the plains for the ransom of the Christian Indians of the Picuríes nation."[30] In contrast to the Spaniards' punitive raids against Pueblos and Apaches in pre-revolt days, the governor intended that this expedition would demonstrate the Spaniards' new style of humane governance. That humanity may have been lost on the various pueblos that suffered under the Spanish reconquest, but the Spaniards' believed they had changed their ways. Their survival and perhaps the comfort of their consciences rested as much on the olive branch as the sword.

In June 1706 Sergeant Major Ulibarrí mustered nearly thirty presidials, a dozen militia, and more than one hundred Pueblo allies for his journey to El Cuartelejo. One of the militia is noteworthy. The "Spaniards" of New Mexico always included a smattering of French, Flemish, and other European exiles. Juan de l'Archévèque now joined Ulibarrí's expedition. L'Archévèque, a native of Bayonne, France, had survived Réne-Robert Cavelier, sieur de La Salle's attempt to establish a French post on the Gulf of Mexico. The young Frenchman reached El Paso del Norte in 1691 and joined the reconquest under Vargas. His presence on Ulibarrí's expedition may reflect Spanish suspicions that his knowledge of the French language would be useful on the northeastern frontier.

On July 13 Ulibarrí's army left Santa Fe, stopped at Santa Cruz to finish preparations, and camped at San Juan Pueblo. The next day the expedition stopped at Picurís Pueblo to acquire blankets and horses that the pueblo dwellers had gathered for their destitute kinsmen on the plains. At Taos Pueblo the Indians warned Ulibarrí that Ute and Comanche warriors were preparing to attack the province. Consequently the Spanish captain waited several days for the governor to confirm his mission to El Cuartelejo. Ulibarrí's sizable expedition and horse herd finally left the pueblo on July 20 and rode east up Don Fernando Creek and over wooded Apache Pass, which lies two miles south of modern New Mexico Highway 64 (which traverses Palo Flechado Pass).

Ulibarrí noted in his journal that after crossing the Sangre de Cristo Mountains that he looked eastward toward his objective. "From this slope the plains can be made out and the unknown land with its trails," he wrote in his journal.[31] Apparently Spaniards had not journeyed to El Cuartelejo since before the Pueblo revolt, though they obviously recalled that trails existed in those "unknown lands." To locate those trails Ulibarrí relied on a native frontiersman named José Naranjo, who had traveled to El Cuartelejo before. Like many frontiersmen Naranjo was illiterate, yet he knew Apache dialects and customs, undoubtedly more valuable to a man in his line of work. Naranjo, who may have been the offspring of an African slave and a Hopi woman, had served under Vargas during the reconquest and in 1704 had fought the Faraone Apaches with the governor in the Sandia Mountains when the latter took ill and died. On Ulibarrí's expedition and for more than a decade afterward he commanded the Pueblo allies who accompanied Spanish expeditions across the frontier.[32]

Though Naranjo officially guided the expedition, Ulibarrí was also assisted by Apaches from La Jicarilla, a native rancheria in the Dry Cimarron Valley in present-day northeastern New Mexico.[33] From Santa Fe to the Dry Cimarron, many place names from colonial days remain in use today, making Ulibarrí's route simple to retrace. By the time he reached Colorado's eastern plains, however, his route is more difficult to trace because he bestowed names on geographical landmarks, most of which are no longer used.[34] Nonetheless Ulibarrí's expedition in 1706 is the earliest well-documented Spanish journey to El Cuartelejo, a route well-traveled by Spaniards since at least the 1640s.

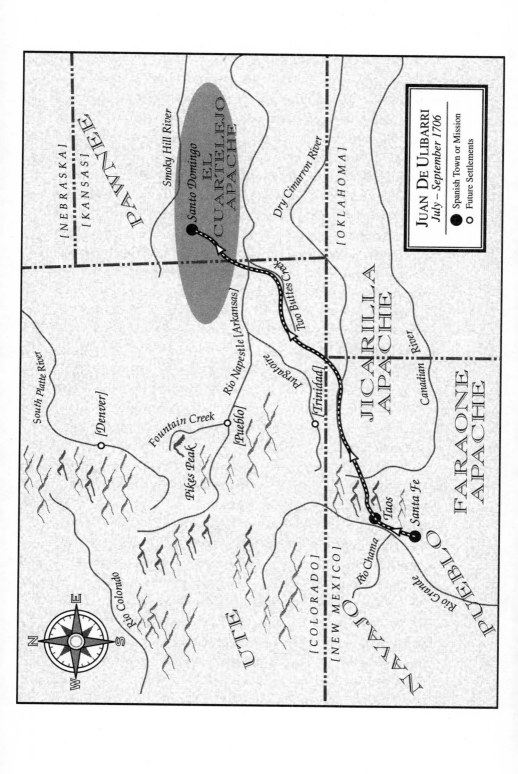

JUAN DE ULIBARRI
July – September 1706

● Spanish Town or Mission
○ Future Settlements

Santo Domingo

EL CUARTELEJO APACHE

PAWNEE

[NEBRASKA]
[KANSAS]

Smoky Hill River

Dry Cimarron River

[OKLAHOMA]

JICARILLA APACHE

Canadian River

FARAONE APACHE

Two Buttes Creek

Rio Napestle [Arkansas]

Purgatoire

[Trinidad]

[Pueblo]

Fountain Creek

Pikes Peak

South Platte River

[Denver]

Río Colorado

UTE

[COLORADO]
[NEW MEXICO]

Rio Chama

Taos

Santa Fe

Rio Grande

PUEBLO

NAVAJO

N E S W

On July 20, having crossed the Sangre de Cristos, Ulibarrí noted in his journal: "We happily succeeded in crossing the first part of the mountain and descended to a very delightful valley which they call La Cieneguilla, eight leagues distant from the pueblo [of Taos]." (The name La Cieneguilla today still refers to a little valley between the Sangre de Cristos and the Cimarron Range in northeastern New Mexico.) The next day, possibly on present-day Urraca Creek, Ulibarrí struck unfamiliar country. He noted in his journal: "To this [stream] I gave the name of Rio de San Francisco Xabier, under whose protection I was marching across unknown land, barbarously inhabited by innumerable heathens."[35]

Naranjo now guided Ulibarrí in a near-beeline for El Cuartelejo. The expedition crossed the Cimarron Range, then headed east across the headwaters of the Canadian River, which Ulibarrí called the Rio de Santa Catalina. On the Canadian River, or nearby, the expedition met Conexeros, Acho, and Rio Colorado bands of Apaches, who frequented Taos trade fairs. Ulibarrí noted "all the tribes were very happy that we Spaniards were coming into their lands and among their rancherias without doing them any injury." In keeping with the tenor of his mission, Ulibarrí distributed "much tobacco, knives, pinole, corn, biscuits, and ... suitable presents." What a change from a half-century earlier, when Spanish slave raids on the Apache were common!

Near northeastern New Mexico's Laughlin Peak, at a spot the Spaniards dubbed Ojo de Naranjo ("Naranjo's Spring"), Jicarilla, Flechas de Palo, and Carlanas Apaches came down from the Sierra Blanca, possibly Johnson Mesa near today's New Mexico–Colorado state line. These Indians also were understandably pleased to meet peaceful Spaniards. To demonstrate Spanish good will Ulibarrí entrusted worn-out horses to the Apaches, to be retrieved on his way home. Ulibarrí next crossed a modest saddle he named El Paso de Buena Vista ("The Pass of the Good View"), which provided a magnificent look back toward the Sangre de Cristos. He passed La Jicarilla, then present-day Capulin Volcano, and dropped into the Dry Cimarron Valley, which he modestly dubbed the Cañon de Ulibarrí. In his journal the Spanish captain admired his namesake canyon: "A fairly large pleasant stream runs its entire length, bordered with poplar groves, many prunes, a fruit resembling a cherry, with wild grapes." Penxayes Apaches approached with trepidation, but Ulibarrí assured them of his benign intentions. On July 26, east of Raton Mesa, Ulibarrí climbed out of the Dry Cimarron Valley, crossed today's New Mexico–Colorado state line, and skirted the eastern end of Mesa de Maya in southeastern Colorado. Here on the mesmerizing, broken plains, Naranjo had trouble finding his way.

The expedition picked up the headwaters of Two Buttes Creek, Ulibarrí's "stream of San Valentine," and camped on it. The next day, July 28, the expedition met a Penxaye man, woman, and three boys heading toward the Sierra Blanca to join their kinsmen. The Apaches warned Naranjo once again that the Utes and Comanches would soon attack the region. Off in the distance to the east, Ulibarrí saw "two little hills very much alike, sharp and pointed. I called them Las Tetas de Domínguez" ("The Breasts of Domínguez"). (These landmarks correspond to the Two Buttes in Prowers County, Colorado.) The next day the party was reassured to reach the large river that all the tribes called the Napestle, today's Arkansas River, close to the present Kansas border. Ulibarrí seemed to reflect Spanish or Pueblo knowledge of the river's headwaters north of Salida, Colorado, when he added: "It runs from north to east."[36] Ulibarrí looked upon the Napestle with covetous eyes: "[This river] is much more than four times as large as the Rio del Norte and bathes the best and broadest valley discovered in New Spain. It has many poplar trees and throughout the upper part most beautiful open stretches. The plain on our side is ... extremely fertile as is shown by the many plums, cherries, and wild grapes which there are on it. ... Having crossed happily from one side to the other, we passed the night."[37]

After crossing the river Naranjo warned Ulibarrí that "we would [now] undergo much suffering because there was no water," and "the trail ahead was only open land." Near the Colorado-Kansas state line north of the Arkansas the Spaniards tried to follow piles of grass that El Cuartelejo Apache set out for themselves as landmarks but they got lost anyway. Though the Pueblo allies became despondent, Ulibarrí wrote, "I, the sergeant-major, used all possible measures and placed myself under the patronage of Our Lady the Virgin Mary, conqueress of this kingdom and of the Glorious Patriarch, San Ignacio de Loyola, because of its being his happy day." Whether by divine intervention or otherwise, scouts located a distant spring and the news "filled the whole camp with joy."[38] Two weeks after leaving Taos the party reached the outskirts of El Cuartelejo's principal settlements. The Apaches too were overjoyed to meet peaceful Spaniards and had erected a cross atop a small hill to please their visitors. Ulibarrí met with the Apaches and a Picurís leader, Don Lorenzo. As more than one hundred forty, heavily armed men under Ulibarrí's command stood by, the Apaches pledged their cooperation.

The occasion called for solemn ceremony and Ulibarrí's campaign journal describes a fascinating scene that unfolded in the Apaches' settlement.

> Fray Domínguez de Aranz took in his hand the most holy cross and intoned the Te Deum Laudemus and the rest of the prayers and sang three times the hymn in praise of the sacrament. After these holy ceremonies were over, the royal ensign Don Francisco de Valdés drew his sword, and I, after making a note of the events of the day and the hour on which we arrived, said in a clear, intelligible voice: "Knights, Companions and Friends: Let the broad

new province of San Luis and the great settlement of Santa Domingo of El Cuartelejo be pacified by the arms of us who are the vassals of our monarch, king and natural lord, Don Philip V— may he live forever." The royal ensign said: "Is there anyone to contradict?" All responded, "No." Then he said, "Long live the king! Long live the king! Long live the king!" and cutting the air in all four directions with his sword the ensign signaled for the discharge of the guns. After throwing up our hats and making other signs of rejoicing, the ceremony came to an end.

Though the Apaches cooperated in rounding up all Picurís Indians, Ulibarrí diplomatically traded a dozen footsore horses to a chief to secure five Tewa and Tanos Indians. Gathering the scores of Picurís involved sending Spanish detachments to two other rancherias, one of them forty leagues distant. Ulibarrí waited five days for his men to return.[39] During this time Ulibarrí questioned his Apache hosts, who wore "very old" crosses, medals, and rosaries. How had they obtained these Spanish items and why did they wear them? Ulibarrí asked. The Apaches replied that for many years they had traded with the Spaniards.[40] When the Apaches fought their enemies and became tired, "they remember the great Captain of the Spaniards who is in the heavens and then their weariness leaves them and they feel refreshed." Ulibarrí also noted in his journal the prospects for settlement in this region. "Because of the fertility of the land, the docility of the people, and the abundance of herds of buffalo, and other game, the propagation of our holy Catholic faith could be advanced very much," he wrote.[41]

The Apaches described five large rivers found north and east of El Cuartelejo where "other Spaniards" lived, from whom the Apache obtained iron implements like hatchets, swords, even muskets. When Ulibarrí asked about "the seas to the north and east," perhaps hinting at the long-sought Strait of Anián or dim rumors of the Great Lakes, the Apaches replied that they knew of those seas only by hearsay, but that they weren't far. The Apaches in turn asked Ulibarrí for help against the French and Comanches and against the Pawnees to the north. They told Ulibarrí that only days prior to his arrival they had killed a Frenchman and his wife and confiscated a rifle during an aborted French-Pawnee attack on El Cuartelejo. Ulibarrí secured the French rifle; he needed evidence to bolster the shocking news in his report to the governor. Mid-August found Ulibarrí departing El Cuartelejo with three score of rescued Pueblo Indians in tow, after giving the "staff of command" to one Apache he deemed worthy.

The day after Ulibarrí's departure from El Cuartelejo, the expedition got a taste of high plains weather. "This evening we had the greatest of storms, rain, wind, thunder, and lightning, that one can imagine," Ulibarrí noted. "We put ourselves under the protection of the Queen of the Angels, the most holy Mary, because it was the eve of her Glorious Acceptation, who came to our rescue like a mother with serenity and peace." The next day the weather relented, and the men killed and butchered six buffalo. Ulibarrí arrived back at Santa Fe on September 2, having returned the Picurís and others to their pueblos.

The Spaniards had indeed reclaimed New Mexico and established more humane policies toward the Pueblo Indians along the Rio del Norte. They had reasserted their presence on the northern frontier among the Navajos, Utes, and Apaches. Now at the start of the eighteenth century they faced a new challenge. Using Colorado's eastern plains as their base, mounted Comanches made daring, deadly raids on settled New Mexico for horses, livestock, and human captives. Beyond the Comanches on the far northeastern frontier lurked Frenchmen whose proximity awakened old fears.

French and Comanche Threats
1682-1752

T HE RIVALRY BETWEEN Spain and France naturally extended to the New World, where it ebbed and flowed for centuries. That contest often involved winning the allegiance of native peoples, and the two nations pursued that fundamental strategy in distinctly different ways. Spain sought dominion over the continental interior by maintaining far-flung settlements such as New Mexico, from which it could conduct frontier diplomacy. Spaniards sought to create dependency in nearby tribes through the peaceful trade of nonlethal goods and to enlist friendly tribes against their mutual enemies. In contrast, French traders sought to gain native alliances through an unfettered trade in guns, often to New Mexico's neighbors. The situation was ripe for confrontation. A French presence in the Mississippi Valley in the first half of the eighteenth century had the practical effect of drawing Spanish expeditions to cross the high plains to discern the enemy's intent.

This New World contest had a long history. France immediately disputed Spain's claim to the Americas after Pope Alexander VI divided the new lands between Spain and Portugal late in the fifteenth century, and sent expeditions overseas to America. In the New World, Spain and France engaged in war and simple piracy in the West Indies, in Florida, along the eastern seaboard, and on the high seas. In 1559 the treaty of Cateau-Cambresis established a pragmatic premise: clashes on the high seas should not imperil peace on the European continent. "This paradox of peace at home and war in America lasted for two centuries," noted the late Henri Folmer, foremost student of this New World rivalry.[1] French successes in the 1620s–1640s in taking islands in the West Indies advanced their ambitions in the Gulf of Mexico, a thrust that would reverberate on the frontier of landlocked New Mexico.[2]

Events quickened as the seventeenth century wore on. By 1678 René-Robert Cavalier, sieur de la Salle, set out to find the mouth of the Mississippi River and establish a French harbor that could provide a staging ground for an invasion of Mexico. That same year, a notorious former governor of New Mexico, Don Diego Dionisio de Peñalosa Briceno y Berdugo, reached Paris. Don Diego had emigrated to avoid the Inquisition's review of his venal governorship in New Mexico in 1661–1664. At the French royal court he proposed to conquer the "kingdoms" of Teguayo and Quivira—those mythical lands in the Colorado region—by attacking from the Great Lakes. Or, he suggested desperately, he would attack the Spaniards' Mexican coastal province of New Biscaye and seize its mines. The French took the turncoat Peñalosa with a grain of salt; his motives were suspect and his ideas were hardly novel. French ambitions in the last quarter of the seventeenth century focused, after all, on nothing less than the conquest of New Spain.

To further that end La Salle sought and found the mouth of the Mississippi in 1682. A later effort to establish a colony foundered in 1687 at a lonely outpost on Matagorda Bay on the Texas coast. It was here that La Salle's men mutinied and murdered him. Spanish officials were unaware of La Salle's fate, but learned of his intentions, which fueled their anxieties for decades. In 1689 a Spanish expedition under Alonzo de Leon finally located La Salle's forlorn fort and rescued several Frenchmen, including a teenager named Jean L'Archévèque, who eventually settled in

New Mexico. Meanwhile, in 1686, Frenchman Henri Tonti had descended the Mississippi from the Illinois River in a failed attempt to find La Salle. Upon his return upriver, Tonti established a French post at the mouth of the Arkansas River (the Spaniards' Rio Napestle), the first French settlement west of the Mississippi. Reports even reached New Mexico governor Don Diego de Vargas in 1695, via the Apaches, that Frenchmen were ascending the Rio Napestle in force.

When the French erected forts at Biloxi Bay near the mouth of the Mississippi in 1699, France finally had a foothold in Louisiana. The ascent of a Frenchman, Phillip D'Anjou, to the Spanish throne in 1700 (he became Felipé V of Spain) nurtured a French presence in the Gulf of Mexico. This peaceful lull in Franco-Spanish relations lasted only so long as the two nations were allied against England in the War of the Spanish Succession.[3] Peace between Spain and England in 1714, however, rekindled Franco-Spanish rivalries west of the Mississippi. So when Juan de Ulibarrí in 1706 learned at El Cuartelejo about French movements on New Mexico's frontier, the news once again provoked paranoia about foreign encroachment. But based upon precarious settlements such as New Mexico, Spain's claims always far outstripped its ability to hold them. Paranoia proved to be the partner of such grandiose claims.

From settlements like New Mexico, Spanish officials sought peaceful trade and alliances with the *indios barbaros* as a buffer against French encroachment. In that respect the unfettered French traders held an advantage, for they would trade anything to gain influence with frontier tribes. Spanish policy in contrast forbade trading weapons and horses to the indios barbaros. The frontier trade that emanated from New Mexico chiefly dealt in the exchange of iron implements and produce for buffalo meat, furs, and hides. New Mexicans—Spaniards, Pueblos, mestizos, or *genízaros*—

traveled up the Rio del Norte to Ute country for this trade, or to the plains. Despite prohibitions, Spaniards also traded horses, guns, and slaves. In December 1712 this traffic prompted Governor Juan Ignacio Flores Mogollón to issue an *auto*, or order, that specifically prohibited settlers from "visiting the ranches of the wild Indians for the purposes of barter and trade."[4]

West of the Mississippi, Frenchmen kept busy supplying firearms, powder, lead, and other war-making tools to the region's tribes. Early in the eighteenth century French traders extended their influence up the Platte, Arkansas, and Red rivers to the wide prairies that stretched across New Mexico's northeastern frontier. French guns emboldened the Pawnees, Comanches, and others, who in turn pressed down upon the Apaches on New Mexico's perimeter. A few documented French movements in the continental interior fueled rumors that reached New Mexico in this period. In 1713 French trader St. Denis founded Natchitoches on the Red River of present-day Texas, and in 1714 he appeared at the Spanish presidio of San Juan Bautista two hundred miles upriver from the Rio del Norte's mouth. These movements propelled Spanish efforts at colonizing Texas.

Frenchman Etienne Bourgmond reached the Platte in 1714 and within three years had gained a Pawnee alliance and forged relationships with other Indian tribes along the Platte and Kansas rivers, just beyond New Mexico's northeastern frontier. Word of these activities reached Santa Fe via intervening tribes and from Spanish and Pueblo traders who reached the high plains for illicit trade. In 1719 the viceroy of Mexico, Marquis de Valero, was alarmed to hear of a French detachment said to be marching west from the Red River (of Texas) against New Mexico. He ordered New Mexico's governor Antonio Valverde y Cosío to find out "what manner of living [the French] pursued, how many there were and other particulars."[5] Valero told Valverde that "it is necessary to hold this nation" at bay, and that an alliance with the plains Apaches "could inflict considerable damage on the French and block their evil designs."[6]

Valverde, in simple defense of his own province, also had reason to seek the whereabouts and designs of the Utes and Comanches, who in alliance now attacked the province in ferocious raids. When Comanches first visited Taos in 1705 they were already in possession of horses, supreme equestrian skills, and a reputation for fierceness. "Comanches counted themselves as numerous as the stars," writes historian Elizabeth John. "They were a vast set of proud individuals, each man entitled to rise to leadership on the basis of his demonstrated capacities in war, and none bound to accept any authority higher than himself expect by his own choice."[7] As with other frontier tribes, this lack of a hierarchical structure would hamper Spanish diplomacy. The Comanches were said to possess "short legs, squat, ungainly figures, and [an] awkward gait afoot." Yet these fearsome warriors exhibited "graceful mastery astride, when man and horse seemed like one sentient being."[8]

The Utes' alliance with the Comanches about the turn of the century—and their subsequent parting of the ways with the Spaniards—led to audacious, dual attacks upon New Mexico's northern settlements. The autonomy of Comanche bands made the situation harrowing. Peace with one band did not preclude conflict with another. During the administration of Governor Don Joseph Chacón Medina Salazar y Villaseñor, Marqués de las Peñuelas (1707–1712), for instance, the Spaniards signed a peace treaty with one Comanche division that facilitated trade. In late summer 1716, however, a Comanche attack on Taos sent Captain Crístobal de la Serna and a hastily assembled army thirty leagues, or nearly one hundred miles, north of Santa Fe in pursuit. The Spaniards killed many warriors and captured the rest, who were sold into slavery down the Camino Real. If Captain la Serna indeed traveled thirty leagues north of Santa Fe, he would have reached the lower San Luis Valley in the vicinity of today's New Mexico–Colorado state line.[9]

Comanche attacks in 1718 on Jicarilla Apache settlements east of the Sangre de Cristos sent the Apaches into Taos for protection. Friar Juan de la Cruz at Taos's mission wrote to the viceroy and relayed the Apaches' concerns and their sudden desire for baptism. Later that year Comanches descended upon Taos and Cochiti pueblos, killing settlers and Indians. Utes were said to have taken part, too. Despite the Spaniards' expanding geographic knowledge of their northern frontier, Comanche pressures kept actual settlement from expanding. The frontier opened like an abyss just beyond the province's last rancho. The Spaniards had to take the offensive. August 1719 found Governor Valverde, presidial leaders, and settlers gathered in a council of war at Santa Fe. The council determined that for the sake of survival "the military forces should set out to curb the boldness of the enemy."[10]

Governor Valverde, age forty-eight when he traveled New Mexico's northeastern frontier, was a native of Castile, Spain. He must have arrived in the New World at a young age, for at twenty-one he joined the reconquest under Vargas. By 1696 he was an officer at the Santa Fe presidio, and led troops in pursuit of the rebellious Picurís that year. Afterward he returned to El Paso del Norte on the lower Rio Grande, settled, and kept a vineyard. Prior to his appointment to two terms as governor of New Mexico in 1717–1722, he had acquired military experience and business acumen.

Valverde mustered his forces at Taos in mid-September 1719. He led sixty presidials, forty militia, and five hundred allied Pueblo warriors. José Naranjo would guide this army. The expedition later was joined by an additional two hundred Jicarilla Apaches. The expedition's *cavallada* numbered more than a thousand. The presidials were well armed. Of the militia, Valverde wrote in his journal: "To these, on account of the impoverished condition of some, it was necessary to supply powder and balls and distribute among them ten leather jackets. ... [The governor] ordered divided among them a quantity of pinole, and likewise seventy-five horses and mules, all his own."[11]

Governor Valverde's journal opens a window onto the country he passed through, its Indians, flora and fauna, and incidents of travel. This account is spiced with minutiae: as a former vintner, Valverde traveled in style with a few casks of wine, "a small keg of very rich spiritous brandy," glasses, silverware, and melon preserves for celebrating the ubiquitous saints' days.[12] The governor and the bulk of his Spanish presidials and militia rode in the vanguard. A string of pack animals followed, guarded by well-armed men. Pueblo warriors came next, perhaps grouped by pueblo affiliation. A small company of presidials brought up the rear. Scouts rode ahead and to the sides, looking for water, buffalo, campsites, and the enemy.

The distinctions observed between members of the expedition are not known beyond the broad categories of officers, settlers, and Pueblo Indians. Typically, Spaniards and natives camped separately. But a few contemporary social classes might have created further distinctions, for bloodlines no longer were pure. Spaniards born in Spain, referred to as *peninsulares,* topped the social order. Those born in America, called *criollos,* ranked second. Spanish settlers in New Mexico who paid taxes were known as *vecinos.* Presumably, the foregoing had no trace of Indian or black blood, and considered themselves above others. Mestizos (mixed bloods), genízaros, and natives came next in the pecking order. In the most menial role came slaves, either Africans who had been brought by way of the Caribbean and Mexico, or captives from the tribes on New Mexico's frontier.[13]

Valverde's army stretched out over a half-mile of trail. The expedition left Taos on September 20 and rode eight leagues up and over the Sangre de Cristo Mountains "through painful mountain trails, forest, and underbrush," Valverde noted. "The march was attended with much suffering."[14] Valverde and his men continued on to La Cieneguilla, today's Moreno Valley, New Mexico. As he descended the eastern slopes of the Sangre de Cristos to reach the "stream of San Joseph," possibly today's Rayado Creek in northeastern New Mexico, the governor found the trail marked by stones. Obviously this pass over the Sangre de Cristos (at Apache Pass, east of Taos Pueblo) saw regular traffic. Valverde's scouts located a small Apache settlement, whose inhabitants told José Naranjo they had endured repeated Comanche assaults. Valverde declared he would end the raids, and made gifts of tobacco and food, including that effective and seemingly ubiquitous tool of diplomacy—chocolate.

Further east a band of Jicarilla Apaches approached with similar complaints about Comanches and offered to join in chastising the enemy. When the Spaniards came upon the Apaches' irrigated fields of corn, beans, and squash, Valverde (as Vargas before him) forbid his men from pillaging. The Spanish governor sought to reward his friends and punish only his enemies. As Valverde moved on, Sierra Blanca Apaches appeared. Their chief, Carlana, recounted to Valverde his own concerns about Ute and Comanche raids. The Spanish expedition reached the Apaches' Rio Colorado, which Valverde named Rio Nuestra Señora del Rosario— probably today's upper Canadian River. Five days after leaving Taos, the men crossed north over a difficult sierra at today's Raton Pass, and camped near present-day Trinidad. "He crossed a mountain ridge with so many forests, ravines, canyons, and narrow places that it was necessary that day to divide the cavalry into ten groups to get it over such a difficult trail," Valverde's amanuensis noted. "In this the soldiers worked considerably in order not to lose many beasts. With which care and divine favor intervening, they succeeded in bringing the horseherd safely as far as the Rio de las Animas, a name his lordship gave it, where the camp was placed thankfully, because the spot was pleasing."[15]

Although Valverde's amanuensis implies that his governor named the Rio de las Animas, the reference is mysterious. The full name given by the Spaniards to this river—El Rio de las Animas Perdidas en Purgatorio, "The River of Lost Souls in Purgatory"— does not appear in Valverde's journal, and would seem to predate his abbreviated version. He eloquently described its attractions and vexations. "The river was lined with luxuriant foliage and had considerable good water," Valverde noted in his journal. "The many poplars and elders found furnished a supply of wood with which [the men] could warm themselves because they suffered this day from great cold, for the north wind blew with such biting sharpness all had arrived on the spot numb."[16]

The next two days brought snow and rain and the army remained in camp. Valverde distributed extra rations to certain men who, in crossing the Raton Mesa, "were sick from an attack of an herb called ivy, caused strangely by lying down upon it or being near it. Those affected swelled up." The governor, wishing to help, "ordered Antonio Durán Armijo, a barber by trade who had some knowledge of blood letting, to attend and assist them."[17] That day Chief Carlana and scores of Sierra Blanca Apaches joined the Spanish camp. Later, painted with white or red paint, they "danced according to their custom." The following day the weather cleared, and the expedition moved on to an arroyo with little water, probably the Apishipa River near present-day Aguilar, Colorado. Carlana sent out scouts. On September 29 the men observed mass, then moved north to the Rio de San Miguel, probably today's Rio Cucharas near Walsenburg, which cut "a very broad and pleasing valley." Valverde noted in his journal: "In the woods some deer were caught by the Indians who, surrounding them, drove them into camp, at which there was great glee and shouting." Though Valverde's precise itinerary can be debated, there's no doubt he traversed Colorado's Front Range from south to north. For in one passage the governor's amanuensis confirms their basic position: "They always followed the route to the north, leaving a high sierra on the west, with much level ground stretching towards the east."[18]

Chief Carlana's scouts returned to report sign of Comanches to the north, whereupon Valverde ordered the sheep butchered and dressed to expedite his army's movements in preparation for battle. As this enormous army reached a nearby confluence (possibly the Greenhorn and St. Charles rivers) on October 2, however, Valverde's journal reflected no sign of impending combat. "It was leafy here and the command took a nap, enjoying the coolness and shade of the many poplars and deep woods. While they were in this happy state, a bear came out of the thicket and threw the entire camp into an uproar. The people took great delight in teasing it for some time until they killed it." Valverde ordered the march to begin late that afternoon so that the enemy might not see the dust that attended the army's movements. The lengthy procession reached the Rio Napestle that night. Valverde named it Rio de San Antonio, perhaps unaware of its traditional name. "It is an admirable stream much resembling the Del Norte because of its large volume of water and broad, spacious meadows, filled with poplars," Valverde noted.[19]

The next day Apache scouts reported more tracks "on the road ... which goes to the Teguas [Tewas]," the peoples who inhabited the northern pueblos on the Rio del Norte.[20] The men rode northeast to the next stream, which they called El Rio de San Francisco, probably today's Fountain Creek. "Here they hunted and caught many deer and a lot of good fat prairie hens with which they made very delicious tamales," Valverde noted. After supper the governor, Friar Juan del Pino, and certain officers retired to the governor's tent for a libation. "They celebrated together ... the eve of the glorious patriarch San Francisco, having ordered out a small keg of rich spiritous brandy made at the Pass of the Rio del Norte of the governor's own vintage," wrote Valverde's amanuensis. The scribe added: "It was of such good flavor, taste and quality and though vinted without the carefulness with which other wines are made, that that of Castile does not surpass it."[21]

Crossing Fountain Creek on October 4 the expedition ascended the stream's east bank four leagues and camped, probably near present-day Buttes, Colorado. "It is a very cheerful spot, with a beautiful view and excellent springs and many thick poplar groves," Valverde noted. "On the left hand [facing north], about three leagues away, there is a range of mountains and on the right, a very extensive plain in the distance. On this day a mountain lion and a wildcat were killed. At about sunset some Indians came in, running from a bear which plunged into the middle of the camp, throwing the people into confusion. With great shouting and uproar, they killed him with many spear thrusts and arrows. His strength and size were so formidable that the governor was impelled to go with the chaplain to view it."[22] This of course was *ursa blanca*, the white bear, or grizzly, which ruled the region's mountains and plains.

In the next few days the expedition veered away from the mountains, across the southern flank of today's Black Forest Divide, northeast of present-day Colorado Springs. The expedition encountered another bear, probably on the head of Big Sandy Creek. This, too, was a grizzly.

On this day before the halt a bear was met. It was larger than the preceding ones, for its size and height were probably greater than a donkey. One of the soldiers went out and put a spear into him up to the middle of the shaft. The brute, turning around, seized the lance and grasped the horse by the hocks. At the same time another soldier went to the rescue and gave the bear another spear thrust. The bear, seizing the horse by the tail, held him down and clawing viciously, tore a piece of flesh off the rump. Having tied the bear up finally, they finished killing him. The soldiers who were bringing up the rear guard of the cavalry met a female and two cubs, which they also killed.[23]

The expedition moved farther east and ran down a few buffalo. Apache scouts arrived and reported fresh sign of a Comanche camp. Valverde took the precaution of forbidding the men to attack a large herd of buffalo, lest it give them away. On October 10, three weeks after departing settled New Mexico, the governor again sent out scouts to track the Comanches as "he had a great desire to punish their insolence" with the "rigor of the arms of the Spaniards, whose kindness and good nature they had abused." The scouts included two Apache, two Taos, and two Picurís Indians. "All these were quite experienced because of the long time that they wandered among the heathens, for as apostates they fled during the rebellion which they had," Valverde noted.[24] Evidently Picurís who had rebelled in 1696 and been rescued by Ulibarrí in 1706 from El Cuartelejo accompanied Valverde's expedition.

Chief Carlana grew impatient for battle. The expedition turned south and followed a dry tributary to the Napestle. En route a "furious hurricane" forced them into tents, "which it seemed would be uprooted." A taste of the high plains' fury! When scouts reported signs of the enemy to the northeast, Valverde suggested they pursue, but the Apache, Carlana, and the scout, Naranjo, cautioned against it. The trail would be bone-dry, they argued. The moment called for a council of war. Valverde declared himself ready to press on, despite the hardships, but left the decision to his men. The result was predictable. The rank and file had ridden far from home, without pay, for nearly a month. Their families, fields, and flocks lay many leagues behind them. They voted to return to New Mexico, ostensibly for fear of losing the province's best horses in winter weather. "This his lordship well knew, for he was familiar with the rigor of the snow and cold weather, which in these lands is so extreme that it benumbs and annihilates," Valverde's journal noted. He tossed in a few more justifications for his return, just for the record. "To fulfill his obligation in the royal service—since no other person would have penetrated through so many and such unknown lands, never before seen or discovered by the Spaniards, as those his lordship has explored in the present campaign—he has demonstrated his great zeal in the service of his majesty. For these reasons, it appeared that his lordship should suspend following the enemy and retire with his army to the presidio in the center of the kingdom."[25]

That night El Cuartelejo Apaches arrived in camp and reported that their kinsmen were ascending the Napestle to see Valverde. Two days later the expedition reached the Napestle (probably east of Las Animas, Colorado), where "there were great herds of bison so that in the distance they looked like rolling hills."[26]

Three days passed as Valverde awaited the El Cuartelejo Apaches, whom he wished to befriend. When the Apaches assembled one thousand strong on the opposite bank, Valverde and a few officers crossed the Napestle to join them. In exchange for his demonstration of concern the Spanish governor received some useful news of his other enemies, the French. "The French have built two pueblos, each of which is as large as that of Taos," Valverde's account reads. "In them they live together with the said Pawnees and Jumanos Indians, to whom they have given long guns which they have taught them to shoot. ... They also carry some small guns suspended from their belts. All the enemy ... have done [the Apaches] much damage in taking away their lands and that each day they are coming closer. The French have three other settlements on the other side of the large river, and ... from these they bring arms."[27]

Valverde reassured the Apaches that he would assist them and made certain his amanuensis noted this courageous promise in his journal. "He would expel the French and the [Indian] nations with which they were confederated, in order that they could live securely on their land," Valverde's amanuensis noted, admiringly. "He would expel the French from it as the lands belong only to the majesty of our king and lord, Don Philip V (may God guard him many years). The others, he said, were thieves and intruders. ... They would see that the Spaniards were coming with their power and strength to attack and drive the French out of the land and destroy their pueblos and villages." With these high-flown assurances, Valverde gathered his men and rode home to New Mexico "along the Rio Napestle, on which they had been going." Because the remainder of this campaign journal is missing, the return route remains unknown. Due to the difficulty of crossing the Raton Mesa, Valverde may have ridden up the Huerfano River and over Sangre de Cristo Pass to reach the upper Rio del Norte. In any case he arrived back at Santa Fe in mid- or late November, having traveled three hundred leagues, or about eight hundred miles.[28]

Valverde's journey, despite its holiday air and lack of success against the Utes and Comanches, resulted in a detailed record of numerous encounters with settled Apache bands, grizzly bears, buffaloes, and autumn storms—an intriguing picture of Colorado early in the eighteenth century.

Even as Valverde traipsed along the Front Range, learning alarming news about French "pueblos" on the Platte River, war erupted on the Continent. The war of the Quadruple Alliance pitted Spain against France, England, Holland, and Austria over Spanish forays in Italy. With Spain focused on Italy, France and

England believed Spain's New World colonies might be vulnerable. Spanish officials, for their part, believed this to be an ideal chance to clear New Spain's northern frontier of all foreigners. When Viceroy Valero heard from Valverde about French posts on the Platte, he ordered the governor to fortify El Cuartelejo and find the French posts. Valverde responded that "the purpose of the enemy appears [to be] to penetrate little by little into the land." Further, the governor claimed, "I am prepared . . . to attend to the matter personally, or my lieutenant-general will do so, that is, the making of a reconnaissance of the enemy."[29] Valverde requested additional materiel and men.

The viceroy had also received shocking reports from the governor of Nueva Vizcaya on New Mexico's southern flank that thousands of French troops were poised to attack New Mexico. In January 1720 Viceroy Valero and his council decided that Governor Valverde should establish a Spanish outpost at El Cuartelejo, and bolster the Apache presence in the region, as a buffer against the French. Spanish missions and presidios in Texas were given similar instructions. In a reflection of Mexico City's distance from the realities of New Mexico's frontier, Viceroy Valero suggested manning a presidio at El Cuartelejo with a score of men. The viceroy didn't grasp that New Mexico's northeastern frontier stretched from the Front Range of the Rockies to the Mississippi River, an arc of nearly a thousand miles. Twenty Spanish soldiers on El Cuartelejo's wind-scoured plains could never counter a French "invasion," let alone withstand an attack by a modest band of any Plains tribe.

Valverde wrote the viceroy in May to say that his lieutenant governor, Don Pedro de Villasur, would lead another expedition to the plains in search of the French. He added that the Apache rancheria El Cuartelejo was not suitable for a post—too exposed to defend and lacked water and wood. Valverde proposed instead that fifty soldiers fortify a site in La Jicarilla, the tablelands of Raton Mesa on today's Colorado–New Mexico state line. At least that location was close enough to New Mexico's settlements to be bolstered in an emergency.[30]

Don Pedro de Villasur had been lieutenant governor for at least five years and commanded the Santa Fe garrison, though little is known about his practical military experience. Villasur and his men departed Santa Fe in July 1720 with forty-two soldiers, three militia, and sixty Pueblo warriors. The faithful José Naranjo again served as guide and interpreter. Jean l'Archévèque, now known in the Spanish record as Juan Archibeque, joined as an interpreter, should Frenchmen be encountered. Captain Crístobal de la Serna joined, as did Alonso Rael de Aguilar, who had served Vargas and Ulibarrí as amanuensis. Fray Juan Mínguez accompanied the expedition as well. In the interests of diplomacy Villasur brought corn, knives, sombreros, and "half a muleload of tobacco" to distribute as gifts to the native he encountered.[31] The lieutenant governor followed Valverde's example and for his personal use brought silver platters, cups, and silverware. For official reasons he carried an inkhorn, paper, and quills. Because only a fragment of Villasur's diary has been recovered, his route can only be conjectured. But his mission required that he first seek El Cuartelejo to confirm a Spanish-Apache allegiance. After regrouping there he would sweep the frontier. With Naranjo guiding the expedition, it might have taken a route to El Cuartelejo similar to that used by Ulibarrí fourteen years earlier.

En route to El Cuartelejo Villasur made gifts to La Jicarilla and Carlana Apaches. From El Cuartelejo the Spaniards headed northeast to find the rumored French pueblos. Villasur's journey to El Cuartelejo probably took the customary two weeks from Taos. The next leg of his journey required an equivalent distance further north and east, possibly along a route that anthropologist

Donald Blakeslee has dubbed the Pawnee Trail. Villasur crossed the Smoky Hill and Republican rivers of today's eastern Colorado, and on August 6 he reached the "Rio Jesus Maria," today's Platte River, and was probably east of Kearney, Nebraska. Villasur had traveled by his own measure three hundred leagues, although the actual distance appears closer to two hundred. In any case, hundreds of leagues and a month from home, the Spaniards had found no sign of Frenchmen, so Villasur called for a council of war. The council decided to seek the Pawnees and ask about nearby Frenchmen.

Villasur next crossed the Platte, where he noted: "The large number of islands which are in this river makes navigation with pirogues absolutely impracticable."[32] He sent scouts ahead. On August 8 Villasur crossed another stream, probably the Loup River. The next day scouts returned to report a small Pawnee band ahead performing a dance. An exiled Pawnee servant of Captain la Serna's attempted to open a parlay, but the Pawnees' hostility rebuffed him. The next day, August 10, Villasur's men moved east of the Loup-Platte confluence and assembled on the Platte's north bank, opposite the Pawnees. Captain la Serna once again sent his Pawnee servant across the shallow stream to establish the Spaniards' good will. "The lieutenant-general instructed him to tell his nation that he was coming to see them and without any intention of causing them the least injury," Villasur noted in his journal. "Accordingly, they could treat with us in all security concerning the peace and good relationship which was and ought to be between us and them, as brothers and subjects of the same king. The lieutenant-general gave some tobacco to the savage [Pawnee servant] to take to them, which is the reasoning ordinarily used at these conversations."[33] There ends a three-centuries-old fragment of Villasur's diary. According to later testimony the situation quickly unraveled.

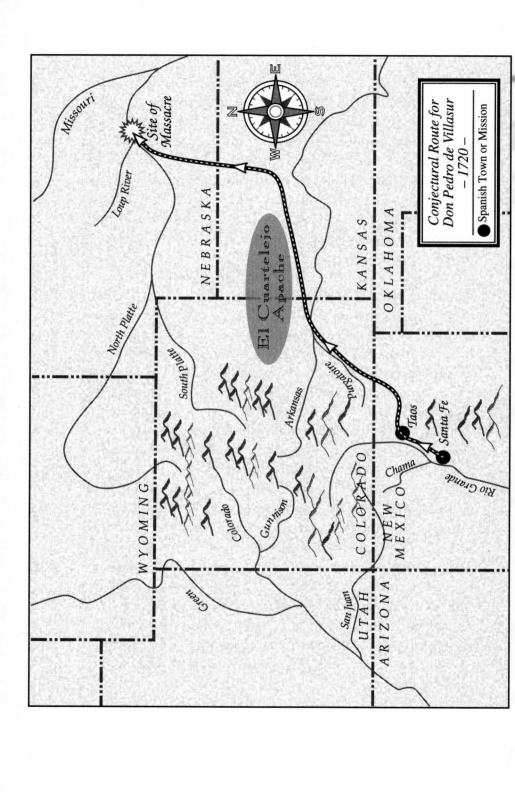

Conjectural Route for
Don Pedro de Villasur
– 1720 –
● Spanish Town or Mission

The next day the Pawnee servant reappeared on the riverbank opposite the Spanish camp and reported that the Pawnees were well disposed. He couldn't learn about the French, however, and his hosts would not let him leave. The Spaniards interpreted that as a hostile act, and the expedition returned to the confluence of the Loup and Platte to camp on a spit between the two rivers. That night several men heard "the barking of a dog and the noise of people ... crossing the river." Villasur commanded his guards to be vigilant. Scouts reported nothing amiss. The next morning, August 13, at daybreak, the Spaniards began to break camp. Men packed baggage and readied the cavallada for loading. Villasur may have been dressing in his tent. "At this very moment a horde of men who were in ambush near them attacked both with guns and arrows and wrought ... havoc," according to testimony given six years later by survivor Alonso Rael de Aguilar. "Although our men defended themselves, considering that they were few in regard to that multitude, it was impossible to hold out. While those who were mounted were sufficient to make that host retreat, the rest were unable to aid, as they were already dead. Those who remained fled, rescuing only the witness, who had nine wounds of great severity. The Indians also cut off a braid of his hair."[34]

According to the testimony of Villasur's amanuensis, Felipe Tamariz, who also survived: "At the time when the soldiers were exchanging horses, an ambush of some five hundred enemies fell upon them with firearms, lances, and arrows. The nearby discharge of the fusillade threw the horseherd into a stampede." Tamariz did not recognize his attackers. He was guarding the horse herd, and so was able to overtake it, but those on horseback "found themselves immediately attacked by a great number of enemies, whom they repulsed three times. The number quickly grew so great that they could not resist longer than to free three of their companions who, badly wounded, had escaped from those in the camp."[35]

From the foregoing descriptions and other evidence, this devastating attack on Villasur's expedition may be reconstructed a bit more fully. Because the Spaniards camped on the spit between two streams, they could be nearly surrounded by attackers crossing the two rivers. Many New Mexicans were engaged in packing and loading baggage near the horse herd that they kept some distance from the main camp, and thus could not wield their rifles. Large numbers of Pawnee and Oto Indians apparently attacked on foot, firing bows and possibly rifles and wielding hatchets and swords. Villasur emerged from his tent only to be struck down by arrows. Jean de l'Archévèque, Naranjo, and most of the Spanish officers died making a valiant defense. Some formed a final circle in the midst of camp and, back to back, fought to the death. Fray Mínguez sustained fatal wounds as he administered last rites to the fallen.[36] Those men nearest the horse herd mounted and rescued several wounded comrades, but their assailants' sheer numbers caused them to retreat. Most Spaniards on the expedition already stared lifelessly at the early morning sky.

Thirty-four soldiers and a dozen Pueblo allies died in this debacle. Only eleven soldiers escaped with a few dozen Pueblo warriors. It is believed that the Pawnees and Otos probably stripped the dead of useful items.[37] The survivors fled with the remaining horse herd back to El Cuartelejo, then Santa Fe, with news of the massacre. Nearly all the expedition's equipment, baggage, and papers lay scattered across a remote prairie, hundreds of leagues beyond settled New Mexico. A Pawnee or Oto warrior apparently retrieved a single page from the Spaniards' journal, which reached a French post and, eventually, archives in Paris. Two centuries later scholars discovered it there and translated and published the document.

New Mexico's lieutenant governor and one-third of the province's best soldiers had been killed hundreds of leagues from home, a devastating loss to New Spain's northernmost province. Governor Valverde, under attack for the loss, insisted that Frenchmen had instigated the massacre—though that contradicted survivors' testimony. More likely, the Pawnees had made a preemptive strike against a large party of well-armed strangers who had suddenly appeared dangerously close to their homes. The severity of the loss propelled a crossfire of accusations. Valverde's enemies faulted him for not pressing his mission in 1719, for not leading the tragic expedition of 1720, and for sending an inexperienced subordinate to his death. Valverde responded that Villasur was a veteran campaigner and had New Mexico's best men with him who, nonetheless, had ill-served their leader. Valverde retired to El Paso in 1722 for four years, but returned to Santa Fe in 1726 to defend himself at trial. He won exoneration, but paid fifty pesos to charity and one hundred fifty pesos to missions at Junta de los Rios, in the name of his fallen countrymen.

When the French Company of the Indies learned of the Pawnee attack on Villasur's expedition, it feared Spanish revenge. But the French also would be ready should peace prevail. So fur trader Etienne Veniard de Bourgmond ascended the Missouri River in 1724 to establish a post that could launch a trade route to Spanish New Mexico. He did not reach his goal.

The tragic story of Villasur's ill-fated expedition eventually led to the creation of a hide painting depicting the massacre. Today this is considered one of the Spanish colonial era's most intriguing artifacts. Charles Bennett of the Museum of New Mexico has called this artifact "the most graphic period illustration of the eighteenth-century rivalry between Spain and France in North America."[38] The painting fills a seventeen-by-four-foot hide canvas. The artist's perspective looks south toward the confluence of the Platte and Loup rivers; two rivers run right to left and join together. Streams of attackers cross the river, left to right, to Villasur's camp on the spit. In the center a ring of Spanish defenders in broad-brimmed hats stand back-to-back, under attack by overwhelming numbers. In the foreground Pedro de Villasur, in blue shirt, lies mortally wounded outside his tent, blood trickling from a corner of his mouth. On the right dark-skinned José Naranjo battles his enemies with sword raised. The balding Fray Mínguez, in blue smock, is wounded by many arrows as he ministers to the dying. On the far right of the huge canvas, Pueblo Indians rally the Spaniards' horse herd.

That portion of the painting is thought to be a relatively accurate window onto the past. But the inclusion of Frenchmen in tri-cornered hats, firing long guns, is thought to be propaganda in support of Valverde's contention that Spain's rivals had instigated the attack. In that respect, this extraordinary painting is also a window onto the contemporary Spanish mindset. Anthropologists and historians believe that sometime after 1720, survivors of the Villasur massacre advised Spanish artists in the creation of this painting, yet its origins remain mysterious. It may have illustrated an official report on the debacle (thus the usefulness of propagandist details), or a wealthy patron might have commissioned a decorative or historical painting of an important event in New Mexico's history.

Whatever its source, the painting's subsequent journey is rather fantastic. In 1758 a Jesuit in Sonora, Father Philipp von Segesser von Brunegg, shipped a package of "three colored skins" to his brother in Switzerland.[39] That package included the hide painting depicting the Villasur massacre, subsequently dubbed, "Segesser II." The paintings remained in the family for two centuries, but in 1945 a Swiss ethnologist named Gottfried Hotz became intrigued by the scenes depicted on the animal hides displayed at the Segesser home. Hotz devoted two decades of study to determine that Segesser II portrayed events in colonial New Mexico history, specifically, he concluded, the Villasur massacre of 1720. In 1985 the state of New Mexico bought Segesser II and two other related hide paintings for nearly a half-million dollars. The paintings now reside at Santa Fe, probably the very town in which they were created more than two centuries ago.

Villasur's demise emphasized New Mexico's vulnerability to foes on a frontier of unimaginable proportions. The province's northern frontier stretched from the high plains northeast of Santa Fe to the Rio Chama on the northwest, an area so vast and relatively empty that enemies could penetrate the province at innumerable places. Conversely, any army that Spanish New Mexicans might send across the northern frontier would be dwarfed by the magnitude of the wild lands, and subject to attack. The Spaniards now had to count the Pawnees among the threats posed by the Utes, the Comanches, and the French. In November 1723 Carlana Apaches visited Santa Fe and again demanded help against Ute and Comanche attacks. Governor Juan Domingo de Bustamente subsequently led a Spanish expedition to the valley of La Jicarilla, on the south side of Raton Mesa. That same year he chased marauding Ute and Comanche warriors beyond the settlements and retrieved scores of Apache captives. Apparently Bustamente made another journey to La Jicarilla in 1727, but few details have survived. It is not known whether Bustamente's expeditions traveled far enough to have reached present-day Colorado.

After a visit to New Mexico in 1726 the viceroy's representative, Visitor Rivera, advised his superiors that a presidio at La Jicarilla would not be necessary. The Jicarilla Apaches could simply settle closer to Taos for protection. (Today the Jicarilla Reservation sits on lands some distance northwest of Taos.) Though this approach seemed practical, it removed the last buffer between the Comanches and settled New Mexico. Two decades later another New Mexico governor would revive the idea of a presidio at La Jicarilla to guard against Comanche attacks, also to no avail.

In the eighteenth century New Mexico served primarily as a defensive province. After abandoning plans for a presidio at La Jicarilla, Spaniards no longer sought to expand the northern frontier of New Mexico or, for that matter, New Spain. During the 1720s and 1730s Spanish officials at Santa Fe continued to hear from Indian sources about Frenchmen on the plains, at El Cuartelejo, and even closer. Governor Bustamente proposed a foray to El Cuartelejo to his superiors, but that expedition seems not to have taken place. Subsequent peace between Spain and France led Viceroy Marqués de Casafuerte to express disinterest in pursuing foreigners on New Mexico's frontier who, he observed correctly, were merely traders.

The real threat continued to come from Ute and Comanche raids, but little detail is available on Spanish activities on New Mexico's northeastern frontier in the half-century following the Villasur debacle. Trade between Spanish *ciboleros* and *comancheros* and peaceful bands of Utes and Comanches may have taken New Mexican hunters and traders across the northern frontier, for in 1735 Spanish officials found it necessary to issue a *bando*, or proclamation, prohibiting the sale of arms to any Indian. Two years later, Governor Henrique de Olavide y Micheleña issued another bando proscribing all trade with frontier tribes. Nonetheless, the frontier slave trade continued unabated. In 1739 a certain Miguel de Salazar was found guilty of trading with frontier Indians and purchasing an Indian girl in the process, though officials suspended his penalty due to his poverty. Slaves, furs, skins, produce, and live elk all traveled down the Camino Real to Mexico as exports from the northern frontier.

Periodic campaigns still crossed the province's frontier in this period to repulse the Comanches of the northeastern plains, and their cohorts, the Utes. In 1737 the governor issued a bando demanding that all able-bodied men in the province, Spanish or Indian, be ready at any moment for campaigns against New Mexico's enemies. In November 1752 Governor Tomás Velez Cachupín led nearly two hundred soldiers, settlers, and Pueblo warriors against the Comanches, chasing the enemy all the way to the Rio Napestle where, it is said, the Indians suddenly sought peace. Another foray against the Comanches, led by Governor Pedro Fermín de Mendinueta, took place in 1768.[40]

The tenor of such campaigns, though undocumented, produced stern warnings to soldiers and settlers from the governor. In 1741 Governor Don Gaspar Domingo Mendoza issued a bando that specifically prohibited ill treatment or sacking of rancherias during frontier campaigns. His successor, Don Joachín Codallos y Rabál, felt compelled to repeat this prohibition. Much of the activity on New Mexico's frontier in this period has escaped the record and can be seen only in the imperfect reflection of these bandos.

Less than two decades after the Villasur massacre, Frenchmen were no longer feared as the harbingers of foreign invasion, and individual French traders from the Mississippi Valley succeeded in reaching New Mexico. Certainly on a grand commercial scale the French Company of the Indies still planned to exploit the Missouri country and win over the allegiance of Plains tribes from the Spaniards, though it never quite succeeded. At the same time, however, individual French traders simply sought the time-honored pursuit of personal profit.

The first Frenchmen to reach New Mexico arrived in 1739. Pierre and Paul Mallet and several companions left the Illinois River country in French Louisiana that year and probably passed down the so-called Pawnee Trail. That route left Pawnee villages on the Platte and Loup rivers—near the site of Villasur's demise—and headed southwest to a traditional ford on the Rio Napestle in today's southern Kansas. The route traversed the Oklahoma and Texas panhandles, where the Mallets followed the Canadian River west to Pecos and Santa Fe, which they reached in late July 1739.[41] After a few months of informal house arrest the Mallet brothers were allowed to leave the province. They reached their countrymen at New Orleans and simply encouraged other French traders to reach New Mexico's starved markets. With France and Spain at peace, officials in New Spain now feared an economic invasion, and continued to proscribe foreign trade. The French at New Orleans, in contrast, hoped to open a contraband trade between Louisiana and New Mexico. Henri Folmer has written that from the early 1740s "pack trains crossed the wilderness each year [from French Louisiana] into the Spanish provinces. The post at Natchitoches and the route of the Arkansas River were the trail whereby French goods entered New Spain."[42]

Between 1748 and 1752 several small parties of French traders reached New Mexico, including one led by Pierre Mallet, but the Spanish attitude to illicit trade had hardened. Mallet's group and those that followed had their goods confiscated and were sent south down the Camino Real and jailed in Mexico City. Some were even sent to Spain. Yet a number of French traders reached New Mexico and escaped with their profits.[43] In February 1748, for example, Fray Antonio Durán de Armijo at Taos wrote to Governor Don Joachín Codallos y Rabál to report the arrival of seven Comanches, who asked for tobacco. The Comanches told the father that their village of one hundred lodges sat on the Jicarilla River forty leagues east from Taos. Recently, thirty-three Frenchmen had visited them and bartered muskets for mules. When the Frenchmen left to return to the Mississippi Valley, two entered New Mexico with the Comanches.

The governor took this report seriously. In a March 1748 letter to his superiors in New Spain, Don Joachín wrote: "It is to be feared that if these Frenchmen insinuate themselves into this Kingdom they may cause some uprising—as was attempted by a Frenchman named Luis Maria, who with eight of his own nation entered this Kingdom in the former year of 1742 ... and for it was shot in the public square in this capital town of Santa Fe, in virtue of sentence by the superior government of this New Spain. There is reason to fear some conspiracy" between French and Comanche forces, Don Joachin continued. "This would be irreparable, by the slight military forces that are in this said Kingdom for its defense. Particularly as the said Gentile Cumanches now find themselves with firearms, which the French have sold them." The governor reminded his superiors of the Villasur massacre, then three decades in the past, where "the French ambushed our said force and killed more than thirty." He resurrected the perennial recommendation that a garrison of fifty mounted soldiers be established "at a point called Jicarilla, distant from the said Pueblo of Taos twenty leagues."[44] His suggestion was met with the perennial response.

Frenchmen kept arriving in the province. A trio of French traders materialized at the Taos fair in 1749, and their identities shed light on the varied backgrounds of these intrepid frontiersmen, as well as on conditions in New Mexico. When Governor Cachupín questioned them at Santa Fe, Louis Febvre, age twenty-nine, professed that he was a tailor and barber by trade. He deserted the French army in New Orleans and had reached New Mexico by ascending the Arkansas River. Pierre Satren, age forty-two and a native of Quebec, practiced carpentry and had served as a soldier before deserting. Joseph Michel Riballo, twenty-four years old, was born on the Illinois frontier, also practiced carpentry, and had deserted. These men had reached New Mexico by traveling through Jumano Indian villages on the Arkansas, then reaching the Comanches, who brought them to Taos. En route from the Arkansas to Taos these would-be traders may well have passed through the confines of present-day Colorado, but the record gives no hard evidence of their route.

Governor Cachupín asked his superiors to grant the three Frenchmen permission to settle in New Mexico, for he noted "there is a lack of members of these professions in this villa and in the other settlements of the realm. ... It would seem to be very advantageous that they should remain and settle in it, because of their skill in their callings, for they can teach some of the many boys here who are vagrant and given to laziness. It is very lamentable that the resident who now is employed as barber and bloodletter is so old that he would pass for seventy years of age; as for a tailor, there is no one who knows the trade directly."[45] Four French traders who arrived in February 1751 may not have possessed useful skills for they did not fare as well. Cachupín arrested them, sold their goods, and sent them south to Chihuahua under guard.

The commodities traded between the Spaniards and Indians have been mentioned earlier. The items Frenchmen brought across the frontier to New Mexico are no less interesting. For clothing and related purposes the French brought yards of coarse woolen, and bolts of silk, muslin, linen, and lace. These traders carried a few cotton shirts, trousers, and dresses, woolen caps, beaver hats, and handkerchiefs. For hardware they toted hatchets, files, augers, awls, knives, and scissors. Oddities included puzzles, combs, paper, and mirrors. Their foodstuffs and spices included wine, pepper, and chocolate. Perhaps the most important category, munitions, often included black powder, iron balls, rifles, and flints.[46] Every one of these items would be eagerly purchased in materially starved New Mexico, if indeed the items reached that remote province.

By 1763 war between France and England—known in America as the French and Indian War, and in Europe as the Seven Years' War—had ended badly for France. France ceded Canada and all of Louisiana east of the Mississippi to England as a result. To Spain France ceded Louisiana west of the Mississippi. The French threat that had enthralled officials in New Mexico and New Spain over the past century suddenly vanished. At this point the Spaniards of colonial New Mexico knew their northeastern frontier at least as far as the Platte, possibly as far as the Missouri River. Spanish traders seeking native commerce may have found the North Platte in Wyoming, even points beyond. North up the Rio del Norte, Spaniards probably had located the river's source and exploited the San Luis Valley's passes, including those later named Sangre de Cristo, Medano, and Mosca east to the plains, Cochetopa west to the Gunnison country, and Poncha Pass north into the Bayou Salado, or "Salt Marsh," today's South Park. Did Spaniards cross present-day Tennessee Pass near the Arkansas's source, or Hoosier Pass by the Platte's source, to reach the Eagle or Blue rivers, both tributaries to the Colorado, the Spaniards' Rio Tízon? So far the record does not provide an answer.

On the northwestern frontier, peace with the Navajos since 1720 had encouraged Spanish traders to renew their efforts up the Rio Chama. Spanish expeditions in that direction produced a few well-documented journeys across southwestern Colorado and into the heart of the Colorado Plateau. As the 1700s wore on, New Mexico's frontiersmen, soldiers, and priests contacted previously unknown tribes in that direction and learned a fantastic new geography.

La Plata and Rio del Tizon
1720-1776

*T*HE SPANIARDS OF New Mexico had been familiar with the high plains on their northeastern frontier since Coronado explored that oceanic grassland in 1541. Spanish soldiers and traders had explored to the source of the Rio del Norte in the Sierra de las Grullas, probably since the early 1600s. In contrast, the country that stretched away on New Mexico's northwestern frontier still held mysteries.

From New Mexico's inception, diplomacy and Christianity had sent modest expeditions up the Rio Chama. But those *entradas* seem to have been limited in scope, given Navajo resistance to the Spaniards' smothering embrace. As war between the Spaniards and Navajos developed in the seventeenth century, however, Spanish armies eventually made forays up the Rio Chama as far as the Navajo's Rio Grande, today's San Juan River on the Colorado–New Mexico border. On the far banks of that river rose the forbidding Sierra de las Grullas, which dominated the northern horizon with snow-dappled peaks. But the westernmost mountains in that chain remained unnamed and unknown. And beyond those mountains? Perhaps early in the eighteenth century no Spaniard knew.[1]

A durable peace between Spaniard and Navajo in 1720 finally opened the way for Spanish traders to ascend the Rio Chama, cross the Navajo's Rio Grande, and reach Ute homelands beyond the northwestern mountains. Despite the hostility of certain Ute bands north of settled New Mexico, by then allied with the belligerent Comanches, many Utes from the northwestern mountains were trusted traders. Long before any Spaniard ever rode up the Chama, Ute bands had descended the river to reach pueblos on the Rio del Norte.

The earliest Spanish entradas up the Rio Chama after the Navajo peace of 1720 probably went unrecorded because frontiersmen typically were secretive as well as illiterate. By the 1740s, however, documents reflect quite a bit of activity on New Mexico's northwestern frontier. Provincial officials had long sought to expand their settlements west of the Rio del Norte, and the Spanish-Navajo peace provided a climate for the establishment of new ranchos and *plazas*. Settlers could obtain modest land grants on New Mexico's margins if they worked the land and could defend it. Success proved elusive, however. Tentative efforts to settle the Chama Valley began after 1720, but repeated Ute and Comanche raids often sent settlers downstream to more defensible homes near Santa Cruz de la Cañada. Those raids, joined by Moache Utes, devastated the Navajos as well. Governors in that period sent missionaries and soldiers to assist their northwestern neighbors, just as their predecessors had done a century before.

As the threat of attack receded, settlers returned sporadically to their abandoned fields and homes in the Chama Valley. Plazas such as Puerto de Santa Rose de Lima de Abiquiu had numerous incarnations as settlers' fortunes ebbed and flowed. Life on this frontier was different. Whereas Spanish settlements in the valley of the Rio del Norte were relatively close to each other, and situated close to Pueblo Indian neighbors, the Chama settlements existed at arm's length from other Spanish and Pueblo villages. *Genízaros* found economic and social opportunity on the physical margin of settled New Mexico, forming a cultural buffer between the frontier tribes and Spanish New Mexico. Visitors to Abiquiu were more likely to come downriver from the wild country than upriver from civilization (such as it was in this province, "remote beyond compare."²). Capote and Sabuagana Ute traders appeared most often at Abiquiu and other Chama settlements. The Capote lived along the northern tributaries of the Navajo's Rio Grande, on the southern flanks of the Sierra de las Grullas. The Sabuagana lived farther north, on the Rio del Tízon, or Colorado River, of western and central Colorado.

In the early eighteenth century both bands made annual journeys to Chama settlements like Abiquiu for trade. Ute traders brought young captives from neighboring tribes to sell to the Spaniards and, in the interests of diplomacy, they released Spanish prisoners they had ransomed from the Comanches. The Utes bartered furs and hides for horses and probably guns, and they exchanged deer and buffalo meat for maize, flour, and other bounty from New Mexico's fields. Eventually New Mexico's frontiersmen followed Utes back to the latter's mountain homes. Though this trade was prohibited, it took place all the same. Profits were greater when traders could obtain furs, skins, and slaves at their very source. Spanish trading ventures up the Rio Chama to the Capote, Moache, Payuchi, Sabuagana, and Tabehuachi Utes were commonplace most likely as early as the 1730s, for in ensuing decades repeated *bandos*, or proclamations, sought to prohibit such journeys.³

Only a smattering of documents describes this seminal period. In February 1745 Governor Don Joaquín Codallos y Rabál took depositions from a dozen frontiersmen who had visited the Navajos' homeland and the unknown lands beyond. Antonio Montoya, age fifty-five, "a laborer and breeder of large and small livestock" and a resident of Puerto de Santa Rosa de Lima, told the governor he had made his first journey to the Navajos more than thirty years earlier (circa 1710–1715) in a time of war. His second journey took place about 1730, when New Mexicans aided the Navajo people, "so much under attack by the Utes and Comanches, who are their enemies." Montoya's third journey, he said, occurred two years before his testimony, in 1743. In that instance, "an Indian called Luis of the Christian Apache nation guided the witness [Antonio Montoya] and many other persons and soldiers that were given permission by the governor [Don Gaspar Domingo de Mendoza, 1739–1743] for the security of those people who were going to discover mines [and] great treasures, which proved to be false." This expedition traveled "through the region of a river called Chama where some Spaniards live," Montoya testified, and it headed northwest some thirty leagues (more than seventy-five miles) through uninhabited country. Such a path could have taken the expedition clear to the Navajo's Rio Grande, at the base of the Sierra de las Grullas. In the region he crossed, Montoya testified, the Navajos were three thousand to four thousand strong and "living in their settlements in little houses of stone and wattle on the mesas and in the mountains, supporting themselves with their crops." He noted further that "they sow much beans and squash in season, and that the natives occupy themselves in raising their livestock, cultivating their fields, and weaving some blankets ... [which they] ... trade for other things which the Indians of this Kingdom [Pueblos of New Mexico], and also Spaniards, give them."[4] Don Santiago Roybal, a secular priest, joined this 1743 expedition. His purpose, he once noted, was to find "a very rich mine, abounding in silver, called Chiquagua, where the inhabitants of this country often go to trade."[5]

Despite the meager record, these expeditions northwest of Santa Fe between about 1705 and 1743 reveal that by midcentury, frontiersmen and soldiers had crossed the Navajos' Dinetah to reach Ute homelands beyond the Sierra de las Grullas. These Spaniards sought more than the Indian trade in that remote land, for the mountains west of the Sierra de las Grullas would one day be called La Sierra de la Plata, "The Mountains of Silver." Yet one more alliance had to fall into place before the Spaniards could, with a degree of confidence, explore or exploit the country that stretched beyond Dinetah.[6]

In about 1748, Comanche access to French guns over the eastern plains strengthened the tribe, and they no longer needed Ute allies. Soon after, Utes arrived in Taos to make peace with the Spaniards and inspire a united Spanish-Ute front against the Comanches. When Don Tomás Velez Cachupín assumed the governorship in 1749, he saw the advantage of such an alliance.[7] To gain the Utes' trust, Governor Cachupín ransomed any Ute prisoners the Comanches brought to New Mexico's trade fairs. The governor allowed Ute chiefs to punish errant warriors who independently raided the Spaniards, rather than let isolated incidents escalate into war between their peoples. New Mexico's frontier Indian policy, fostered by Cachupín, acquired a degree of sophistication over the wretched excesses of the 1600s.

Yet Comanche and Ute raids on the Rio Chama settlements continued and sent settlers retreating for cover along the Rio del Norte. On August 1, 1749, in an effort to bolster the province's northwestern settlements, Governor Cachupín issued a bando that prohibited settlers from abandoning the Chama district. The following year he threatened to revoke land grants on the Chama if settlers did not return to their frontier homes. Cachupín's forceful measures contributed to the valley's subsequent, permanent settlement. In fact, from the 1750s onward, Abiquiu's plaza served as a staging ground for frontier expeditions to the Utes. At Abiquiu expeditionaries could sleep safely one last night before departing for the long trail to Ute country.

Governor Cachupín's five-year administration, 1749–1754, proved successful by two measures. His fairness toward the Pueblo Indians won tranquillity at home, and his discerning diplomacy with frontier tribes earned him a degree of peace abroad. Cachupín's tour of New Mexico in 1751–1752, at the close of his first term, produced a fact-filled and perceptive report on the province's condition. Spanish expeditions heading for the frontier in the mid-eighteenth century departed a different province than their predecessors had a century earlier.

In his report Cachupín noted that hostile nomads such as the Comanches and Apaches posed the gravest threat to his province. New Mexico's population had grown and spread out, which hampered its defense. The few hundred men the province could muster, with limited numbers of horses and guns, could not match the sheer numbers of *indios barbaros*. The Santa Fe presidio had but eighty soldiers and a like number of militia. The town couldn't provide mounts for them all, and only sixty men owned working muskets. Albuquerque, founded in 1705, and Santa Cruz de la Cañada, established in 1695, each had about five hundred settlers and faced similar straits.

Abiquiu, inhabited by one hundred genízaros, could muster a third of its population, but possessed only six horses, Cachupín reported. These genízaros had more than one thousand arrows, but no firearms. Taos Pueblo, finally pushed into the Spanish camp for strategic reasons, could send forth one hundred-fifty horsemen armed with more than two thousand arrows but, again, few firearms. All together New Mexico could muster eight hundred fighting men to counter thousands of predatory Comanches and Apaches. Many Apache bands remained virulently opposed to the Spaniards' presence. Comanches found the Spanish and native settlements on the upper Rio del Norte tempting targets that offered horses, guns, captives, and livestock.

Governor Cachupín wrote in an echo of former governor Vargas that New Mexico was "the most distant and remote of all the provinces of New Spain. ... It is completely exposed to attacks by all the barbarous tribes that surround the province and territory in all directions. ... One fears the depopulation and ruin of New Mexico since the forces of this province are so limited that they do not exceed eight hundred arms-bearing men. ... Mining is also impossible [because of hostile Indians], even though there are known minerals." Both settlers and Pueblos "wage war at their own expense," the governor added ruefully. Only the most meager royal support flowed north to this isolated province along the Camino Real. Spanish oppression in the previous century and perennial attacks by outlying tribes had destroyed many pueblos, Cachupín noted. In truth the province's Hispanic towns hadn't fared much better. "Those [Spanish] settlements [of New Mexico] are pitiful victims of the fury of some enemies so bloody and lascivious that they nurture their spirits with the thought of spilt blood, applying the most extraordinary torture to Spaniards whom they capture."[8] In this way, Cachupín noted, "the old settlements of Abiquiu, Ojo Caliente, Embudo, and Quemado were ruined and completely deserted by their inhabitants because of the frequent attacks and raids of the barbarous nations [of] Utes, Chaguaguas, and Moaches. I dedicated myself to their restoration and succeeded not only in repopulating these settlements but also in pacifying the above-mentioned tribes"[9] Having reported the dangers and drawbacks of life on this distant frontier in order to solicit royal support, Cachupín concluded wistfully: "The province is the most fertile of all of New Spain, with beautiful countryside, favorable to the raising of livestock ... [and it has] abundant hunting."[10]

Three years hence, Governor Cachupín's successor, Don Francisco Marín del Valle, found it necessary to repeat the bando prohibiting frontiersmen from selling horses and weapons to frontier Indians. New Mexico's situation was too dire to tolerate the transfer of such vital military resources to potential enemies. But the illicit trade continued; life on the frontier demanded it. Governor

Marín also had to prohibit the export down the Camino Real of cattle, sheep, and raw wool, due to critical shortages of these basic commodities throughout his province.[11] Tomás Velez Cachupín resumed the governorship in 1762 and again initiated a Spanish-Comanche peace by allowing an unconditional exchange of prisoners and by protecting peaceful Comanche traders at provincial trade fairs.

This era of peace would last five years, allowing further Spanish exploration of New Mexico's northwestern frontier. In 1765 Governor Cachupín sent explorer Don Juan Maria Antonio de Rivera to locate the Utes' favored route to their ford on the legendary Rio del Tízon, today's Colorado River. Over the years, Utes, Zunis, and Jemez Indians had brought word to New Mexico of a great river far to the northwest, which the Spaniards reasoned must be the one known since Coronado's time as the Great Tízon. The name Tízon referred to Indians on the lower river who carried torches, seen by Coronado's men in 1540. Spaniards believed (rightly) that this river originated on the western flank of the great mountains on New Mexico's northern frontier. Once New Mexico's Spaniards had discovered the source of the Rio del Norte, the Rio del Tízon posed the next major question in the geography of the interior continent. Governor Cachupín wanted to know about the nature of people rumored to live on the Rio Tízon's far shores and the truth about silver deposits long sought in the Sierra de la Plata. This sober assessment of the frontier reflected Cachupín's pragmatism, though the governor also asked Rivera to report on legendary Lake Copala.

Aside from Rivera's membership in the Royal Corps of Engineers and his journeys to the Rio Tízon in 1765, we know almost nothing about him, including why he was in New Mexico. But his professional affiliation may shed light on this matter: The Royal Corps of Engineers' role in the New World was to design and build roads and forts, make military plans, and locate and develop mineral resources.[12] Events outside New Mexico may explain Rivera's presence on the frontier. King Carlos III, "the most dynamic, innovative, and America-oriented" of Spain's eighteenth-century Bourbon kings, had reached the throne in 1759.[13] Spain's losses in the recent Seven Years' War inspired the new king to restore and reorganize his New World holdings. This king intended to regain Florida from the British (lost as the price of peace in the last war) and bolster the defense of New Spain. To effect the latter plan, Carlos III in 1765 sent Visitor General Jose de Galvez to New Spain's frontier to assess defenses and recommend improvements. Galvez's mission coincided with a tour of the northern frontier by the Marqués de Rubí and Nicolas de Lafora, a member of the Royal Corps of Engineers.

No documentary evidence yet links Rubi's visit to New Mexico and Cachupín's orders to Rivera. Rubi's impending visit to New Mexico might have pushed the governor to seek hard information on his northwestern frontier, a still mysterious land of Utes and silver. What traders reported had to be verified by reliable, official explorers. Although Rivera's ultimate designs remain obscure, Governor Cachupín's instructions to him on the second of his two entradas in 1765 are found in his journals. Those journals, discovered in 1969 at military archives in Madrid, Spain, are incomplete; some portions have been lost or destroyed. But Cachupín's instructions for Rivera's second entrada imply that the objective of the first journey was to locate the great Rio del Tizon and prospect for silver in the northwestern mountains.

According to Rivera's journal, the latest Spanish interest in discovering silver mines on the northwestern frontier had been sparked by an old Ute who appeared in Abiquiu with a small silver ingot. The Ute sold it to a blacksmith named Jose Manuel Trujillo, who made from it two rosaries and a crucifix. This story, or some version of it, must have spread quickly. Subsequently, a Moache Ute, el Cuero de Lobo, or Wolfskin, met Rivera at Santa Fe. Wolfskin agreed to meet Rivera later that season on the Rio de las Animas and lead the Spaniards to the source of silver. The Rio de las Animas, still so named, flows southwest from the southern flanks of the Sierra de las Grullas and meets the Navajo's Rio Grande, which flows into the Tízon.

Rivera's mission deep into Ute homelands required subterfuge. The Utes understood the Spaniards' predilection for imposing their will and would vigorously oppose Spanish encroachment on their domain. By this time Spanish frontiersmen regularly ascended the Chama and crossed the headwaters of the Rio Grande to reach the Utes for trade. But any sign of martial intent on Rivera's part could spark hostilities. So Rivera and his men proceeded as if they were traders, without armed escort. This would be simple, for the group included frontiersmen such as Gregorio Sandoval, Antonio Martin, Jose Martin, Andres Sandoval, and numerous genízaros. These practical men guided Rivera and probably brought some trade goods to maintain their cover and make the trip worthwhile.

In late June 1765 this expedition began, as most journeys to the northwest frontier did, in the plaza known as Santa Rosa de Abiquiu on the lower Rio Chama. Rivera, his men, and a modest *mullada* followed the winding river northwest, avoided its yawning canyon, then looped north and west to rejoin the upper Chama. They forded the Navajo's Rio Grande near the modern-day New Mexico–Colorado state line and rode across the seven rivers draining the southern flanks of the Sierra de las Grullas and the Sierra de la Plata. Rivera's men knew the way. By early July the group reached the Rio de los Pinos, a stream still so named near Bayfield, Colorado. There the men found ancient native ruins. "We began to see, at the margin of the mountain, ruins of ancient edifices that ... had been a Pueblo ... [and found in them] ... crucibles

Portrait of Don Juan Bautista de Anza, who vanquished the Comanche leader, Cuerno Verde, in 1779. *(Museum of New Mexico)*

Portrait of Don Diego de Vargas, who led the reconquest of New Mexico from 1692 to 1696. *(Museum of New Mexico, neg. no. 11409)*

Ron Kessler fords the Rio Grande where Governor Vargas forded the river on July 10, 1694. *(Author's collection)*

Left: Navajo man and his mother in the early 1870s, photographed by Timothy H. O'Sullivan on the Wheeler Survey. *(Colorado Historical Society, neg. no. 84-192.1587). Right:* Comanche warrior circa 1880. *(Colorado Historical Society, neg. no. F-23, 525)*

Left: Apache warriors in the early 1870s, photographed by Timothy H. O'Sullivan on the Wheeler Survey. *(Colorado Historical Society, neg. no. F-24, 120). Right:* Ute warriors in 1874. *(Colorado Historical Society, neg. no. F-5940)*

Taos Indian runners in race on San Geronimo's Day, 1893. The Pueblo Indians' prowess at long-distance running aided their revolt against Spanish colonial rule in August 1680. *(Pioneers Museum, Colorado Springs, neg. no. A45-33)*

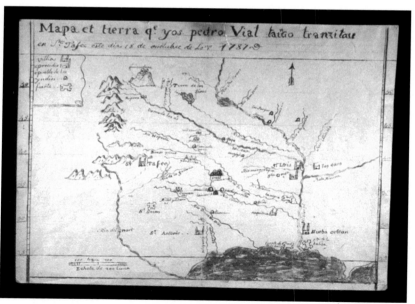

Pedro Vial's historic map of the country drained by the Rio Grande (left) and Mississippi River (right), drawn in 1787, revealed a vast geography known to few individuals. *(Museum of New Mexico, map no. 19052)*

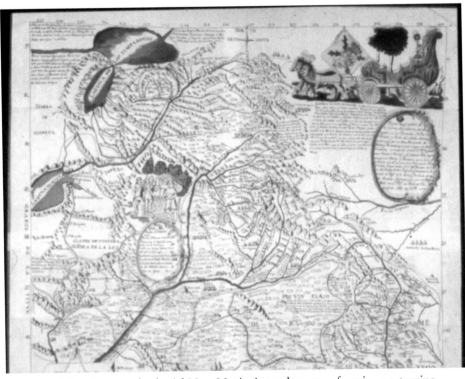

Historic map of colonial New Mexico's northwestern frontier, portraying
the southern Rocky Mountains and the headwaters of the Colorado River,
Rio Grande, and Arkansas River, drawn by Bernardo Miera y Pacheco in
1778. *(Museum of New Mexico, map no. 92063)*

Historic map of colonial New Mexico's northern frontier drawn by
Bernardo Miera y Pacheco following Governor Anza's 1779 campaign
against the Comanches. *(Museum of New Mexico)*

Photograph of native pictograph of Spaniards on horseback on the walls of
Cañon del Muerto, Arizona. *(Arizona State Museum, University of
Arizona, neg. no. 28883)*

Fremont Indian picto-
graph of menacing
anthromorph in
Cañon Pintado in
western Colorado,
perhaps seen by
Dominguez and
Escalante in
September 1776.
(Author's collection)

The late Ken Stanelle of Pueblo, Colorado, examines a Spanish colonial lance point uncovered from the prairie at Pueblo West in 1974. *(Author's collection)*

Photograph of sixteenth-century Spanish chain mail uncovered in Kansas. *(Kansas Historical Society, neg. no. 14MP1-10)*

An immense overhang in a meander on Chacuaco Creek in southeastern Colorado, perhaps similar to one visited by Pedro Vial in the 1790s, early 1800s. *(Author's collection)*

Nineteenth-century Penitente church ruins and cross in the Purgatoire Valley, southeastern Colorado. *(Author's collection)*

Mt. Pedernal is a landmark in the Navajo's historic territory that rises above the Rio Chama in New Mexico. The river provided Spaniards with a route to the Utes on their northwestern frontier. *(Author's collection)*

in which metals had been cast that looked like they had been gold,"
Rivera noted in his journal. "We took some ... to show to the
Señor Governor."[14] Rivera and his men soon reached the Rio de las
Animas near present-day Durango, Colorado, but Wolfskin did
not appear. In subsequent days Rivera met a tangled cast of Ute in-
formants, searched unsuccessfully for silver, and reached as far as
the Dolores River, which he named El Rio de Nuestra Señora de
Dolores, "the River of Our Lady of Sorrows." A Payuchi named
El Chino joined Rivera's camp and warned the Spaniards that the
seasonal heat now made the journey to the Rio Tízon dangerous.

"The said river was far away," Rivera's informants warned him,
"and was through awful country without foliage or water, that
there were many sand dunes that would tire out the horses, and
that we would burn up from the Sun along the trail ... or we
would die from hunger. ... If we really wanted to go, it is best to
go when the leaf of the oak is falling." Even that journey would be
ill advised the Utes told Rivera, "as [the river] is so wide that one
cannot see across it, and on the other side are barbarian white men
dressed in iron suits" and bizarre monsters.[15]

The Utes tried to discourage Rivera, for they had a well-founded
suspicion of Spanish motives and may have sought to retain their
position as middlemen in regional trading patterns. Rivera acquiesced, retraced his steps, and was surprised to find the elusive
Wolfskin camping on the Rio La Plata near present-day Herpe-
rus, Colorado. Wolfskin led Rivera's men upriver on a short jaunt
in search of silver, but apparently they found little if anything of interest. Rivera resumed his homeward ride and reached Santa Fe at
the end of July.

Governor Cachupín's instructions for Rivera's second entrada
were that he meet his Payuchi guides, reach the ford on the Rio
del Tízon, and report on the land and its natives. If he found settlements on the opposite shore of the river, he should identify the

occupants and determine whether, according to Ute tales, white bearded men in European dress lived there. Across the river Rivera and his men should continue to behave as traders, yet discover the truth about Payuchi stories that told of some kind of defensive trough there, and whether it was impenetrable, as rumored. Covertly Rivera should discover if the Rio Tízon began in the Lake of Copala or the land of Teguayo. Cachupín added that once these tasks were accomplished, Rivera could explore La Plata for the virgin silver that the Utes talked about.[16]

In early October, as a chill wind whipped the brown, dry leaves from New Mexico's scrub oak, Rivera rode up the Rio Chama for the second time that year. He crossed the seven rivers of the Sierras de las Grullas and the Sierra de la Plata and met his Payuchi informant, El Asigare, and a Moache, El Cabezon, on the Rio Dolores. They were joined by another Payuchi guide, a grandson of the Ute named El Chino, who earlier promised to show Rivera to the Tízon's ford. The Payuchis agreed to guide Rivera as he desired, but the Moaches dissented. They wanted no part of Spanish intrusion into their land. A Moache and a Payuchi even wrestled physically over the matter, until El Asigare stepped in and said that the grandson of El Chino would guide the Spaniards.

Rivera left the Rio Dolores in early October and headed northwest into new territory. Along the trail the Spaniards met El Chino, who confirmed that his grandson would lead them to the Rio Tízon's ford. The next day, at a spot he dubbed "el Puerto de San Francisco," Rivera reached the present-day Colorado-Utah state line south of the Rio Dolores.[17] A brother of El Asigare, whose name has escaped the record, caught up with the group; he had been sent to lead them to the river. The Spaniards thought this a gesture of goodwill, but were mistaken. It was a ruse.

El Asigare's brother now led Rivera on elaborate detours to dissuade him from his goal. Perhaps the Moaches and Payuchis had

had second thoughts about the Spaniards' mission. The direct route through this rugged country to the sought-after river crossing might have taken only two days. But the brother of El Asigare led Rivera over ridge and through canyon to the camp of a Tabehuache, El Tonampechi, who tried to convince the Spaniards to turn back. El Tonampechi's camp probably lay somewhere south or east of the La Sal mountains in present-day eastern Utah.

El Tonampechi told Rivera that his people did not know the route, and that ahead lay insurmountable dangers. Rivera countered that "our Captain ordered it … and although they might kill us we were required to go on. … Why [we asked] for what reason had it been [necessary] to fool us and cause us to come [so far] with such great difficulty? Do friends and comrades change their minds?" At this point the Utes generally acquiesced, assigned Rivera a new guide, and invited him to dance and feast for several days. In order to rest his men and horse herd, and join the Utes in a face-saving, peace-making gesture, Rivera agreed. Rivera's small group resumed its journey in mid-October. To avoid the badlands south of the La Sals, the expedition probably traversed the mountains' pine-clad upper flanks. The men camped that night in a cramped pass with little grass or shelter, but plenty of firewood. "That night we suffered a furious storm of wind and rain," wrote Rivera, "[so] we called this camp El Purgatorio."[18]

Two more days' arduous work through canyons and cactuses brought the Spaniards to the river that the guide identified as the Rio Tízon. "The guide agreed to send our [Indian] servants, who had accompanied us, to call to the people of the mountain on the other side so that they would come to trade with the Spaniards who were there in peace," Rivera noted. "And it was done, and Gregorio Sandoval and I went with them to reconnoiter the river, passing into the only ford that is there. The water came to the edge of the saddle of the horses, and leaving it came up over their rumps. The width of

the ford is about 60 to 70 *varas* [about two hundred feet]. Throughout most of it is very boxed-in, and is of two to three *estados* [about
fifteen feet deep] of water where it is very narrow. Upriver ... we
left a *bronce* [plaque]." Upon his return Rivera insisted to his guide
that this river was not the Rio Tízon they sought. The guide, taken
aback, assured him other Indians could verify its identity. Later,
Sabuagana Utes did so. The guide warned Rivera that beyond the
Rio Tízon he would encounter "a species of people who, because of
the lack of food ... eat their own children." Another day's travel
would bring him to "another people, very white and with hair of
washed-out-pearl color." Two days' travel further "there is a very
large lake ... and that there live people more numerous than
stones." By taking a trail along a nearby mountain range in that region, the guide continued, "one sees the Spaniards who live on the
banks of a pretty little river ... where they make houses like ours.
And they are Spaniards, for they speak like us, our same language.
They are fair-skinned, bearded, and they dress in chamois." When
Rivera expressed a desire to go there, the Tabeguache guide and a
companion frowned. These peoples would kill the Spaniards and
the Tabeguaches. "[The Tabeguaches said] our Captain ... should
send many people ... and only that way should we go there, any
other way would be impossible."[19]

The Tabeguachi messengers Rivera had sent into the hills on the
west bank of the Rio Tízon soon returned with five Sabuagana
Utes, who said their people were hiding from the Spaniards. Some
years earlier they had killed several Spaniards and now feared ret-
ribution.[20] (This places Spanish traders in eastern Utah well before
1765.) Rivera assured them his interest lay only in trade. The
Sabuaganas in turn invited Rivera to their encampment a few
leagues upriver, where Rivera met El Capitan Cuchara (Captain
Spoon), and the two pledged cooperation. The Sabuaganas told
Rivera of a trail that led to the lower Tízon, and a trail that led
northwest seven days' ride to the Timpanogos Utes, probably at

today's Utah Lake in northern Utah.[21] By pointing out the trails west from the Tízon's ford, these Indians may have planted a seed in Spanish minds: a land route might be possible between New Mexico and the distant Pacific Coast. Before Rivera turned back, he "left on the banks of the Gran Rio de el Tíson in a new growth of white oaks [aspen], as a sign, a large cross with a viva Jesus a la Cabeza, my name, and the year, at the foot, so that anyone can at any time benefit from our arrival there."[22] The inscription read: "Long Live Jesus at the Head of the Cross!" a traditional battle cry during the Spaniards' fifteenth-century reconquest of Iberia over their Muslim enemies.

Rivera returned to Santa Fe along his outward route and reached home in mid-November. Later records hint that Rivera may have made other journeys to La Plata and beyond, possibly the following year. Over the next decade traders who had accompanied Rivera in 1765 and others continued to travel the same trail to reach the Utes. Rivera's expedition simply represented an official, recorded effort in a burgeoning tradition of Spanish travel across New Mexico's northwestern frontier.

Having acquired vast Louisiana from France, Spain sent the Marqués de Rubí in 1766 to make a two-year inspection of New Spain's northern frontier. Rubí reached New Mexico in the year following Rivera's entradas, where he found that Governor Tomás Velez had maintained peace with the Comanches, Utes, Navajos, and some Apache tribes. Governor Cachupín pointed out to his visitor that the Comanches were better armed than New Mexico's presidials.[23]

Rubí later recommended administrative changes on New Spain's northern frontier that would affect future Spanish expeditions out of New Mexico. Before the Spanish bureaucracy could put Rubí's recommendations into action, however, events on the distant Pacific Coast propelled another ambitious expedition across New Mexico's northwest frontier. The Dane, Vitus Bering, had sailed for Russia and discovered Alaska in 1741. This news led Spanish officials to fear challenges to their claim to the Pacific Coast of North America. Captain James Cook's reconnaissance along the northern Pacific Coast for the British in 1776–1780 aggravated that fear. So as Spain planted settlements along the California coast—San Diego in 1769, Monterey (then spelled "Monterrey") the following year—officials sought ways to bolster the empire's position. From New Mexico to Alta (upper) California, solitary explorers and major expeditions now set out to connect Spain's far-flung claims and make new ones.

In 1773 Viceroy Bucareli authorized Captain Don Juan Bautista de Anza, presidio commander at Tubac in northern Sonora, to establish an overland route from that landlocked desert province clear to Monterey on the Pacific Coast. Anza's father had dreamed of finding such a trail, but died fighting Apaches before he could achieve it. Bucareli also approved another overland exploration, from Santa Fe to Monterey, in hopes that linking New Mexico and California would strengthen both. Whether Spanish officials really understood the distances involved is open to question. Certainly they had an idea. Yet distance alone never seemed to inhibit Spaniards bent on spreading their empire. In fact the next few years would find expeditions crisscrossing the length of what is now the American Southwest.

In 1774 Captain Anza, Friar Francisco Garcés, and thirty men reached Monterey from Sonora, a roundtrip of two thousand miles. That year the Spanish sailor Juan Perez supplied San Diego and Monterey by sea, then reached the coast of British Columbia before turning back. His goal had been Russia. The following year Juan Francisco de la Bodega y Quadra sailed as far north as Juneau in today's Alaskan panhandle. Meanwhile, in late 1775, Captain Anza again left Sonora, this time with more than two hundred settlers. His men reached San Francisco Bay early the next year and founded the area's first settlement. In 1776 Father Garcés left San Gabriel Mission near present Los Angeles, crossed eastward over the Mohave Desert and the lower Colorado River, and reached the Hopis. The year before, Father Silvestre Vélez de Escalante had journeyed from Zuni Pueblo on the western outskirts of New Mexico, as far west as the Hopis. Escalante learned firsthand of the Hopis' enduring hatred for Spaniards.

In three short years Spanish soldiers, padres, and frontiersmen had connected Sonora and upper California, established a colony at San Francisco Bay, and nearly tied California to New Mexico. At that critical juncture, two Franciscan priests offered to trek west from New Mexico in hopes of connecting their isolated province to California. They would take Rivera's route up the Chama to avoid the Hopis, arc northwest, then southwest across the Great Basin to reach the coast.

This ambitious plan arose simultaneously and independently in two inquisitive and pious minds. Fray Silvestre Vélez de Escalante had been born in Treceño, Santander, northern Spain, in June 1749, and had traveled at an early age to the New World, joining the Franciscan order in Mexico City in 1767. Although no portrait or description survives, one historian has suggested that based on his origins in Santander he may have been fair-haired and grey-eyed. [24] The young father suffered from a recurrent kidney ailment that sometimes incapacitated him. Silvestre Vélez, or Father Escalante, as he is popularly known, was ordained as a priest and sent to distant New Mexico to serve the mission at Zuni Pueblo. He arrived in January 1775. In an echo of Vargas and Cachupín, Escalante frankly described his post as "this out of the way place [situated] at the end of Christendom in this New World."[25]

Escalante noted that Nicolas de Lafora's recent map showed Monterey and Santa Fe at nearly the same latitude. "Therefore in my opinion the Yutas Payuchis are in the same latitude as

Monterey," he wrote. "[Thus] the journey to Monterey seemed to me more feasible via the Yutas than via the Cojninas [at Hopi Pueblo]." The Payuchi Utes, of course, were reached via the old trace up the Rio Chama. Further, Escalante noted, twenty men would form a large enough group to reach the Tízon, though perhaps not Monterey, "which according to what I conjecture, is a long distance from the Rio del Tízon, and the character and number of the intervening tribes are unknown."[26] This sober assessment of the difficulty of traveling overland from Santa Fe to Monterey seems to have been lost in the excitement of subsequent events. At this juncture Fray Francisco Atanasio Domínguez arrived in the frontier province from Mexico City to inspect New Mexico's missions. A native of New Spain's capital, he had joined the Franciscan order in 1757 at age seventeen. He too left no portrait.

At Santa Fe Father Domínguez and Governor Pedro Fermín Mendinueta discussed a route to Monterey. Domínguez then made a three-month inspection of the province's missions, and wrote a scathing report that earned him the enmity of his fellow Franciscans. By chance, as Domínguez requested archival materials from Governor Mendinueta, he received word of a visit by a Father Escalante from Zuni who wished to examine the same papers. By such coincidences history is created. Domínguez learned of Escalante's intent to reach Monterey and eagerly anticipated a meeting. Escalante arrived in Santa Fe in early June and reiterated his desire to make the arduous journey. Domínguez later wrote: "That very night we made a pact for the two of us to undertake the journey and to seek out persons who might be useful to us in the enterprise."[27] This would be a grand adventure in the service of both Church and Crown, and quite unlike two centuries of official expeditions before it. Governor Mendinueta agreed to underwrite the modest cost of the journey.

The fathers planned to leave July 4, 1776, at the height of summer, but events postponed their departure for more than three weeks. They may have had news that British colonies nearly a thousand leagues to the east were uniting against their monarch, though it seems doubtful, given the vagaries of the information flow over the Camino Real. The reverse could not have been true. In the weeks following the signing of the Declaration of Independence at Philadelphia, two Spanish fathers set out from the ancient capital of Santa Fe deep in the unknown interior of North America to seek the Rio Tízon and the terra incognita beyond it. The fantastic geography they would encounter had intrigued Spanish frontiersmen for two centuries. Those lands were simply beyond the ken of distant British colonists, suddenly swept up in a revolutionary storm.

The very morning he set out, Escalante wrote in a letter to his superiors: "I am not without hope of reaching Monterey."[28] In trying to sound optimistic, he revealed his doubts.

The group numbered ten upon departure. Fray Atanasio, age thirty-five, led the party while Fray Silvestre, age twenty-seven, acted as amanuensis for the requisite journal. A veteran artillery officer and cartographer, Captain Don Bernardo Miera y Pacheco, a native of Spain in his mid-fifties, hankered to see the unknown and signed on. A genízaro trader from Bernalillo, Andres Muñiz, acted as interpreter. The prior year, he had traveled the Chama Valley to reach the Utes. His brother, Antonio Lucrecio Muñiz from Embudo, joined the group, too, as did Don Pedro Cisneros, alcalde mayor of Zuni, and his servant, Simon Luceros. Don Joaquin Lain, a friend from Father Escalante's days at Zuni, also joined. Lorenzo Olivares of El Paso del Norte and Juan de Aguilar of Bernalillo completed the party.

Domínguez and Escalante's journal reflects the personal dynamics of this diverse group. Captain Miera's skills and experience might be useful, Escalante noted, if the captain kept in mind who led the expedition. The men from Zuni he knew and could trust. The genízaro traders, though coarse men, spoke the Ute language and had traveled to the Ute homelands; their experience would be critical, as would their cooperation. Escalante noted that all the men were told to leave behind weapons and trade goods so the natives might understand that they had higher motives than war or commerce. This remarkably varied group of individuals was bound together primarily by the newfound friendship of the two Franciscans. Although modern accounts of this expedition tend to romanticize it, the diversity of the group's characters and their motives held seeds of conflict. These people would make a grueling journey of great distances over waterless *jornadas*, cactus-studded arroyos, and obstacles yet to be imagined. Nonetheless, the two fathers, with unstinting belief in their religion and the need to save heathen native souls, managed to impart to their journey the flavor of a minor crusade.[29]

In July's last days the men made final preparations in the plaza at Santa Rosa de Abiquiu. On July 29 they rode up the Rio Chama with their modest *cavallada*, turned north at the river's gaping canyon, reached the upper river, and headed northwest along a variant of Rivera's route. For guidance, besides their genízaro companions, they carried a copy of Rivera's diary. In their own journal Escalante kept careful note of the distance and direction traveled, and described geography and daily events on the trail. Domínguez and Escalante named each of their campsites, in Spanish frontier tradition, though early on they used geographic names that had been in place since before Rivera's time. Beyond familiar landmarks, they bestowed their own choice of names on rivers, mountains, valleys, and passes. The meticulous journal kept by Escalante allows close reconstruction of their route.

In early August the men crossed the seven rivers draining the Sierra de las Grullas and the western La Plata mountains. Of the La Plata River Escalante wrote, "[It] descends through the same

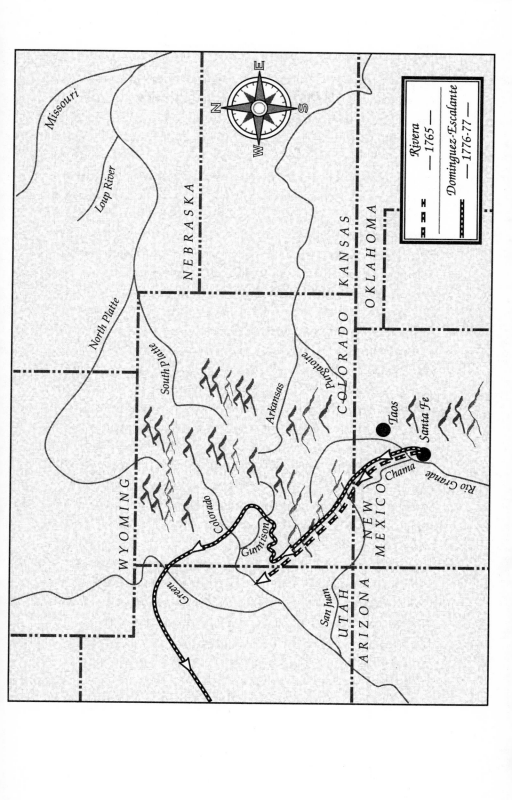

Rivera
— 1765 —

Dominguez-Escalante
— 1776-77 —

canyon in which there are said to be veins and outcroppings of metallic ore. … The opinion which some formed previously, from the accounts of various Indians and from some citizens of the kingdom, that they were silver ore, furnished the sierra with this name."[30] The group reached a great bend in the Rio Dolores, which created a deep canyon that twisted northwest. Eleven years earlier Rivera had camped nearby. "Here there is everything that a good settlement needs for its establishment and maintenance as regards irrigable lands, pasturage, timber, and firewood," Escalante wrote. "Upon an elevation on the river's south side, there was in ancient times a small settlement of the same type as those of the Indians of New Mexico."[31] Here two genízaros from Abiquiu, Felipe and Juan Domingo, overtook the group, hoping to join it. The fathers reluctantly agreed. Their adventure had just begun.

Each afternoon, summer thunderstorms doused the men. When the Muñiz brothers faltered over the precise route, Escalante derided them in his journal: "We paused to rest in a small arroyo which the experts thought had water, but we found it completely dry."[32] Apparently impatient at the guides, and showing some disdain for the expedition's nominal leaders, Captain Miera rode ahead on August 16 to find the way. Three days later, on a high plateau northwest of present-day Dove Creek, Colorado, the Spaniards faced a choice. The guides disagreed on whether the desired route lay northwest, or northeast toward the Sabuagana Utes. As Escalante noted in the journal, "We put our trust in God and our will in that of His most holy Majesty; then, after begging the intercession of our thrice-holy patron saints that God might direct us through where it would be more conducive to His most holy service, we cast lots."[33] The results pointed northeast towards the Sabuaganas. Here the party departed from Rivera's earlier route to the crossing of the Colorado, only two days' ride to the northwest and a sure shot at California.[34]

The small procession forded the Dolores and San Miguel rivers and crossed the southern end of the Uncompahgre Plateau in western Colorado. A Tabehuachi Ute overtook the party on the plateau and the next day brought several Ute families to meet the Spaniards. "They thought we were here to trade, and so they brought cured deerskins and other things to barter," Escalante wrote. "We gave them to understand, although they did not wholly believe it, that we were not here for what they thought, or carried goods for trading."[35] The two parties shared mutual gifts of jerked deer meat, dried *manzanita* [crab apples], and bread. The Spaniards gave their Ute visitor two knives and sixteen strings of glass beads to guide them to the Sabuaganas.

The group descended the plateau's northeast flank and reached a river "among the Yutas called Ancapagari" [Uncompahgre], "[where] there is a very wide and well-beaten trail," Escalante wrote. "La Sierra de las Tabehuachis, which we have finished crossing, runs toward the north. … It abounds with good pasturages and is very moist and has good lands for farming without irrigation. It abundantly produces piñon, ponderosa pine, spruce, scrub oak, various kinds of wild fruit, and flax in some places. On it deer and roe and other animals breed, and certain chicken fowl. … West of this sierra is the one of La Sal, which likewise appears small. To the west-southwest [is a sierra] they call La Sierra de Abajo."[36] Unbeknownst to the Franciscans, the gap between the Sierra de la Sal and Sierra de Abajo led to the Colorado River crossing they sought.

Domínguez and Escalante reached the Gunnison River, which they named El Rio de San Francisco Xavier, and noted that the Utes called it Tomichi, a name preserved today on an upper branch. Here Utes warned them that Yamparica Comanches would kill them if they proceeded. (The Yampa River that flows through Steamboat Springs and Craig, Colorado, may reflect, by

its name, part of this band of Comanches' contemporary territory.)
The Spanish fathers, however, hoped to reach the Timpanogotzis,
or Laguna Utes, to the west. They sent Muñiz and Atanasio, the
Sabuagana guide, ahead to alert the Sabuagana encampment that
Spaniards approached. They had reached the limits of their party's
knowledge and needed a guide. Muñiz and Atanasio brought five
Sabuaganas and one Laguna Ute back to camp. Warnings about the
Comanches were repeated, until the fathers offered the Laguna a
woolen blanket, knife, and glass beads to lead them onward. He
accepted, but insisted that the Spaniards first visit an important
Sabuagana encampment.

The group crossed the Gunnison, noting that "the water reached
the mounts well above the [horses] shoulder blades," and ascended
the river's north fork near present-day Paonia, Colorado. There
they turned north and ascended present-day Grand Mesa. The
group reached the top on the first day of September. There they
were met by eighty Ute warriors. "They told us that they were
going out to hunt, but we figured that they came together like
this, either to show off their strength in numbers or to find out if
any other Spanish people were coming behind us or if we came
alone," Escalante noted. The Spanish fathers finally reached the
Sabuagana's camp atop the mesa. Before inquiring the way to the
lower Tízon, however, Father Domínguez asked the Ute chiefs to
gather their peoples. "When those ... had been assembled, he an-
nounced the Gospel to them through the interpreter," Escalante
noted in their journal. "All listened with pleasure. ... When the
padre saw the evident joy with which they heard him, he suggested
to the chieftain ... that if ... they would accept Christianity we
would come to instruct them and set them in a way of living that
would lead to baptism. He replied that he would propose it to his
people, but he did not return all afternoon to provide further cause
whereon to base a likely hope of their accepting the proposal."[37]

The Franciscans admonished individual Lagunas for having animal names and for taking multiple wives, and gave them Spanish names. They then asked to exchange their footsore horses for fresh mounts. "The chief, some very old men, and many of the others [however] ... began trying to persuade us to turn back from here, exaggerating anew and with greater effort the hardships and perils to which we were exposing ourselves." In response, Escalante noted: "We ... told them that the one God whom we worshipped would expedite everything for us and would defend us, not only from the Comanches but also from all others who might intend to do us harm, and that we feared not a thing ... [because] His Majesty was on our side."

The Sabuaganas told the padres that if they didn't turn back, no horses would be exchanged. Further, the Utes asked the padres to write a letter to "the great chief of the Spaniards," noting that the Sabuaganas had done them no harm. Domínguez told the Indians they would proceed anyway, "because under no circumstances would we turn back without knowing the whereabouts of the padre our brother who had been among the Moquis and Cosninas and might be wandering about lost." Here Domínguez invoked a story of Father Garcés's journey to the Hopis in 1775 to impress the Utes with the Spaniards' resoluteness.

The Sabuaganas, in turn, "prompted by those of our very own who understood their language and were underhandedly giving us a rough time, [said] that the padres could not get lost because they carried drawn on paper all the lands and routes of travel," Escalante noted with asperity. Finally, exasperated with his own companions, Escalante stated the problem:

Ever since La Villa de Santa Fé, we had reminded all of the companions [they] were not to take along any goods for trading. ... All agreed not to bring a thing, nor any purpose other than the one

we had, which was God's glory and the good of souls. ... But some
of them failed in their promise by secretly carrying some goods we
did not see until we were near the Sabuaganas. And here we
charged and begged them all not to engage in commerce, so that
the infidels might understand that another motive higher than this
one brought us through these parts.

We had just been telling the Sabuaganas that we needed neither
arms nor men because we placed all our safety and defense in
God's almighty arm, and Andres our interpreter, with his brother
Lucrecio, proved themselves to be such obedient and faithful
Christians that they peddled what they secretly brought along
and most greedily sought weapons from the infidels, telling them
that they badly needed them because they were about to pass
through the lands of the Comanches. In this way, to our own sorrow, they betrayed their meager faith or lack of it, and how very
unfit they were for ventures of this kind.[38]

The padres' stubbornness prevailed, and they left the Ute encampment the next day with "utmost pleasure." Father Domínguez took along on his horse a Laguna boy who wished to return
home. A seasonal chill was in the air, and at night "we were feeling
the cold very much," Escalante wrote. The group descended the
mesa's north flank and reached the Colorado River, "which our
own call San Rafael and the Yutas Red River. ... We crossed it and
halted by its northern edge on a meadow. ... On this side there is a
chain of high mesas which are of white earth from the top down
to the middle and from the middle down evenly striated with yellow, white, and not too deeply tinged red ocher." (These are the
austere Roan Cliffs near present-day Debeque, Colorado. In summer's harsh sun these bluffs can mesmerize a traveler.) "This river
carries more water than El Norte," Escalante observed. "It comes
down, according to what they [Sabuaganas] told us, from a great
lake which lies in the high Sierra de los Sabuaganas next (toward
the north) to La Grulla."[39]

Silvestre, the Sabuagana, now led the men up Roan Creek, a stark, hypnotic landscape of colorful mesas. The men argued yet again. Some believed they were being misled to discourage them, or to enter a Sabuagana or Comanche trap. They met a group of Sabuaganas who said the Comanches had moved east to the Rio Napestle. That news eased tensions. The Spaniards ascended a branch of Roan Creek, dismounted, and scrambled up an incline they dubbed La Cuesta del Susto, "Shock Hill." Beyond they traversed a pass that today abounds with towering, old-growth aspen. The group dropped down into a labyrinth of creeks, the main branch leading north. "Halfway in this canyon toward the south there is a quite lofty rock cliff on which we saw, crudely painted, three shields," Escalante wrote. "Farther down on the north side we saw another painting which supposedly represented two men in combat. For this reason we named it El Cañon Pintado [Painted Canyon]"[40]

The Spaniards' subsequent journey may be summarized. They crossed the Rio Blanco east of Rangely, Colorado, and headed northwest to the Green River crossing upstream from present-day Jensen, Utah. By traveling west along today's Strawberry River, at the base of the Uinta Mountains, the Spaniards reached Laguna Ute villages just east of Utah Lake at present-day Provo, Utah. There, natives described to the priests the Great Salt Lake and the natives along its shores. Later, Escalante would equate Salt Lake with the Lake of Copala. The party then headed southwest, meeting the "Yutas *barbones*," the bearded Utes.

Early October brought a fearsome snowstorm. Hunger, cold, and the unknown terrain ahead gave the padres pause. Lain, Miera, and Andres Muñiz argued to continue on. The frustrations, the forced camaraderie, the hardships of the journey now accentuated differences among the small but diverse group. Dissent grew bitter. For the second time the priests resorted to drawing lots to avoid a disastrous rift. The men put two slips of paper in a hat, one marked

"Monterey," and one "Cosninas," for the Hopis, implying a return
to Santa Fe. The drawing again favored the padres, and they returned south, then east and southeast to a remote ford on the
Tízon, where they cut steps in the rock to reach the river and
emerge on its far bank.[41]

The group continued on to the Hopi, Zuni, and Acoma pueblos
en route to the Rio del Norte and Santa Fe, which they reached on
the second day of January 1777. They had made an incredible circle of perhaps five hundred leagues—more than a thousand miles—
over a period of five months. They had seen the region's numerous
tribes and lands, which they felt were ripe for missions and settlements. Yet they missed the Ute ford on the Rio Tízon and failed to
discover a workable trail to the lower river and California.[42]

Domínguez and Escalante's recommendations for new missions
and settlements on New Mexico's northern frontier were ignored.
The empire was strapped, and New Mexico was preoccupied with
its grim defense against the Comanches. Governor Pedro Fermín
de Mendinueta, among others, pointed out the uselessness of new
lands, when the empire could not even protect those already settled. Yet the sheer amount of country crossed by the two fathers
pushed back the frontier, exposing myths. That benefited Spanish
traders who subsequently reached Rivera's ford on the Tízon and
pushed on to the edge of the Great Basin.

Escalante later served at San Ildefonso Pueblo, and wrote the
Extracto de Noticias, a history of the province from the Pueblo revolt to 1717. He left New Mexico in 1779 for Mexico City for
kidney treatment, but died at Parral, April 1780, about age thirty.
Domínguez spent from 1777 to 1788 at El Paso del Norte, then
served as chaplain at Carrizal in New Spain. "His meticulous report on the missions of New Mexico was filed with a sarcastic notation and forgotten," one historian has observed.[43] In the 1790s
Domínguez served again at El Paso del Norte, then Janos, Sonora,
where he died in 1805, at age sixty-five.

Perhaps this journey's most lasting legacy was the map that Captain Miera produced soon after his return to New Mexico. Miera modestly titled it, "Geographic map of the region newly discovered to the north, northwest and west of New Mexico, surveyed by me, Don Bernardo de Miera y Pacheco, who entered [this land] to effect its discovery." This remarkable map depicts with a surprising degree of accuracy the Rio del Norte and its source mountains, and the locations of the Sierra de las Grullas, the Rio Napestle, the Sierra Mojada (our Wet Mountains), even the Rio de las Animas (today's Purgatoire River) that cuts Colorado's eastern plains. The plains are dotted with tipis marked "Cumanche"; a legend describes their origin and danger to the province. The map sweeps west and shows the "Provincia de Nabajoo" northwest of settled New Mexico. Beyond it the seven rivers of the Sierra de las Grullas flow into the Rio de Nabajoo, which joins the Rio de Zaguagana, then the Rio Colorado. Miera locates the Moache, Payuchi, Sabuagana, and Utes Barbones where Domínguez and Escalante's party encountered them. The summit of the Rockies is marked, "This mountain range is the backbone of North America, since the many rivers that are born of it empty into the two seas, the South Sea [Pacific] and the Gulf of Mexico." In the southwest corner of the map, where the Colorado leaves the frame, appears this notation: "This river flows through a canyon of red, rocky and steep cliffs." The Grand Canyon!

Miera made errors certainly; he could not resist exaggeration. El Cerro Azul, also known as the Sierra Azul, sought for centuries, crops up on his map just downriver from the Yutas Payuchis, and north of the Hopis. (This legendary source of silver and mercury was never located.) Taken in sum, however, Miera's map shows that Spaniards knew far more about the northwest frontier than that gleaned by the Franciscan fathers' circular trek in 1776. Frontiersmen in New Mexico must have contributed generously to Miera's knowledge, for his map seems to reflect a great deal of unrecorded travel across the province's northern frontier. One inscription reads: "The Timpanogos Indians say that the people who live on the other side of their lake, and [in] a high range of mountains that they can see from their houses ... make the tips of their arrows, lances and swords of a yellow metal, according to old reports."[44] Spanish officials didn't jump at this vague allusion as they might have in earlier centuries. A lack of money and manpower throughout New Spain crippled New Mexico. Chasing chimeras had fallen out of style. Comanche raids now demanded whatever resources this exposed province could muster. As the ink dried on Miera's map, the Spanish-Comanche rivalry would come to a head.

Provincias Internas
1776-1803

ETWEEN 1756 AND 1763 England and France fought a war known in Europe as the Seven Years' War and in America as the French and Indian War. Fought, in part, over the two nations' conflicting claims in America, the war had repercussions well beyond the two direct antagonists. In the tumult, Spain suffered severe losses on both continents. Yet Spain's fortunes in the New World rebounded with Spain's acquisition of Louisiana from France in 1763. In Spanish minds this near-mythical land expanded the already incalculable reach of New Spain's northern frontier and, by extension, New Mexico's to unimaginable proportions. Spain now claimed all lands from the Pacific to the Mississippi, as far north as the Yellowstone River country in present-day Montana.

King Carlos III recognized the need for vigorous administration of that sprawling claim, so he reorganized New Spain's northern provinces into the Provincias Internas, or "Internal Provinces." Local conflicts could not be solved by administrators in Mexico City. Rather, effective administration on the frontier required decisionmakers to live on the frontier itself. This strategy worked. In New Mexico the appointment of Don Juan Bautista de Anza to the governorship brought a concerted effort to end the chronic Comanche threat to that province. To accomplish that difficult task Governor Anza would have to make full use of his countrymen's knowledge of the geography of their northern frontier.

The threat to New Mexico from the *indios barbaros* waxed and waned over the centuries, but the recent assessment by the Marqués de Rubí and Nicolas de Lafora in 1766 echoed an earlier provincial governor who noted that "New Mexicans lived in a state of 'never ceasing war ... with the barbarians.'"[1] As to contemporary knowledge of the northern frontier, Lafora later reported that Spaniards were familiar with it for "a hundred leagues above New Mexico."[2] Although this estimate might have been a bit conservative in describing Spanish experience on the high plains, it might have been generous with respect to Spanish penetration of the northern mountains, or the lands beyond the Sierra de la Plata to the northwest. The mountains and canyons on the province's northern and northwestern frontiers had always challenged Spanish expeditions to those quarters. Explicit documentary evidence to support Lafora's statement is slim, but Don Bernardo Miera y Pacheco's extensive 1778 map of New Mexico's northern frontier implies that it is substantially accurate.

The perennial complaint about hostile frontier tribes, echoed by Rubí and Lafora, were focused at this point on Apache bands south and southwest of settled New Mexico. These Apaches had in fact harried Rubí and Lafora on their trek to New Mexico. (In contrast, Navajo, Ute, and Comanche bands made peaceful trade visits during Rubí's inspection, which coincided with the enlightened term of Governor Tomás Vélez Cachupín.) Rubí returned to Mexico City in 1768 after a wide-ranging tour and reported that he had seen "the tremendous damage His Majesty's subjects suffer daily from the barbarians."[3] He recommended to the king an evenly spaced string of presidios, each some forty leagues (roughly one hundred miles) apart, stretching from Texas to California. This vain attempt to impose the orderliness of geometry on unruly terrain ignored the realities of the northern Sonoran Desert and southern Rocky Mountains, not to mention the nomadic nature of the indios barbaros. Rubí's ideal presidios would each be staffed by forty presidials, each of whom would supply their own equipment, firearms, and a half-dozen horses. He did not say, however, where on the materially starved frontier Spain would find such generous men. Yet some of Rubí's recommendations eventually were embodied in the Regulations of Presidios, issued in 1772, which governed frontier policy until the end of the colonial period. The regulations marked a change from a two-century-old policy, begun in 1573, of peaceful expansion on the frontier. Harmonious coexistence with frontier tribes remained important, but now frontier governors were given official backing to make war on hostile peoples. In practical terms this had been the policy in New Mexico since the province's inception.

Rubí's recommendations and the new regulations aside, the Spanish empire could no longer afford to expand settlements on New Spain's northern frontier, nor could it create or support a string of new presidios to protect a province like New Mexico. But it could address chronic threats to security on the northern frontier. Even as Rubí began his tour of that frontier, the king's Council of the Indies had already decided to remove New Spain's northern provinces from viceregal control based at Mexico City. The frontier provinces would henceforth fall under a commander general who could devote his sole attention to their security and administration. Carlos III soon appointed Teodoro del Croix, a French-born Spanish army veteran, to the new post. Croix's considerable bailiwick included Louisiana, Texas, Coahuila, New Vizcaya, New Mexico (including present-day Colorado), and Sonora—in essence, much of northern Mexico and the present-day American Southwest.

Meanwhile, far from the Internal Provinces, the recent revolt among the British colonies on the distant eastern seaboard afforded Spain a chance to reassert its American claims. Spain could assist the rebellious colonists and reclaim land by ejecting England from the lower Mississippi Valley and from Florida. (New Mexicans even paid a war tax to finance Spanish assistance to the American rebels.) Yet Carlos III was not blind to a potential backlash. Ultimately, the success of the Americans' revolution could pose a threat to his own colonies in Texas and New Mexico.

Commander General Croix made his frontier headquarters at Arispe, Sonora, and named Captain Juan Bautista de Anza, fresh from establishing a colony at San Francisco Bay, to lead the presidio at nearby Tubac. When the governor of New Mexico, Colonel Don Pedro Fermín de Mendinueta, resigned in 1777 Croix appointed Lieutenant Colonel Anza to lead that northernmost province. Anza's considerable skills as an Indian fighter and military strategist were in dire need, for the situation in New Mexico had changed since Rubí's visit a decade earlier. The Comanches made relentless raids on the province's outlying pueblos, ranchos, and missions. They had already swept Colorado's high plains clear of Apaches. Three distinct branches of the Comanche people now made their homes in the region: the Yamparicas lived in northern Colorado and southern Wyoming; the Jupes held the plains north of the Arkansas; and the Cuchanecs inhabited the Rio Colorado (Red River) of eastern New Mexico and west Texas. The Jupes in particular preyed on New Mexico's settlements, and the fury of their raids baffled and terrified the province's settlers. The Spanish province offered horses, to be sure. Yet the Jupes attacked New Mexico as if bent on destroying all things Spanish.[4]

Contemporary Spanish knowledge of the Comanche nation is reflected in a legend on Bernardo Miera y Pacheco's map of 1778 depicting the lands that stretched across New Mexico's northern frontier. In an area that corresponds to Colorado's Front Range, the map reads: "This Comanche nation first appeared in the land of the Utes a few years ago. They say they left the region farther north breaking through various nations, and the said Utes br-zought them to barter with the Spaniards; they brought many dogs loaded with their hides and tents. They obtained horses and iron weapons, and they have acquired so much skill in handling both that they excel all nations in their dexterity and hardiness. They have made themselves the lords and masters of all the buffalo country, taking it from the Apache nation. ... [The Comanches] have destroyed many of the Apache nations, pushing those that were left to the frontiers of our King's provinces. This has caused a great deal of suffering."[5]

Don Bernardo erred on one point. Comanches actually first appeared at Taos with Ute allies in 1705. So by the time he drew his map in 1778 these Indians had traded in and warred upon the province for the better part of a century. From the beginning of this troubled relationship Spanish captains had mustered the province's best soldiers and pursued Comanche raiders northeast clear to the Napestle, or Arkansas River, on present-day Colorado's eastern plains. Documented Spanish counterattacks rode northeast over the mountains in 1716, 1718, 1719, 1752, and 1767. Between 1753 and 1767 Governor Tomás Vélez Cachupín managed to maintain peace with the Comanches by freeing Comanche prisoners and allowing Comanche leaders to punish their own warriors who threatened the peace. But hostilities resumed when Captain Don Pedro Fermín de Mendinueta assumed the governor's office in 1767. That summer Governor Mendinueta mounted a Spanish expedition across the northeastern frontier to chastise his Comanche nemeses, but this foray is not well documented. Although the governor hoped to find peace, he sensed the difficulty of dealing with the autonomous nature of the Comanches' three divisions and numerous bands.

Mendinueta's misgivings led him to post fifty men—presidials, militia, and Pueblo warriors—at the exposed settlement of Ojo Caliente, on the west side of the Rio del Norte. This post sat just five leagues from a ford often used by Comanches to attack the town. On the first day of June 1768 Mendinueta received disheartening news at Santa Fe. Comanche chiefs had reached Taos flying a white flag, and their tribe soon arrived for a brisk trade. Mendinueta suspected treachery and rode hard for Taos with his presidials. His instincts were good. These Comanches hoped to draw settlers away from Ojo Caliente for the Taos trade. A party of one hundred warriors had already split off to attack Ojo Caliente while its settlers traveled to Taos.

This time the garrison that remained at Ojo Caliente surprised the approaching Comanches and sent the Indians into flight. Even valiant native warriors understood the wisdom of living to fight another day. A month later Mendinueta and an army of five hundred rode north in search of the offending Comanches, as far as "a little river which flows into the Napestle"—conceivably Fountain Creek, at Pueblo, Colorado, a prehistoric crossroads. In early August, still on the high plains, the governor's scouts reported a nearby group of Comanches. But when Ute and Apache allies prematurely rushed to attack, the mounted Comanches simply vanished. "Pursuit and the success of the expedition based on surprise was impossible," Mendinueta wrote to Viceroy Bucareli.[6] In fact, the difficulty of surprising the Comanches in open country had always hobbled Spanish counteroffensives.

The pivotal drama of this difficult year unfolded after Mendinueta's return to Santa Fe. On September 26, 1768, a score of Comanches attacked Ojo Caliente but again were repulsed by the new garrison. At daybreak four days later, five hundred Comanches descended upon the isolated *plaza*. "A troop of the enemy advanced, commanded by one who wore as a device a green horn on his forehead, fixed in a headdress or on a tanned leather headpiece," Commander General Croix wrote later. Spaniards managed to kill this man though his distraught comrades retrieved his body. As Governor Mendinueta later learned, "a barbarian has raised himself up among that nation with the appearance and accouterments of those of a little king." During the October 30 confrontation at Ojo Caliente the Comanches' effort "to carry away the body of the one who commanded them, the one who carried the ridiculous device, and the feeling they showed at his loss are very suggestive that he may be the little king."[7]

The "little king's" death meant no end of trouble. The term *Comanche* referred to myriad, autonomous peoples bound chiefly by speech and custom. Some customs were indelible, inviolable, and universal. "Vengeance was a tribal imperative," according to a modern authority. The death of a relative had to be avenged by obtaining at least one enemy scalp. And "the death of a distinguished chief ... could spark an extended, bitter vendetta, which required many scalps and horses to satisfy Comanche honor," as one writer has observed.[8] The Comanche chief's death at Ojo Caliente sparked such a vendetta among the Jupe Comanches against the Spanish. Leadership of the warring parties that rode against New Mexico now devolved upon another warrior, also known as Cuerno Verde, or Green Horn. It has often been assumed that the first and second Cuerno Verde were father and son, but that is not necessarily so. The relationship could have been a simple passing of command and title, though the younger Cuerno Verde's subsequent decade of terror strongly suggests kinship.[9]

"Green Horn" reflected the Spaniards' name for these charismatic figures. Among the Comanches themselves, the younger was Tabivo Naritgant, meaning "Man Who Holds Danger," or "Dangerous Man." In fact, he may have been as dangerous to his own tribesmen as he was to his enemies. Cuerno Verde probably used coercion—as well as courage, daring, and indifference to hardship—to seize and maintain his leadership. He proved to be a thorn in the side of other Comanche bands that preferred peaceful trade to hostile raids.[10]

During the year 1774 five Comanche attacks on New Mexico took a devastating toll. In June Comanches attacked Picurís Pueblo, then Nambé. At Nambé, however, Pueblo warriors counterattacked so effectively that the Comanches had to escape into "the wilds of the sierras," according to one contemporary account.[11] In July one thousand Comanches wreaked havoc on Santa Cruz de la Cañada. And in August one hundred Comanches attacked Pecos, though the pueblo's defenders repulsed them and gave chase. The subsequent testimony of a witness to this last encounter sheds light on the shifting fortunes of frontier life and its human dimensions. According to this witness, the Comanches, after seeing a couple Spanish scouts, made a successful retreat based on the advice of "a soldier (who was twelve years a captive among [the Comanches] and who spoke their language perfectly) who told them that ... the [Spanish] command would arrive momentarily."[12]

The following month Carlos Fernandez, alcalde at Santa Cruz de la Cañada, led six hundred soldiers, militia, and Pueblo allies fifty leagues east from Santa Fe in pursuit of a Comanche raiding party. Though many escaped, Fernandez's group trapped scores of the Comanches in a thicket and annihilated them.[13] Given the Comanches' predilection for revenge, this event simply heaped fuel on an already raging fire. Governor Mendinueta wrote to Viceroy Bucareli the following summer with a grim assessment and a desperate plea: "I count some six hundred guns and one hundred and fifty pairs of pistols of fair condition in all the realm. [But] the rearing of the animals has been destroyed by the enemy. We do not have the tame horses with which to defend ourselves from the three enemies [Comanches, Apaches, and Navajos] who surround us. Thus, most excellent sir, if the kindness of your excellency and your strong desire to develop this province do not provide this unfortunate and valiant community with a horse herd on the account of the king, perhaps to the number of fifteen hundred horses, I fear its desolation will follow."[14] Mendinueta would leave office in 1778 without a solution to the Comanche menace. The new governor, Don Juan Bautista de Anza, inherited a volatile and rapidly deteriorating situation.

Born in 1735 at Fronteras, Sonora, in Mexico, Anza grew up the scion of a distinguished family of Basque lineage. His grandfather served thirty years on the northern frontier of New Spain and died fighting the Apaches. His father, former presidio captain at Fronteras and temporary governor of Sonora, also lost his life to Apache fury when his son was just a boy. Perhaps understandably, Anza volunteered at his local presidio at age seventeen and within three years reached the rank of lieutenant. Four more years' service elevated him to captain and command of the Tubac presidio. He distinguished himself in several Apache campaigns before making his historic journey across the desert to Monterey in 1774, an expedition that earned him the rank of lieutenant colonel. It was on the heels of his successful journey to the Pacific Coast to found San Francisco that Commander General Croix named him commander of Sonora's forces. "It is apparent," Croix wrote later, "that this officer, during the time he held the ... Commandancy of Arms of Sonora, discharged his obligations with creditable zeal, skill, efficiency, and felicity, as he failed at nothing."[15]

Two portraits of Anza exist, but neither has a firm connection to its subject. The painting, in possession of the Museum of New Mexico, was given to the museum by the Anza family of Spain, which insists that it is in fact a portrait of the New Mexico governor. It shows a thickly bearded man in profile. Another painting, commissioned by the Tumacacori National Historic Park in the 1930s, is a face-on portrait, purportedly based on the earlier work.[16]

Upon his arrival in the remote province of New Mexico, Governor Anza undoubtedly questioned the most perceptive of New Mexico's veteran soldiers and frontiersmen. He saw firsthand the devastation wrought by continuing Comanche and Apache raids. He realized that Ute and Navajo bands also simmered on the frontier. Anza had pressing orders to open a land route from Santa Fe to Arispe, Sonora. The frequency and savagery of Comanche attacks instead demanded his immediate attention. The new governor decided to take the offensive and attack his enemies in their own country. In midsummer 1779 Anza mustered eighty soldiers, more than two hundred militia (mainly settlers), and two hundred-fifty Pueblo warriors. The expedition's horse herd numbered more than a thousand. On August 16, 1779, Anza reviewed more than five hundred troops at San Juan de los Caballeros, Juan de Oñate's old capital. He ensured that each of his nearly ninety soldiers had three horses each and arms and food for forty days. These were *soldados de cueras*, or "leather-jackets." Most were creatures of the frontier, and likely mestizos. They depended on muskets, lances, and swords for offense, and used layered leather jackets and shields for protection. These men were courageous, crack marksmen. Of the settlers and Indians, in contrast, Anza noted in his campaign journal: "Because of their well-known poverty and wretchedness ... I supplied the most needy, each with a good horse from the two hundred that I have extra in the herd at the presidio and all of them with firearms with ten ball cartridge belts."[17]

Anza led the expedition's vanguard. He placed a rear guard under a first lieutenant, and the middle guard under a second lieutenant. The pack train of supplies ambled between vanguard and rear guard; soldiers flanked it. This enormous army stretched out fully half a mile along the trail. As Governor Anza articulated his strategy in his journal: "I am directing the present expedition along a route and through regions different from those which

have been followed previously. Thus I shall not suffer what has always happened so often, that is, to be discovered long before
reaching the country in which the enemy lives, as they inform me
this is very common and is the reason for the failure of most of the
campaigns."[18]

Governor Mendinueta and his predecessors typically had
reached the high plains by crossing the Sangre de Cristo Mountains east of Taos, then traversing north over Raton Mesa on the
present-day New Mexico–Colorado state line. Anza's plan to attack the Comanches in their own country required judicious use
of the geographic knowledge he gathered from the province's
frontiersmen. He would travel north up the Rio del Norte into
the mountains, then traverse passes to reach the plains to launch a
surprise attack on the Jupe Comanches where they typically
gathered. In modern terms, that meant ascending the western
margin of the San Luis Valley, crossing Poncha Pass at the valley's
northern end, traversing South Park to the east, and descending
Ute Pass on the northern flank of Pikes Peak.

On August 17 Anza led his enormous army west across the Rio
del Norte at a traditional ford, just upstream from the mouth of
the Rio Chama. The men turned north up the Rio Ojo Caliente
and camped by the deserted settlement. Anza noted in his journal
that the town's scattered layout was poorly suited to defense. Ojo
Caliente officially marked the northern terminus of the Camino
Real, extended by Governor Oñate nearly two centuries earlier.
To the north stretched the frontier, familiar yet still wild.

Two days later Anza's army reached the Rio San Antonio,
which rises just west of the mountain of the same name, south of
the present-day New Mexico–Colorado state line. Another day's
ride brought the army to the Rio de los Conejos. The expedition
could cover about seven or eight leagues (perhaps twenty miles),
each day. Anza's casual use of these familiar names in his journal

reflected their traditional use long before his arrival. At the Conejos two hundred Ute and Apache warriors arrived in the Spanish camp and asked to join the expedition against their mutual enemies. Anza assented after receiving the natives' agreement on a peaceable division of war spoils. Specific agreements on this point had long been a feature of Spanish forays against frontier enemies, in America as on the Iberian Peninsula.[19] Expedition leaders could not risk chaos or anarchy in hostile country.

The next day's march took the army over the Rio de las Xaras (La Jara River) to the Rio del Pino. Anza's journal reflected his understanding of Indian wariness and his own determination to make this a decisive foray. "It was necessary to make the next march at night so that the enemy might not descry the dust of our troop and horseherd from the sierra, not very distant, which we are keeping on our right," he wrote.[20] (Anza referred here to the Sangre de Cristo Range, fifty miles east of his position.) The army traveled another night's march to reach the Rio del Norte, "where the ford was named El Paso de San Bartolome."[21] Anza kept to the western margin of the San Luis Valley not only to avoid detection by Comanche scouts, but also to circumvent the marshes that plagued the central valley in that period. He then forded the great river just east of present-day Del Norte, Colorado. Here the governor recapitulated contemporary Spanish knowledge of New Mexico's northern frontier.

> This river, as is known, empties into the Mar del Norte and the Bay of Espiritu Santo. It has its own source fifteen leagues more or less from this place in the Sierra de la Grulla, which is that on the skirts of which we have been traveling since the 17th, it being the one to the west and closest on this route to the principal Villa [Santa Fe] of this government under my charge. The Ute nation which is accompanying me, who reside at said source, and three civilians who have explored it, tell me that the river above proceeds

from a great swamp, this having been formed, in addition to its
springs, by the continuous melting of snow from some volcanos
which are very close. The same persons also assure me that after
fifteen leagues on the breadth of the sierra, one sees seven rivers in
a very short distance. These united form in the same way one
[river] of considerable size which flows to the west. For this reason
and others which I omit, I judge this river to be that which they
call the Rio Colorado, which merging with the Gila, empties into
the Gulf of California.[22]

Anza had seen enough of the Southwest in the past four years to
correctly piece together its basic geography. (The seven rivers of
the Sierra de las Grullas, crossed by Domínguez and Escalante
just three years earlier, actually flowed into today's San Juan River,
which then meets the Colorado.) Few contemporary Spaniards
had such a comprehensive view. The most tantalizing aspect of this
passage, however, may be his reference to three "civilians," obviously frontiersmen who had reached the source of the Rio del
Norte and traversed the seven rivers. These frontiersmen must
have enjoyed good relations with the Utes of the northern mountains, whether those visits were legal or not. They might have
hunted, traded, and explored in those regions over the past
decades. Anza was wise to take advantage of their knowledge.

Governor Anza's army again marched at night, and all the men
"suffered from bitter cold." At the end of the day's march they
planned to kindle fires, but the appearance of fires to the east initially dissuaded them. As it turned out, these campfires marked a
traditional Ute camp, though Anza didn't know that until the next
day.[23] Twelve days after leaving Santa Fe the army crossed Poncha
Pass at the great valley's north end. "We forced our way through a
very narrow canyon with almost inaccessible sides," Anza noted in
his journal. "It being rarely crossed, cost us considerable work to
conquer."[24] This casual notation that unnamed Poncha Pass was

rarely crossed underscores that Spaniards had indeed reached Colorado's central basin, today dubbed South Park. New Mexico's frontiersmen must have done so secretly, for officials had just issued a *bando* prohibiting Spanish and Pueblo traders from visiting the Utes.[25]

The army forded the Rio Napestle, which Anza correctly observed came from the northwest. Anza's men then crossed "another medium-sized sierra," perhaps the small range north of Salida, Colorado, known today as the Arkansas Hills. They continued east through hills in the midst of South Park that they dubbed Las Perdidas, because, as Anza wrote in his journal, "of the trouble we had from the snow and fog which beset us before nightfall." Here, probably in the eastern part of South Park, before the rugged trail re-entered the mountains, the men paused to dress fifty buffalo they had killed. On Monday, August 30, two weeks and 113 leagues from Santa Fe, Anza noted, "we began to force our way over Sierra Almagre, which is very rough with its ravines and thick woods, route to the east."[26] This traditional trail is most likely today's Ute Pass, on the northern flank of the Pikes Peak massif. Spaniards knew that range as the Sierra del Almagre, or Mountains of Red Ochre. Although Anza apparently did not bestow the name, his diary is the earliest known record of its use.[27] After threading Ute Pass, Anza readied his men at the edge of the plains.

The next day Anza's scouts reported "clouds of dust three leagues distant." The source of that dust could only be the Comanches they sought. By marching at night up the San Luis Valley and taking Ute Pass to the plains, Anza had finally reached the Comanches' homeland without being detected. Suddenly, scouts reported, the Comanches had wind of the Spaniards' presence. The Indians hurriedly broke camp and fled east across the plains. "I resolved to attack without delay," Anza wrote. Leaving his baggage train and horse herd in the rear, Anza sent his best men to attack. He sent forth a right and left column to apply a pincer movement. The Comanches raced away but, after a few miles of hard riding, members of the Spanish army caught up. A running battle took place over several miles before the Spaniards secured complete victory by killing most of the warriors. The Spaniards recovered five hundred horses, but estimated, based on the number of tents, that the Comanche group should have been much larger. Finally, perhaps under torture, two Comanches told Anza that Cuerno Verde had left two weeks earlier to raid New Mexico. "I determined, although the time was propitious for my return, to follow the trail of Cuerno Verde, to see if fortune would grant me an encounter with him," Anza noted grimly.[28]

Anza descended Fountain Creek, which he dubbed the Rio de Sacramento, and forded the Napestle at present-day Pueblo, Colorado. At this juncture, without notice, the Utes rode off for their mountain homes. In his journal the Spanish governor noted: "Along the same route five more leagues were made."[29] It is likely that from here on Anza followed an Indian trail that hugged the Sierra Mojada, or Wet Mountains, to the southwest, a path later known as the Taos Trail. That afternoon, resting the army in an arroyo, Anza got word from his scouts that Comanches appeared on the horizon. It could only be Cuerno Verde returning from New Mexico. Anza hid his baggage train and horse herd in a ravine and led his men to the attack. The Comanches took flight. On this undulating, broken terrain the Spaniards could not immediately press for a decisive battle. Anza returned to his baggage and horses, and spent the night there against the advice of veterans, who pointed out the danger of ambush. Anza showed both courage and a degree of foolishness in disregarding this advice, but his gamble paid off. The Spanish army slept undisturbed.

At daylight on Friday, September 3, Anza moved his men out to the south. Ahead gathered the Comanches at the edge of a wood.

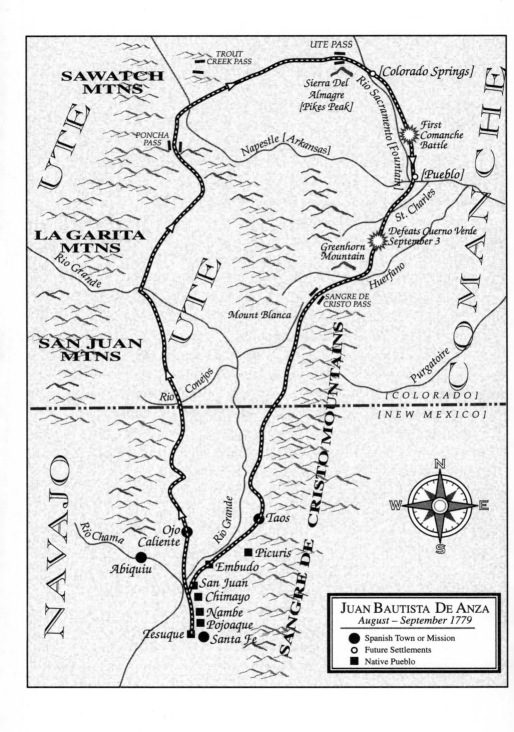

JUAN BAUTISTA DE ANZA
August – September 1779

● Spanish Town or Mission
○ Future Settlements
■ Native Pueblo

Apparently they wished to head north along the same trail Anza now held. The Comanches could have withdrawn and looped south, then east, to reach their country without a confrontation. But they had learned of their brethren's defeat the day before and vengeance or death seized their minds. Historian Elizabeth John has suggested that Cuerno Verde, after a decade of attacks on New Mexico, might have been prepared to "end it all."[30] Anza again sent forth his men to surround the enemy. "At the wood the enemy had already increased to more than forty, and they drew almost within gunshot, firing off their own muskets," Anza wrote. "In this way was recognized from his insignia and devices the famous chief Cuerno Verde, who, his spirit proud and superior to all his followers, left them and came ahead his horse curvetting spiritedly. Accordingly, I determined to have his life and his pride and arrogance precipitated him to this end."[31]

As Anza prepared to surround the Comanches, Cuerno Verde read his plans and began a tactical retreat. The Spaniards managed to trap the chief and his closest warriors in a gully. "There without other recourse they sprang to the ground and entrenched behind their horses made in this manner a defense as brave as it was glorious," Anza noted later, still in awe of his foes' raw courage.

Notwithstanding, the aforesaid Cuerno Verde perished, with his first-born son, the heir to his command, four of his most famous captains, a medicine man who preached that he was immortal, and ten more. ... A larger number might have been killed, but I preferred the death of this chief even to more of those who escaped, because of his being constantly in this region the cruel scourge of the kingdom, and because he had exterminated many pueblos, killing hundreds and making as many prisoners whom he afterwards sacrificed in cold blood. His own nation accuse him, ever since he took command, of forcing them to take up arms and volunteer against the Spaniards, a hatred of whom has dominated him because his father who also held the same command and power met death at our hands. All of our people and the prisoners say his death will be greatly lamented but I believe that their regret will not exceed the pleasure our people have had in it. ... From some of the dead [Comanches] were taken five muskets, today an article which is plentiful among these heathen.[32]

Though tradition, local historians, and various plaques claim this battle took place at different sites on Greenhorn Creek between Rye and Colorado City, Colorado, no credible evidence has yet been discovered that establishes this battle's location. Anza returned to the upper Rio del Norte by following a native trail up today's Oak Creek, a branch of the Huerfano River, and crossing Sangre de Cristo Pass, southwest of Badito, Colorado. The long procession, flush from victory, crossed the saddle in brisk, early fall weather. "It was extremely fatiguing from its constant alternations of ascents and descents and to this was added a violent wind and fog," Anza noted. On the south side of the pass the men were once again in the San Luis Valley. On September 5 the army reached the Rio de la Culebra, site of Vargas's encampment nearly a century earlier, and hurried south to see how their province had fared against Cuerno Verde in their absence.[33]

At Taos the men heard that Anza's strategic precautions had served well. The settlers had gathered together inside the northern valley's cluster of plazas and pueblos, built defensive bastions, and fought valiantly. Cuerno Verde's attack, with two hundred-fifty warriors, had been repulsed with minimal losses. Governor Anza reached Santa Fe on September 10, twenty-six days and more than two hundred leagues after departing. Anza's victory had not necessarily been a decisive military defeat of the Comanches. Individual bands continued sporadic raids. The governor recognized, however, that the death of Cuerno Verde in effect would stop the Jupe Comanche threat to New Mexico. It also seemed to quell an intra-tribal split between the Jupes, who favored war against the Spaniards, and the other two bands, which sought consistent, peaceful trade.

Anza later sent Commander General Croix in Arispe a copy of his campaign diary and the headdress taken from Cuerno Verde. This well-documented act produced a fascinating modern story that flourished among Southwestern historians two centuries later. According to this tale, so far unsubstantiated, Cuerno Verde's headdress had been passed along to the viceroy, then the king of Spain, who in turn sent it on to the Pope, who purportedly stored it at the Vatican.[34]

In the year following Anza's Comanche expedition, mapmaker Don Bernardo Miera y Pacheco drew a detailed map of the province's northern frontier and the region traversed by the governor's campaign. This map, which reposes in the Archives of the Indies in Seville, Spain, purported to show the provincial frontier from the Rio Chama's source on the west to the plains on the east, from Santa Fe on the south as far north as the fortieth degree of latitude. It has both a remarkable degree of accuracy and a critical mistake that many would repeat.[35]

Miera's map showed the Rio del Norte and its tributaries in the San Luis Valley and reflected both the traditional names used in Anza's diary as well as those Anza himself bestowed. The Cerro de San Antonio, for instance, is clearly marked in the correct spot. But Miera mistakenly depicts the Rio del Norte heading in the northern end of the valley, rather than in the mountains to the west. This suggests that Miera hadn't accompanied Anza's expedition, or at least hadn't read the governor's remarks about the three civilians who explored the river's source in the Sierra de las Grullas.[36] At the top of the map are the mountains split by Poncha Pass, and at top, right, is the Sierra del Almagre, or Pikes Peak massif. Miera correctly depicts the Napestle as heading between two high ranges and flowing east towards the plains. Miera shows the Rio de Sacramento, today's Fountain Creek, flowing south into the Napestle at present-day Pueblo, Colorado. Teepees with flags indicate Anza's encounters with the Comanches. Anza's route southwest from Pueblo to Sangre de Cristo Pass parallels a river Miera identifies as the Rio de Dolores; from the 1800s onward this stream has been known as the Huerfano.

In a note on the legend of his map, Miera characteristically claimed that the land north of Ojo Caliente and Sangre de Cristo Pass was newly discovered on Anza's campaign. Clearly that was not the case; frontiersmen had traversed that country for a century or more. Miera may have meant that an official expedition had not passed that way before, though even that would be hard to believe. Perhaps he simply exercised the prerogative of the chronicler and sought greatness for his governor and perhaps, by extension, for himself. A year earlier he had named an enormous lake in the far northwest, described by Fathers Domínguez and Escalante, the Laguna de Miera.

Miera's map of the northern frontier reflected the essential geography traversed by Governor Anza and more. Yet his map could not reflect New Mexico's continuing fragility. In 1780–1781, as Governor Anza consolidated the province's missions, perhaps five thousand Pueblo Indians died of smallpox, many of them at Hopi pueblos sixty leagues to the west of the Rio del Norte. The province's terrible isolation could suddenly grow at the whim of outside events. In a letter from Commander General Croix to Governor Anza in March 1780, Croix forewarned that no mail would soon be forthcoming. The most recent ship from Spain, pursued by an English corsair, had been forced to throw overboard excess weight, including bags of correspondence for denizens of New Spain. In August a royal decree commanded that every Spaniard in the province contribute two pesos, and Indians one, to a provincial war fund. Though the Comanche threat now receded, Apache attacks remained a condition of life in New Mexico.

United action by New Mexico's inhabitants, regardless of financial recompense, would be their only salvation from attacks by indios barbaros, but a complaint lodged by a *genízaro* in 1780 sheds light on the Spanish armies of the day and reflects the tenuous commitment of the rank and file. Bentura Bustamente, a lieutenant of genízaros at Santa Fe, formally complained to the governor that he and thirty-three of his peers had been taken from their fields to fight on the Comanche frontier. Bentura declared this unjust and threatened to flee the province and join the Comanches.

Spanish officials tried in vain to stem illicit trade across the northern frontier in this period. In February 1783 a number of Abiquiu residents were tried for trading with the Utes without permission. The commander general at Chihuahua subsequently proclaimed that no settler or Indian could leave his or her district or mission without permission. This proclamation, however, could not stop the traffic. In the spring of 1785 a citizen, Vicente Serna, was tried for illegally trading with the Utes. A man named Marcellino Manzanares landed in court for the same offense, as did Salvador Salazar, Santiago Lucero, and Francisco Valverde.[37] New Mexico remained a tenuous outpost deep in the wild, continental interior. The dangerous frontier trade lured many New Mexicans away from their homes out of sheer necessity.

In the aftermath of Cuerno Verde's death Anza pressed for a treaty with a Comanche "nation," which truly didn't exist. In a reflection of their own hierarchical society, the Spaniards sought to deal with one supreme chief, rather than dozens of bands. In the winter of 1785–1786 various Comanche bands met at Casa de Palo, or House of Wood, on the Napestle to discuss peace with the Spaniards. (This site probably is the so-called Big Timbers near Lamar, Colorado, later known to William Bent.)[38] They agreed that one among them, named Ecueracapa, should negotiate for all Comanches. Comanche representatives subsequently met with

Anza and other Spanish officials at venerable Pecos Pueblo to sign a treaty. Peace provisions included a Spanish pledge of material assistance to the Comanches and an alliance against Apaches to the south. At Pecos Governor Anza presented silver-headed canes, uniforms, and flags to Ecueracapa and other chiefs to cement the new alliance.

Viceroy Bernardo de Galvez now departed from past Spanish policy and allowed New Mexicans to trade firearms to frontier tribes. In his "Instructions for Governing the Interior Provinces of New Spain, 1786," Galvez wrote: "Powder should be supplied with regular abundance, in order that the Indians put the use of the firearm before that of the arrow and begin to lose their skill in handling the bow. ... Consequently, they would be forced to seek our friendship."[39] This directive reversed a two-centuries-old policy of trying to keep one of the Europeans' crucial military advantages out of native hands.

Spanish-Comanche relations soon took a wholly unexpected turn. In July 1787 a Comanche representative named Paruanarimuco twice visited Taos with an "anxious entreaty" to Governor Anza to assist his people in settling in villages on the Napestle.[40] The source of this proposal is not known. But by August Anza granted thirty laborers, tools, and a craftsman named Manuel Segura to build a settlement to be known as San Carlos de los Jupes. This settlement may have risen at the confluence of the Rio San Carlos—today's St. Charles River—and the Napestle, about ten miles east of present-day Pueblo, Colorado. So far, however, no archaeological evidence has established the exact site, said by contemporary documents to lie near a spring with good lands. Within two months the group had erected nineteen houses in a traditional plaza layout, but extant documents do not say of what materials, though one assumes adobe. Spaniards and Comanches apparently also labored over irrigation ditches at San Carlos de los Jupes. Soon after completion of the plaza Governor

Anza provided the Comanches with sheep, oxen, maize, and seeds to aid them in agricultural pursuits.

Anza's actions met with belated approval by the new commander general, Don Jacobo Ugarte y Loyola, who authorized successive governors to follow suit. This prompted certain Ute bands to demand a similar level of material assistance for a settlement to be situated between Abiquiu and the Rio del Norte, but for various reasons—perhaps due to the proposed settlement's close proximity to the Spanish settlements, or merely due to cost—this request was denied. Within weeks of San Carlos's creation, however, news that Governor Anza would leave the province at the end of his term prompted the Comanches to mistakenly conclude that Spanish support had ended. Manuel Segura and his men returned home with their tools. The Comanches themselves remained until the following January when they abruptly abandoned their new plaza. As Anza's successor noted, the death of a woman close to Paruanarimuco precipitated this move, as the Comanches were "full of superstitions."[41] The commander general and viceroy vowed never again to expend monies in a similar fashion. The cost of establishing San Carlos de los Jupes could have been spent on needs closer to home. Although the Spanish did not attempt a repeat of the San Carlos experiment, the Comanches continued to receive gifts to maintain their allegiance in the face of French or American traders pushing west from the Mississippi Valley.

Anza's spectacular success in saving New Mexico from the Comanches did not shield him from controversy. His firm consolidation of New Mexico's outlying settlements and missions to improve defense ran counter to the settlers' penchance for independence and it ruffled the clergy's sense of autonomy. Critics who fled the province in 1783 even succeeded in obtaining Anza's censure from Commander General Croix' successor.[42] By 1786 Anza himself requested a transfer south due to deteriorating health. He left the province for the last time in November 1787 bound for

Sonora, where Anza briefly commanded the troops at the Tucson presidio and sent an associate to open a direct route between that settlement and Santa Fe. He died at Arispe on December 19, 1788, and may have been buried beneath the floor of a side chapel in the church of Santa Iglesia Nuestra Señora de la Asuncion.[43]

The Americans, with Spanish and French assistance, had succeeded in their revolution against the British Crown. Of course that conflict played out an impossible distance beyond New Mexico's most remote horizon, yet news of the American revolution and the colonists' fledgling democracy reached far and wide. Spain had backed the colonists in their revolution somewhat hopeful that the new United States of America would limit its western growth. After all, for centuries the balance of power in the New World derived in part from diplomatic agreements forged in European capitals. Such restraint was not the emerging American way. Spain's grandiose claims to swaths of country it could not settle or protect no longer sufficed. After their successful revolution Americans no longer faced east toward Europe. They now turned west.

Commander General Ugarte urged Anza's successor, Governor Don Fernando de la Concha, to look into settling the abandoned San Carlos community with Spanish families. Ugarte argued that such a move would afford a bird's-eye view of Comanche movements, provide a defensive buffer against invaders, and serve as a supply point for plains expeditions. There is no evidence to suggest that this settlement ever took place, though it would have been the only known Spanish colonial settlement in present-day Colorado. The suggestion itself, however, reflects that the Spaniards' concept of New Mexico's practical frontier now extended to the Napestle on the northeast, the San Luis Valley due north of the province, and at least as far as Abiquiu on the northwest. The modest nature of Spanish settlements in those outlying areas reflected the traditional gap between Spain's geographic knowledge and claims and pesky reality. The "Province of New Mexico," though a grand sweep of high plains, mountains, and mesas in the Spanish mind, continued at this late date to comprise a modest string of pueblos, *villas,* ranchos, and missions along the upper Rio del Norte.

In the decades following Anza's enduring peace with the Comanches on New Mexico's northeastern frontier, the provinces' *comancheros,* those who traded with the Comanches, and its *ciboleros,* or buffalo hunters, traveled the familiar passes that led from the Rio del Norte to the plains to secure meat and hides. These frontiersmen often met their native counterparts at the confluence of the Rio Sacramento and the Rio Napestle (Fountain Creek and the Arkansas River at present-day Pueblo, Colorado). Often the roles of comancheros and ciboleros were interchangeable. Hunters took trade goods and gifts—they could not pass otherwise—and traders joined a buffalo hunt when opportunity arose. Of course the plains trade with the Comanches represented only a part of New Mexico's frontier economy in this period. The traditional trails that stretched north up the margins of the San Luis Valley and northwest up the Rio Chama still took New Mexicans to Ute homelands. Though sporadic hostilities with Apache, Comanche, and Ute bands on the northern frontier infused these expeditions with a degree of danger, commerce now dominated the largely peaceful frontier. Still, the frontier had not grown appreciably safer from the vagaries of the wild. The fearsome grizzly bear still roamed the Sangre de Cristos, Sierra del Almagre, and Sierra de las Grullas. Fat diamondback rattlers could repose in any patch of sun. Sudden storms still lashed out at travelers in the mountains or on the open plains. Because these Spanish trading journeys across the northern frontier remained forbidden, they went largely undocumented. Yet indirect evidence makes it clear that regular, clandestine trading ventures continued throughout the Spanish colonial period on all fronts.[44]

Not all contemporary frontiersmen were illicit traders. A rare breed also traversed the frontier in the royal service, largely for diplomatic reasons. One such man, Pedro Vial, traveled much of the region between the Mississippi and the Rio del Norte in this era, opening trails that linked Spain's frontier settlements. His sometimes solo travels covered epic stretches of country. In his background one senses the ingredients for footloose ways. Pierre Vial was born about 1746 in Lyon, France, but that date is uncertain.[45] Vial himself may not have known the year. Nothing of his early life is known, nor how and when he reached the New World. By 1779 Spanish officials in Texas learned of his presence among natives on the Rio Colorado, today's Red River, near present-day Natchitoches, Louisiana. Vial subsequently moved upstream to reside with the Taovayas division of the Wichita Indians, who valued his mastery with firearms. In fact, his gunsmithing skills and aptitude for native languages guaranteed him full-time employment on any American frontier.

In the winter of 1784–1785 a certain Juan Baptista Bousquet, a veteran Louisiana trader in Spain's service, discovered Vial living among the Wichita on the upper Rio Colorado near the present-day Oklahoma-Texas state line. Bousquet managed to convince Vial to take up residence in the Spanish community of San Antonio to the south, as gunsmiths were too valuable to be allowed to roam loose on the Spanish frontier. Pierre Vial become Pedro Vial. His official role in Spain's service was that of "interpreter," a catch-all phrase that combined actual interpreting with the roles of diplomat, trailblazer, and guide. His pay was modest but steady.

By this time Vial spoke his native French, a smattering of Spanish, fluent Comanche, and several dialects of Wichita. In 1786, as

Governor Anza orchestrated a regional peace, Vial extended a Spanish olive branch to Comanche divisions in Texas on the governor's behalf. Later that year he opened a trail from San Antonio northwest to Santa Fe, where he conferred with Governor Anza in person. While in New Mexico Vial drew a map of the region with which he was familiar. Though only a crude sketch, it covered a staggering amount of country, from New Orleans north to the three forks of the Missouri River, from the Rio del Norte clear across the plains to the old French town of St. Louis.[46]

Having conferred with Governor Anza, Vial attempted to ferret out a more practical route between the New Mexican capital and San Antonio and made a round trip between the two settlements in 1788–1789. On these dangerous journeys Vial typically traveled alone or with a single companion. This approach allowed him to pass through territory where an army, on the same mission, might have provoked native resistance. At least once in the course of his solitary wilderness travels Vial was taken prisoner and tortured until a native friend intervened. No physical description of Vial, nor a sketch of his character has come down to us. But he was without doubt a remarkable man. "You had to have a certain personality and a great deal of flexibility to adapt yourself to the Indians' culture," Donald Blakeslee, a Wichita State University anthropologist, has said. "Absolute personal bravery was essential. There weren't too many Spaniards on the frontier who could command that kind of respect."[47]

In May 1792 Vial blazed a route from Santa Fe to St. Louis by heading east out of New Mexico. He met with Osage Indians, then turned north across the plains. After wintering at St. Louis, Vial returned to New Mexico via the Pawnee villages still ensconced on the Platte River. (Vial's visit came three-quarters of a century after the Villasur massacre.) After arranging a Pawnee-Comanche peace he departed for distant New Mexico. He may have followed what Blakeslee has dubbed the Pawnee Trail, upon his return to the Spanish frontier. That route dropped south from the Platte through present-day Kansas before turning southwest along the Cimarron River to reach New Mexico's Spanish settlements, bypassing present-day Colorado.[48]

The speed with which Vial made his return from St. Louis to Santa Fe alarmed Spanish officials. If a lone horseman could cover that incredible distance in so little time it meant footloose Americans on the United States's western frontier were uncomfortably close. The northern frontier of colonial New Mexico suddenly shrank. The matter caused serious deliberation in Spanish quarters. A few years later Commander General Nemesio Salcedo wrote to New Mexico Governor Joaquin del Real Alencaster: "Take the most effective steps to strengthen the friendship with the Pawnee nation ... [and] implant in their minds a horror of the English and Americans, [who] have no other views than to root them out of their lands in order to take possession of them."[49] In fact Salcedo's view was prescient. Vial may have made another journey to the Pawnees in 1795. Four years later he retired from Spanish service and returned to residence among the Comanches. His Spanish employers considered it desertion.

Spanish officials in New Mexico, at Arispe, and Mexico City had for two centuries fended off frontier tribes, sent expeditions into the mysterious north, and maintained vigilance against European rivals to their northernmost province. At the turn of the nineteenth century, however, events both within and without New Spain would undermine the Spanish empire's grip on the Americas. New Mexico, "remote beyond compare," would be all but forgotten. This very moment had been anticipated and feared for centuries. Strangers now appeared on the province's doorstep.

Interlopers

1803-1821

B Y THE BEGINNING of the nineteenth century New Mexico's northern frontier had developed into a busy place. In spring, as the likelihood of dangerous winter storms receded, frontiersmen led carefully packed *muladas* up the Rio del Norte, up the Rio Chama, or across the mountains to reach native homelands. Utes, Comanches, Apaches, and Kiowas likewise traveled into settled New Mexico for trade fairs at the province's outlying settlements. Only November's wintry threats curtailed this annual, two-way traffic so vital to the isolated province's well-being.

New Mexico's frontier traders faced the unenviable choice of poverty at home or danger abroad. The frontier offered opportunity to *genízaros*, mestizos, and Pueblo Indians, as well as settlers of predominantly Spanish descent. Class distinctions, though less important in New Mexico than in New Spain, may have pushed the lower strata of New Mexico society into the frontier trade. But beyond the frontier, certainly, social status provided no protection from the dangers of the wild. On the frontier, courage and ability alone could earn a man distinction and a living. These men dressed in wool and buckskin, could ride like Comanches, and probably were expert marksmen with either bow or rifle. Some had undoubtedly learned fighting skills as soldiers or militia in times of strife. Beyond the province's outlying settlements traders traveled in numbers great enough to give pause to any group they encountered. Few of their travels were chronicled because the traders themselves most often were illiterate and their work illicit. We often know of their movements only through court proceedings against them. The slim documentary evidence suggests that in the early years of the nineteenth century they pushed beyond the reach of earlier, officially documented expeditions on the high plains, into the central mountains, and across the broken mesas and canyons of the Colorado Plateau.[1]

These traders carried valuable commodities from New Mexico's fields and workshops to native homelands. For two centuries New Mexicans had raised woolly churro sheep in abundance, and certain pueblos and Spaniards excelled at spinning yarn and weaving it into blankets and serapes. Hispanics and Pueblo Indians alike raised crops and made wheat flour and corn meal that could be efficiently packed for the frontier trade. That trade relied in part on the strong backs of burros and the art of the muleteer. *Arrieros*, or muleteers, blindfolded their pack animal to calm it, then threw a *salea* (sheepskin) and a *jerga* (wool blanket) over its back. An *aparejo* (packsaddle) came next, then a load of up to several hundred pounds could be added and cinched into place. Practiced muleteers could load a pack train in minutes and move a laden mulada five to ten leagues (more than twenty miles) in a day. A month's travel could take New Mexico's traders deep into the wilderness of their northern frontier.

The traders' native neighbors desired blankets, produce, flour, and precious items such as horses, guns, balls, and powder. In turn, the Utes, Apaches, Kiowas, and Comanches possessed hides, bows and arrows, meat, and slaves for trade. New Mexico's surplus goods were exchanged for the bounty of the frontier. Provincial governors apparently shared in the proceeds from this illicit trade, particularly in the lucrative market for slaves.[2] During trade fairs at Taos, Abiquiu, and Pecos, natives of the hinterland might bring in Spanish or Pueblo individuals who had been snatched away from home in a raid, thereby winning the release of a relative or comrade in Spanish hands. The exchange of prisoners and the slave trade itself were ancient practices that long predated the Spaniards' arrival in the New World, though the Spanish eagerly joined it.

At the turn of the nineteenth century New Mexico's frontiersmen continued to ride up both margins of the San Luis Valley north of Taos and Ojo Caliente to reach Ute homelands on the headwaters of the Rio del Norte and in the Bayou Salado. They traversed Cochetopa Pass to find Sabuagana Ute homelands in the Gunnison country. And they crossed Sangre de Cristo, Mosca, and Medano passes to reach the valleys of the Rio Napestle and the Rio Chato, today's Platte River, to meet Comanches, Apaches, and Kiowa Indians—as well as the newly arrived Cheyennes and Arapahos. New Mexican and native traders probably agreed to meet annually at familiar locations like the confluence of the Rio del Almagre and the Napestle at present-day Pueblo, Colorado, the grassy enclosure of Bayou Salado, the Sabuagana summer camp atop Grand Mesa, or the traditional ford on the Rio Tízon. This Spanish-Indian frontier trade flourished after Governor Anza's 1786 Comanche peace, creating a busy regional commerce.

Frontiersmen still possessed the perennial Spanish drive for discovery, and a number of expeditions that departed Santa Fe in this period reached farther north and northwest than ever before. At the same time, events outside the province sent Spanish spies and soldiers across the northeastern frontier to intercept westering Americans.

Outside isolated New Mexico the world began to change more rapidly than within the ancient province. Napoleon Bonaparte of France sought world domination. The Spanish Crown faltered, besieged by war and intrigue. English harassment of Spanish ships that traveled back and forth between Spain and its New World colonies disrupted the Spanish economy and hurt Spain's American colonies. Little if any material support from Mexico City reached Santa Fe in these years. Under such conditions the province's frontier trade assumed even greater importance.

In 1802 Spain relinquished its claim to the country the French had called Louisiana, which stretched north and east of settled New Mexico clear to the Mississippi. That immense sweep of land had formed a strategic part of New Mexico's frontier for two hundred years. Inhabited by the *indios barbaros*, it had provided a healthy buffer between New Spain's northernmost province and lands claimed by its European rivals. Now Spain returned Louisiana to French hands with the stipulation that it not pass to the Americans, who might be tempted to expand their western frontier. Spain's wishes went unheeded. Less than a year later, Napoleon's double-dealing and need for cash delivered that territory to the burgeoning United States for fifteen million dollars. The Americans' western frontier suddenly grew by a thousand miles and thrust up against the northeastern frontier of New Spain where the vague limits of the two became entangled. Impoverished, remote New Mexico would have to defend Spain's interests and its ancient frontier against footloose American frontiersmen and the soldiers and settlers who were certain to follow. Under orders from the south, New Mexico's governors in the opening years of the nineteenth century sent spies and soldiers north into the Colorado region to catch American interlopers. The old frontier exploded with activity.

When France and the United States consummated the Louisiana Purchase in Paris in April 1803, that territory's western boundary was left poorly defined, in part due to the region's still vaguely understood geography. On maps that France and the United States used to determine the borders of Louisiana, that enormous wedge of country began at the mouth of the Mississippi River, ran north along that river a thousand miles, turned west, and came down the spine of the Rocky Mountains to a river running southeast to the

Mississippi. That unspecified river might have been the Arkansas, the Canadian, the Red, or the Pecos. The question of which river France and the United States had agreed upon would be disputed by Spain and the United States for sixteen years and contribute to conflict on New Mexico's frontier.

President Thomas Jefferson had already chosen his private secretary, Meriwether Lewis, to lead an American expedition up the Missouri and west to the Pacific Ocean. Lewis would examine part of the new territory and solidify American claims to the Columbia River and the Oregon country against British rivals.[3] Jefferson's westward thrust had ramifications for Spanish-American relations as well. News of Lewis's expedition immediately raised Spanish hackles. Although Lewis would ascend the Missouri and travel west from its headwaters, Spain claimed that Lewis would be trespassing on New Mexico's frontier, which reflected the expansive Spanish concept of that province. Jefferson had downplayed the importance of Lewis's mission by suggesting that it would simply expand "the boundaries of knowledge, by undertaking voyages of discovery, and for other literary purposes." Spanish officials weren't fooled.[4]

In December 1803 Meriwether Lewis and William Clark reached St. Louis, where Spain's former lieutenant governor of Louisiana, Carlos Dehault Delassus, fired off warnings about the Americans to Spanish authorities at New Orleans and Mexico City. At New Orleans in March 1804 former Louisiana governor Casa Calvo in turn wrote to the commander general of the Internal Provinces, Nemesio Salcedo, to express his outrage.

This move of the United States in the very act of taking possession of the province of Louisiana: their haste to inform themselves and to explore the course of the Missouri, whose source, they claim, belongs to them; setting their eyes on the Sea of the South

[Pacific Ocean], forces us of necessity to become active and to hasten to cut short the great steps of our neighbors if we wish, as is our duty, to maintain unharmed the dominions of the king and to prevent the ruin and destruction of the Interior Provinces and the kingdom of New Spain. The only course is to arrest Captain Merry Weather and his party, which can hardly avoid passing among the neighboring [Indian] nations to New Mexico. ... A decisive and vigorous blow will prevent great costs. ... We should not lose a moment.[5]

In so many words, this stance reflected Spain's policy on New Mexico's northeastern frontier for the next two decades: intercept all scheming Americans!

Commander General Salcedo wrote to New Mexico governor Fernando Chacon in May and urged him to send Don Pedro Vial to stop Lewis and Clark, "as he is the most experienced in those territories. ... [Advise] him to keep an exact journal."[6] Vial had been mining in the District of Ste. Genevieve, near St. Louis, but he returned to Santa Fe in July 1803 to again offer his services as an emissary to the indios barbaros. Vial's offer was gratefully accepted and his "desertion" forgotten. In 1804, in an action often overlooked in American history, Pedro Vial launched an effort to intercept Lewis and Clark. He followed a familiar route from Santa Fe northeast to the Pawnees on the distant Rio Chato, or Platte River. The precise detail Vial recorded in his account of that journey—including place names still in use today—makes it possible to discern that he crossed southeastern Colorado.[7] That region of austere mesas and red rock canyons is known today to few outsiders.

On the first day of August 1804 Vial left Santa Fe, paused at Taos to gather ten well-armed settlers and ten Taos Indians, and with this modest party traversed the Sangre de Cristo Mountains to the plains. The group rode to the northeast across the headwaters of today's Canadian River and reached the Dry Cimarron River just south of the New Mexico–Colorado state line. Vial and his men then crossed into present-day Colorado by traversing the eastern spurs of Raton Mesa. On August 15 Vial wrote, "We entered the canyon of the Casa Colorada, having traveled approximately 8 [leagues that day]."⁸ Vial now entered the confines of Chacuaco Creek, which cuts a canyon en route to its confluence with the Rio Animas, today's Purgatoire River in Las Animas County. Casa Colorado, an as-yet unidentified landmark somewhere in this drainage, obviously had reminded Vial or one of his predecessors of a red house, certainly a welcome image to a man in the wilderness.

Vial and his men followed the red dirt meanders of Chacuaco Creek until they reached "the Rio de la Anima[s], which, due to a very heavy rainstorm which had fallen the previous night, was quite high and rapid."⁹ Vial followed the Anima to the Napestle through rugged canyons and over open plains. From that confluence at present-day La Junta, Colorado, he cut northeast to reach the Rio Chato by early September. He had traveled more than two hundred leagues in a month to reach the Pawnees, as he had a decade earlier. American traders had preceded him to the Pawnees and distributed gifts, urging the Indians to relinquish symbols of their allegiance to Spain. "I have ordered all of the said chiefs of the country not to return the [Spanish] medals nor the patents," Vial noted, in a reference to prior Spanish gifts and pacts. "[I told] them that they do not yet know the Americans but that they will know them in the future."¹⁰ The Pawnees had no news of Lewis and Clark, who had passed within a few days ride along the Missouri only weeks earlier. Vial returned to New Mexico with a Pawnee chief to cement Spanish-Pawnee relations. On his return Vial wrote laconically, "We took the same road until we reached the mouth of the Rio de la Casa Colorada, where about 100 Comanches met us." Vial reached Santa Fe in early November and reported on his journey to Governor Chacon. The "Señor Gobernador," Vial noted, "gave the [Pawnee] Captain a medal, a horse, and a rifle, gunpowder, and bullets [as a reward] for his journey [to New Mexico]."[11]

Vial's services remained in high demand. In June 1805 Governor Alencaster asked him to travel to Taos to escort an American carpenter and two Frenchmen who had arrived with "Cuampes," probably Kiowa Indians, to the Palace of the Governors.[12] The American, Kentucky-born James Purcell, was the first of his nation to reach New Mexico. Purcell told the governor that he had left St. Louis the previous June to trap and trade on behalf of fur trader Regis Loisel. Purcell and several companions ascended the Platte, fended off Kiowas, and fled upriver, sustaining themselves on fish. After many hardships he joined another band of Kiowas on the headwaters of the Platte's southern branch in present-day South Park, Colorado, then traveled south to reach New Mexico.

Purcell, like a few of his fortunate French predecessors, brought valuable carpentry skills to New Mexico and thus was allowed to remain. Purcell's two companions, Andres Terien and Dionisio Lacroix, soon were joined by others of French descent. That included Baptiste Lalande, who had left Missouri for the frontier in 1805 with trade goods provided by a Kaskaskia merchant named William Morrison. Lalande reached New Mexico and settled without returning his employer's investment, much to Morrison's chagrin.[13] As for the Kiowas' arrival in New Mexico, Governor Alencaster wrote to his commander general, "They say that the object of their coming is to ask for peace, alliance, and commerce with this province and the Spanish nation, as they have had it with Louisiana, and that they ask for said peace also in the name of the Sayenas [Cheyennes] and the Aas [Crows], two tribes with whom they are allied."[14] The Kiowa Indians once occupied the Yellowstone River area in Montana, and moved south as other tribes pressed in from the north and east. Tradition said the Crow Indians taught the Kiowas to ride and hunt buffalo, forging a bond between the two tribes. The Kiowas first arrived on the Platte River sometime in the late 1700s, and after a generation of war with Comanches they became established on Colorado's plains and later moved south of the Arkansas River as the Comanches themselves moved further south into Texas. The Kiowas and other tribes became dependent on New Mexico for horses and guns in this period, just as Viceroy Bernardo de Galvez had wished back in 1786.

Concerned about American encroachment—particularly Lewis and Clark's whereabouts—and eager to maintain an alliance with the Pawnees, Governor Alencaster sent Vial back to the Pawnees in October 1805. This time Vial took cohort Joseph Charvet and fifty men under carabineer Juan Lucero to accompany him across the northeastern plains.[15] Several Frenchmen, residents of Santa Fe, joined the group. Vial planned to winter with the tribe, and he brought medals and silver-headed canes to demonstrate Spanish goodwill. "Vial [will] inspect the condition and progress of Captain Merri's [*sic*] expedition, and also ... see if he can influence [the Pawnees] in any way against them," New Mexico's Governor Alencaster wrote to his commander general.[16]

Vial's journal of this mission is once again a terse but informative document. Vial and his men left Santa Fe in mid-October, stopped at Taos, and crossed the Sangre de Cristos as before. At the campsite on the east side known as the "Cieneguilla de la sierra" he remarked that he halted "as usual," a reflection of his familiarity with the route and its established camps. The men crossed over the east end of Raton Mesa and headed northeast for Chacuaco Creek. The small Spanish army descended Chacuaco Creek's canyon until bad weather forced them to stop for a day at a large underhang in the red rock meanders, a place Vial dubbed the "Cueva del Chacuaco."[17] Two days later the men reached the Rio de Animas, today's Purgatoire River, and again camped "as usual." The next night a scout thought he spotted three men near camp but the strangers disappeared. The group reached the confluence of the Rio de Animas and Napestle (the Purgatoire and Arkansas rivers) near present-day La Junta and, fearing an ambush, stopped to reconnoiter. After Juan Lucero reported signs of heavy traffic on the Arkansas's north bank, the men spent an uneasy night. The next morning six men appeared on the far bank but ominously vanished as Vial entreated them to draw near. That night strangers attacked the Spanish camp. "The men who attacked us must have been about a hundred and some in number," Vial wrote, "because after having pillaged the encampment, they gathered to take horses to make their escape, but both our citizens and carabineers and the Frenchmen proved themselves to be courageous."[18]

Vial rallied his men and tried to move camp to higher, defensible ground. The unknown enemy harassed them for three leagues before riding off. "At the end of it all, we were not able to recognize which tribe it was because they neither spoke nor cried out in any language; they only gave, while fighting, a very extraordinary shout," Vial wrote. His attackers were not Pawnees, he noted, because they had attacked on horseback; Pawnees fought on foot. They weren't Kiowas, for that tribe fought nearly naked. Vial claimed his attackers had been "fully dressed in the colors of white, red, and blue, with a cloth tied on their heads." "They had no arrows, but all had firearms," he noted. "Finding ourselves devoid of munitions for our defense, we all decided to return to Santa Fe. I traveled all night."[19] In closing his diary of this interrupted journey, Vial suggested, "For the security of our province, it is advisable to construct a fort on the Arkansas River in order to subdue all the tribes, as well as to avoid the entrance of the Americans, because the Anglo-Americans place all their strength to attracting all the tribes to their side."[20] Vial's advice echoed that of Spanish officials in the prior century who had feared a French invasion of New

Mexico's northern frontier. And his reference to the Arkansas, as opposed to the Napestle, marks a shift in Spanish usage for that river.

Governor Alencaster continued to send out Spanish parties to win tribal alliances. In December 1805 he sent interpreter Alejandro Martín down the Red River of eastern New Mexico and west Texas to win over the Yamparica Comanches. In both 1805 and 1806 the governor sent Vial's protégé Juan Lucero to the Kiowas, a mission that may have taken him far down the Arkansas in eastern Colorado and western Kansas. In early 1806 Vial and Charvet were once again sent to the Pawnees on the distant Platte. Somewhere on the frontier, however, their men deserted and they were forced to turn back. Vial's two consecutive failures eclipsed his role as New Mexico's leading interpreter.

The commander general of the Internal Provinces, Nemesio Salcedo, took seriously the American threat to New Spain. From Arispe, Sonora, Salcedo sent Lieutenant Facundo Melgares and one hundred men to bolster the Santa Fe presidio. Melgares had distinguished himself in recent Apache battles on Sonora's frontier and upon his arrival in New Mexico he would be sent to complete Vial's mission to the Pawnees. Melgares would lead the largest expedition to traverse New Mexico's frontier in colonial times. The Americans had to be stopped decisively and the indios barbaros awed by Spanish might.

At Santa Fe in late summer 1806, Lieutenant Melgares mustered four hundred New Mexican militia, one hundred Pueblo Indian warriors, and a *cavallada* two thousand strong. First, he and his army descended the Rio Colorado (today's Red River) far to the east of Pecos to stop a rumored American expedition under Americans surveyor Thomas Freeman and Peter Custis. Melgares encountered Comanches on the Rio Colorado, though not Custis and Freeman, and then turned north. He left half his men encamped on the Arkansas River in present-day Kansas and continued on to reach Pawnee camps on the Platte. This route probably took him closer to Coronado's route across the high plains two and a half centuries earlier than to Vial's recent dashes across southeastern Colorado.

Melgares repeated to the Pawnees the dire warnings about Americans that Charvet and Vial had delivered in prior years. Ironically, just as Melgares exhorted the Pawnees, Lewis and Clark quietly descended the nearby Missouri to reach St. Louis in early September.[21] Despite Spanish officials' concern over Lewis and Clark's mission to the Pacific, they had not intercepted the Americans. Perhaps the frontier was too big, perhaps the deed too great, too full of portent. In one historian's view, "Each official in the upper echelons of the Spanish hierarchy waited for someone else to assume the awesome responsibility of stopping Lewis and Clark."[22]

As the weather began to turn, Melgares returned south to the Arkansas and reunited with his men. The enormous army ascended that river to present-day Pueblo, Colorado, where Melgares probably followed the traditional trace over Sangre de Cristo Pass to the Rio del Norte. His huge expedition had scoured the frontier and found no one. But just as Lewis and Clark returned to civilization another American party headed west. Nearly three centuries after Coronado first reached the high plains by traveling north from Mexico, a young American explorer named Lieutenant Zebulon Montgomery Pike cautiously made his way up the Arkansas River from St. Louis. Pike zigzagged across the prairie to deliver a message of peace and harmony from America to the Osage and Pawnee Indians. Pike's message, naturally, was diametrically opposed to the one recently furnished by Melgares. And Pike had other business.

General James Wilkinson, governor of upper Louisiana and a top U.S. Army officer, had sent Pike west. (President Jefferson learned about Pike's mission only after the latter's return from New Spain.) Wilkinson was a scoundrel. He apparently conspired with Aaron Burr to seize Louisiana, and he received remuneration from the Spaniards for reports on American intentions. Thus, his purpose in sending Pike into Spanish territory seemed designed to gather intelligence on New Mexico, possibly reflecting treachery against his secret sponsors. Events themselves reflect that his young lieutenant set out to find the Red River—purportedly the western boundary of ill-defined Louisiana—and reconnoiter Spanish strength at Santa Fe.[23] To achieve this, Pike would use subterfuge. Once his party reached New Mexico's frontier, one of his men, Dr. John Robertson, would take Kaskaskia merchant William Morrison's claim against Baptiste Lalande to Santa Fe for payment. Dr. Robertson's visit to Santa Fe might provide a pretext for Pike to visit as well. What Wilkinson or Pike thought might happen after that remains unclear.

Pike and his men left St. Louis in July 1806. After reaching the Osage and Pawnee Indians in present-day Kansas, the Americans headed south to reach the Arkansas River. They followed the abundant signs of Melgares's passage west to the mountains, a noticeable trace Pike referred to as the "Spanish road." Gazing at the western horizon on November 15 Pike noted, "I thought I could distinguish a mountain to our right, which appeared like a small blue cloud."[24] "In half an hour, they appeared in full view before us. ... With one accord [we] gave three cheers to the Mexican mountains." This was the Sierra del Almagre known to the Spaniards for two centuries. Pike camped at the confluence of the Arkansas and Fountain Creek, which he dubbed the "grand forks," and set out to climb "to the high point of the blue mountain ... to be able from its pinical [*sic*], to lay down the various branches and positions of the country"—in a move that reflected American idealism and his own personal zeal. Unfamiliar with the atmospheric clarity of the high plains, Pike supposed it would take a day to reach the mountain and a day to climb it.[25] Four days later, on November 27, on the summit of a nearby, lesser mountain, Pike wrote, "The summit of the Grand Peak … now appeared at the distance of 15 or 16 miles from us, and as high again as what we had ascended. … I believe that no human being could have ascended to its pinical."[26]

Pike subsequently rode into South Park, crossed Trout Creek Pass to the upper Arkansas, and split up his party, some of whom encountered the stupendous canyon of the Arkansas River known today as Royal Gorge. In January 1807 the Americans passed down the Valley of the Sierra Mojada (the Wet Mountain Valley) to cross the Sangre de Cristo Mountains at Medano Pass. En route Pike left behind two men with frostbitten feet. His men were lightly clad and suffering from cold and hunger; only the occasional buffalo saved them. Spaniards and Pueblo Indians, long familiar with the Rockies' fierce winters, would never be caught in such a precarious situation on the frontier.

Pike found ubiquitous, even confusing signs of Melgares's army, which had sent out scouting parties in every direction. As he crossed Medano Pass into the San Luis Valley in late January 1807, Pike noted "that there had been a road cut out, and on many trees were various hieroglyphicks [*sic*] painted." Perhaps *comancheros* and *ciboleros* had left sign of their passage. At the western base of the pass the Americans found "sandy hills," a bizarre landscape known today as Great Sand Dunes National Monument. Pike marched his men southwest to the Rio del Norte and descended that river about eighteen miles to the Rio Conejos, where the men built a crude stockade of cottonwood logs. It was early February and bitter cold. Dr. Robinson departed for Santa Fe as planned. Ute scouts must have been watching, for Governor Alencaster soon dispatched Lieutenant Ignacio Sotelo to arrest the Americans and bring them to Santa Fe. A journal of Sotelo's journey has never surfaced, and he can be glimpsed only through Pike's writings.

Although Pike became famous in American history for blundering about the area now known as Colorado in the winter of 1806–1807, little attention has been paid to the man who probably saved his life by arresting him.[27] Sotelo's life before his encounter with Pike remains obscure. He appears in Santa Fe in 1803 as a second lieutenant. The following year he traveled to Chihuahua as a courier, returning in early 1805. In February 1807 he led a party of one hundred presidials and militia north up the Rio del Norte to Pike's miserable camp on the Rio Conejos. To reach that forlorn post, the Spanish lieutenant rode across the Rio del Norte at the traditional ford by San Juan Pueblo and followed the old trail north to Ojo Caliente and beyond. In February's frigid temperatures, buffeted by winds off the Sierra de las Grullas to the west, Sotelo's undertaking would be simple though arduous. His modest army reached Pike's camp in four days, and the two sides parlayed. Pike feigned surprise when informed of his true position on the Rio del Norte. He suggested instead, probably disingenuously, that he was on the Red River. He had little choice but to surrender. Don Bartholemew Fernandez led the Americans south via Ojo Caliente to Santa Fe, while Lieutenant Sotelo rounded up Pike's stragglers. The record does not reflect whether Sotelo selected Medano Pass or another gap to reach the valley of the Sierra Mojada.

Governor Alencaster questioned Pike, who secreted his notes in his gun barrel, then sent the Americans south to Chihuahua. They were released in April and by July had arrived at Natchitoches on the Mississippi. Before Pike left Santa Fe, however, James Purcell mentioned to him that he had found gold nuggets on the headwaters of the Platte's south branch in Bayou Salado, present-day South Park, Colorado. Purcell added that he had successfully guarded this knowledge from his hosts. Ironically, Spaniards had sought gold in the interior of North America for three centuries, and missed the rich placers and hard rock veins on their northern frontier. Pike's report, published in 1810, introduced the "Grand Peak" and descriptions of New Mexico and Chihuahua to Americans hungry for news about western Louisiana and New Spain. His narrative and its detailed geographic descriptions would guide American frontiersmen who followed.

In light of Pike's appearance, New Mexico's Governor Alencaster had to remain vigilant for Americans. In an April 1807 letter to Commander General Nemesio Salcedo, the governor described scouting parties that he had sent north. "[I am] attempting to prevent the entry into this Prov[ince] of any substantial party of Anglo-American Troop[s] when the snows cease. ... Noting on the 12th a great improvement in the weather, I gave the appropriate order that there go out from the jurisdictions of Taos, Canada and Pecos very small scouting parties, and that Lieut. D. Nicholas de Almansa, with a Corporal and eight Soldiers, and an auxiliary force of up to 30 men counting Citizens and Yndians, and Lieut. D. Ygno. Sotelo, with a similar party, make ready to go out."[28]

Lieutenant Almansa rode east to the Conchas River on New Mexico's eastern plains, while Lieutenant Sotelo rode north "to make observations from the point called the Sangre de Christo [Pass] and the Rio del Almagre [Fountain Creek]."[29] These sweeps of the frontier would continue to the end of the colonial period in 1821. In early spring 1810, for instance, Don Esteban Garcia led forty men to the upper Napestle to check a rumor that a handful of trappers had appeared. Soon after, two large trading parties of one hundred men each traveled to the Napestle and Platte to meet the Kiowas, Arapahos, and Comanches. In fall 1810 the soldier José Orion and three native companions rode northeast to inspect the confluence of the Rio Almagre and Napestle, at present-day

Pueblo, where Americans were rumored to be building a fort. Orion found no Americans but scoured the front range anyway. He met Spanish traders and traveled as far north as Arapaho and Kiowa camps on the Platte. There the Spaniards were informed that American traders had been seen in that country, trapping and trading.

Americans such as Manuel Lisa already were exploiting the abundance of beaver on the upper Missouri River and its tributaries. Lisa, a Spanish-born American and partner in the Missouri Fur Company with St. Louis's Chouteau family, operated Fort Mandan on the upper Missouri in present-day North Dakota. From there he sent Jean Baptiste Champlain in 1811 to open commerce with the Arapahos on the Platte and to seek "the River of the Spaniards"—probably a reference to the Rio del Norte—and open trade with New Mexico. Champlain reported to Lisa that Spanish traders he met on the Platte were regular visitors to the area.

In 1811 Champlain, Jean Batiste Lafargue, Ezekial Williams, and others traveled from Fort Mandan south to the Arkansas where they trapped through the winter. They returned to the Platte in the spring and the party split up. Lafargue headed to Santa Fe; Champlain and the others trapped the upper Arkansas. Lafargue's group was arrested in Santa Fe and sent south to jail at Arispe, Sonora. In 1812, with no word of Champlain's whereabouts, Lisa sent Charles Sanguinet south with a letter addressed to "the Spaniards of New Mexico." The letter reached its destination and amazingly was found in Spanish archives in Chihuahua in the twentieth century. In his letter Lisa expressed a desire "to engage in business and open up a new commerce."[30] But Lafargue's treatment showed that Spain's age-old prohibition against foreign trade remained intact. Matters could have been worse. Of Champlain's trappers, only Ezekial Williams emerged from the mountains alive in spring 1813 to paddle down the Arkansas to civilization.

The New Mexicans continued to patrol their northern frontier and, occasionally, they actually caught someone. Juan Lucero became familiar with Colorado's Front Range on repeated visits to the Kiowas and Comanches on the Rio Almagre and upper Napestle in 1807–1810. In March 1810 Lucero encountered a small group of American traders under Joseph McLanahan, Reuben Smith, and James Patterson, and took them to Santa Fe. Governor Don José Manrique promptly sent them down the Camino Real to Chihuahua where they were jailed for two years.

At this juncture a shock wave of revolt rippled throughout the Internal Provinces. In Mexico City Father Miguel Hidalgo y Costilla's demand for rights for the country's peasants had escalated to a cry for independence from Spain. On the eve of success, however, Father Hidalgo's movement faltered. Royalist troops seized the priest, beheaded him, and placed his severed head on public display in the capital as a warning to like-minded souls. Father Hidalgo's fate had little effect on New Mexico. The frontier province was a land apart, still so terribly isolated in its perch at the northern tip of the Camino Real.

Traders still rode up the Rio del Norte and the Rio Chama each year to reach Ute homelands. In 1805, for instance, a genízaro from Abiquiu named Manuel Mestas made a monthlong journey to present-day central Utah to retrieve stolen horses from the Utes. Apparently Mestas and his comrades were familiar with that region and the trail to it. Mestas himself turned seventy that year and had spent a half-century in service as an interpreter to the Utes.

Though the "search for the fabulous" had faded, Governor José Manrique still sought to locate "a Spanish settlement which the Yutas have always asserted lay beyond their territory."[31] In 1811, Don José Rafael Sarracino, New Mexico's postmaster, reportedly made an epic journey northwest of New Mexico, perhaps for that very reason. "After having traveled for three months, he was finally stopped by a large river," according to Don Pedro Bautista Pino, writing in 1812. Sarracino found among the Indians "knives, razors, and awls" of European manufacture, but could not find a ford across the wide river. The Indians indicated that the metal implements came from a people that lived farther northwest.[32] Sarracino may have reached the Rio Tízon, or Colorado River; he may have reached far beyond it. Too little is known of his journey to say with certainty.

In 1813 Mauricio Arze and Lagos Garcia left Abiquiu in March with seven other traders; they returned four months later. They had reached the Timpanogos Utes at Utah Lake and the bearded Utes west of the Sevier River in western Utah. That country had been crossed by Domínguez and Escalante thirty-seven years earlier, and was depicted, though vaguely, on Bernardo Miera's 1778 map. Upon their return to New Mexico the governor demanded testimony on their activities and subsequently charged them with unlicensed trading. Their testimony did not describe the route from Abiquiu to Lake Timpanogos perhaps because, as one historian has suggested, "that route was so well known that nothing needed to be said."[33]

The American tide continued to rise. In 1812, under the mistaken impression that Father Hidalgo had succeeded, Americans Robert McNight, James Baird, and Samuel Chambers left St. Louis and led a small pack train to Santa Fe. Upon arrival, however, they were arrested, relieved of their trade goods, and sent to jail in Chihuahua. Despite the disappearance of several westbound trading parties, however, Americans remained interested in fur trapping on the upper Arkansas and the Platte. In May 1814 the resilient Ezekial Williams and several companions ascended the Arkansas River to retrieve the furs he had cached the year before. In his company were eighteen trappers under Joseph Philibert. Williams returned to the Mississippi Valley with his furs, but Philibert continued upriver and set his traps. In spring 1815 he descended the river to obtain trade goods and bring horses to the upper Arkansas to carry out his own fur cache. Philibert returned up the Arkansas in company with St. Louis traders Auguste Chouteau and Jules DeMun. These men had left St. Louis on September 10, 1815, and reached the Arkansas six weeks later. DeMun remarked in his journal that "the country offers no diversity to the view; always the prairies, as far as one can see without a single tree to arrest the eye of the traveler." Occasionally "many buffalo" and "a great quantity of wild horses" crossed their line of march. By November, two months after setting out, the weather had turned cold and mountains materialized on the western horizon. DeMun scribbled, in an echo of Pike: "During the course of the day we discovered the mountains; as yet they appear like clouds on the horizon."[34] Before they reached the upper Arkansas where Philibert's men wintered, Chouteau and DeMun caught up with yet another party of Americans. Caleb Greenwood, a former employee of Manuel Lisa, had preceded them with a handful of trappers. Spanish fears were well founded.

Chouteau and DeMun, Philibert, and Greenwood reached the confluence of the Arkansas and Huerfano rivers to find that Philibert's men had wintered at Taos. DeMun probably crossed Sangre de Cristo Pass to reach Santa Fe, where he asked Spanish governor Don Alberto Maynez for permission to trap on the province's northern frontier. The governor passed the request along to his superiors and DeMun returned to St. Louis to resupply his men, who remained to trap the headwaters of the Arkansas and Rio del Norte. By this time New Mexico's governor had received orders from his commander general that Americans "ought to be viewed with distrust and suspicion, [and made to] return to their country by the way they came."[35] The alcaldes, or Spanish administrators, at Abiquiu, Taos, and San Miguel del Vado east of Pecos—traditional routes to and from the frontier—were notified of this policy in May 1816.

When DeMun attempted to enter New Mexico in 1816 Spanish officials stopped him at Rio Colorado, north of Taos, and he was rebuffed. Chouteau and DeMun seem to have made a base camp on the upper Arkansas and the following spring DeMun tried again. This time the governor arrested him and sent a Spanish army of two hundred men north to investigate a rumor that the Americans were building a fort at the confluence of the Arkansas and the Rio de las Animas, and that "twenty thousand men [had there at the confluence] many cannons and ammunition."[36] This rumor proved false, but the Spaniards sent two hundred men to check on it, a reflection of heightened tensions.

DeMun gained his release. Nevertheless, Spanish troops returned to the Arkansas under Sergeant Mariano Vernal and arrested DeMun's entire party of Americans. The Spaniards seized the Americans' traps and furs, which DeMun later valued at more than thirty thousand dollars, "the fruits of two years' labor and perils."[37] Governor Don Pedro María de Allande angrily lectured these trappers that American Louisiana did not extend past the distant Mississippi Valley.

At this juncture Secretary of State John Quincy Adams negotiated Louisiana's border with Luis de Onis, Spanish minister to the United States. In 1818, in the midst of these discussions, Onis was alarmed to see a document in English that described New Mexico's defenses. Titled "Notes concerning the Province of New Mexico Collected on My Mission to the West," the unsigned report gave damaging details. (Historians have since attributed it to Luis DeMun, Jules's brother.) It read, in part: "There is no stronghold in the province, even Santa Fe ... is not fortified. ... The people are generally poor, having neither industry nor commerce. ... They also have some (trade) with the savages who live throughout the mountains on the waters of California [the Utes on the Colorado], and also with those who live to the east of the mountains on the waters of the Arkansas. ... One can cross into the province only at three points." The writer went on to describe the traditional passes over the Sangre de Cristo Mountains as well as San Miguel del Vado southeast of Pecos. He added: "I consider New Mexico, in its present position, as one of the most vulnerable points of the Provincias Internas."[38]

Onis forwarded a copy of the "Notes" to Viceroy Juan Ruiz de Apodaca, Condé del Venadito, who ordered New Mexico's governor to fortify the passes mentioned in the document and report on the frontier. Governor Melgares complied with both requests in spring and summer 1819. His report is a succinct description of New Mexico's frontier geography.[39] Melgares assured his superiors that he would fortify the passes into his province—that is, the traditional pass east of Taos, Sangre de Cristo Pass due north of Taos, at El Vado east of Pecos Pueblo, and perhaps at the mountain saddles known today as Mosca and Medano passes.[40]

Rumor of an impending American and Indian invasion again reached Spanish officials. At the end of August 1818 a trader named José Manuel Cayetano Hernandez brought word from his native contacts that Americans were planning to attack New Mexico with Kiowa and possibly Pawnee allies. Those various elements would gather in the fall at La Agua Gerbidora, possibly present-day Manitou Springs, Colorado. In response, Governor Melgares sent Second Lieutenant José Maria de Arze across the mountains to search for the source of the Rio Almagre and posted additional soldiers at Taos and El Vado east of Pecos.[41] Arze led an army of more than one hundred seventy men over Sangre de Cristo Pass to the Rio Huerfano, where he waited for reinforcements.

On September 12 Arze wrote in his journal: "I ordered a detachment of twenty-five horsemen under the command of the settler, Don José Antonio Martinez of the Pueblo of Taos, to go off and reconnoiter the pass which they call the Gap of the Sierra Blanca [Mosca or Medano Pass] and the valley of San Luis. ... If he did not find anything, he should reconnoiter where the Rio Napete

[Napestle] comes out of the sierra, all the Sierra de Almagre, and where the water boils, and ought to unite with me at the junction of the Rio del Almagre with the Napete."[42] (This is the earliest known reference to the San Luis Valley by that name.) Arze dispatched another scouting party north to the head of the Rio Almagre and on to the distant Rio Chato. His men advised him to check the confluence with the Rio de las Animas, and he did so, though he found no foreigners. When Arze finally turned homeward, he probably crossed the eastern end of Raton Mesa, then turned southwest for the pass to Taos. He reported to Governor Melgares on October 10, 1818, having made a comprehensive, six-week sweep of the frontier.[43]

By October 1818 alarming news again reached Spanish officials, this time based in fact. The Americans' planned to send the so-called Yellowstone Expedition to the headwaters of the Missouri River in steamboats. Viceroy Venadito ordered Governor Melgares to spy on the Americans' movements. The Americans intended to explore the upper river and foster an alliance between its natives and the United States, an aggressive move considering that Adams and Onis had yet to sign a treaty setting Louisiana's borders. But in the worried minds of Spanish officials the Americans purportedly intended to attack New Mexico.

Josef Charvet took fifteen men north along Colorado's Front Range to reach clear to the Yellowstone River in present-day Montana. Charvet reported later that the river was more distant from Santa Fe than St. Louis. In fact he had expanded the documented reach of Spanish expeditions north of New Mexico by more than one hundred leagues.[44] Of the Americans' Yellowstone Expedition, however, Charvet learned nothing. A scientific corps under Major Stephen H. Long led the vanguard and ascended the Missouri only as far as the mouth of the Platte River, not far from the site of Don Pedro de Villasur's demise a century earlier. The Americans' experimental steamboats choked on the muddy river water and the expedition foundered. That winter Congress cut the group's funding and the expedition ground to a halt.

In summer 1819, with Spanish concern over American movements still high, Governor Melgares had his men build an outpost on the north side of Sangre de Cristo Pass. This structure—the location of which has bedeviled modern historians and anthropologists—arose on an Oak Creek tributary to the Huerfano, the first and only documented Spanish colonial building to rise on Colorado soil. By October, however, Governor Melgares had to write Commander General Conde that "a band of one hundred men dressed as Indians" had massacred a party of Spanish scouts and overrun the fort. Melgares subsequently sent three hundred settlers to bolster the fort's defense. Sometime not long afterward the exposed fort was abandoned. When it was attacked and by whom is not known, though circumstances suggest it could have been the Pawnees; Melgares's comment seems designed to suggest Americans.[45] The fort's construction and its abandonment were omens of change on the old frontier.

Secretary of State John Quincy Adams and the Spanish minister, Luis de Onis, finally signed a treaty on February 22, 1819, that settled on the Arkansas River as the new international boundary.[46] This treaty resolved other issues: Spain would cede Florida to the United States, which would relinquish claims to Texas. The new border between New Spain and Louisiana Territory would begin at the mouth of the Sabine River and run up the Red River, shoot due north to the Arkansas, then follow the Arkansas to its mountain source near present-day Leadville, Colorado. From there a line ran due north to the forty-second parallel, then due west to the Pacific. Beyond that line both the United States and Britain claimed the Oregon country.

The new agreement between Spain and the United States seems not to have affected Major Stephen H. Long's orders in 1820 to ascend the Platte and locate the sources of the Platte, Arkansas, and Red rivers. Long's expedition, which arose from the ashes of the Yellowstone Expedition, would send him south of the Arkansas, directly into territory Secretary Adams had just agreed would remain in Spanish hands. Secretary of War John C. Calhoun even wrote to Long before the latter's departure that "the farther you can extend your route to the West with safety, the more interesting and important it will be, as it will take you into a portion of our Country heretofore less explored."[47] Calhoun's orders and the outlook they represented would have outraged Spanish sensibilities. The ink on the Adams-Onis treaty had barely dried, but the American aspiration to be a continental nation had already taken root.

Long took his men up the Platte, then the South Platte to reach Colorado's Front Range. He turned south and begrudged his botanist, the young Edwin James, three days to ascend the Grand Peak mentioned by Pike, the Spaniards' Sierra del Almagre. Long split his party in two after James's successful climb. Half descended the Arkansas to Fort Smith while Long himself led the rest south to the Canadian River, which he mistook for the Red. Amazingly the two American parties encountered no Spanish patrols, or native contingents of any size. In fact, Spain's imperial energies in the New World were spent. For a decade, since Father Hidalgo's uprising, independence movements wracked New Spain. On the continent, in the wake of the so-called Riego Revolt, King Ferdinand VII was forced to accept a new constitution. But that document's liberal and anti-clerical provisions disturbed the upper classes in New Spain, which feared a loss of power. When the newly appointed viceroy of New Spain, Juan Ruiz de Apodaca, arrived to implement the new constitution, rebellion mounted among the ruling classes in New Spain. Agustín de Iturbide, an officer once involved in suppressing Father Hidalgo's movement, articulated the growing opposition to the new constitution. His Plan de Iguala demanded protection for the Catholic religion, equal terms for Spaniards and Mexican *criollos* (American-born Spaniards), and, finally, nothing less than independence for Mexico.

Iturbide met the new viceroy at the port of Vera Cruz and forced him to capitulate to Mexican sovereignty. The Treaty of Cordoba was signed August 24, 1821, and, despite initial denial by the Spanish king, Mexico effectively achieved independence. News of this treaty spread like a wind over the open prairie and took only three weeks to reach New Mexico. Word that Iturbide had entered Mexico City reached the remote province the day after Christmas. New Mexicans officially celebrated independence from Spain, though with mixed emotions, on January 6, 1822. The people would not change, nor would their isolation. Their perch on the upper Rio del Norte would demand the same dedication to survival it had demanded for more than two hundred years. This new political distinction would be honored, but it had little practical impact on daily life. About six thousand Hispanics lived at Santa Fe, the province's largest *villa,* at that time. Thousands of Pueblo Indians lived as they had lived for the past century, in uneasy acquiescence to a Hispanic New Mexico. But the outside world marked a milestone. For more than three centuries Spain had held a sizable portion of the New World in its steely grasp. That tenacious grip now was broken. As Spain's fortunes ebbed, a rising tide of Americans flowed west.

In the June 10, 1821, edition of the *Missouri Intelligencer* at Franklin, William Becknell advertised for men "to go westward for the purpose of trading for Horses and Mules, and catching Wild Animals of every description."[48] Becknell and five companions gathered in August at a Missouri farm belonging to Ezekial Williams, who must have briefed them on the geography of the western country. It seems that Becknell always intended to reach

New Mexico, for November found him threading a canyon pass at the east end of the Raton Mesa and heading toward the Spanish settlements. At that moment, Captain Don Pedro Ignacio Gallego and an army of hundreds rode east to the plains, passed south of ancient Pecos Pueblo, and probably crossed the Rio Pecos at El Vado. These Spaniards and their Pueblo allies sought to punish a predatory band of Comanches. Just east of El Vado this Spanish army met Becknell's Americans and their small *cavallada*. Captain Gallegos sent Becknell on to see Governor Melgares, who informed the American that his province would henceforth be open to foreign trade.[49] Thomas James and another party of Americans arrived on Becknell's heels in December 1821. Hugh Glenn and Jacob Fowler appeared in February 1822. Behind them came William Wolfskill, Ewing Young, Benjamin Cooper, and others, first in a trickle, then a torrent. Ceran St. Vrain, Kit Carson, and the Bent brothers were not far behind.

For more than two centuries after Oñate's first settlement on the upper Rio del Norte, the Spaniards of New Mexico had traced the rivers, passes, and canyons of their province's stupendous northern frontier. According to the voluminous record, they had begun by crossing the daunting openness of the high plains and ultimately reached the Platte, the Yellowstone, and the Missouri on New Mexico's far northeastern frontier. To the north, Spaniards had explored the headwaters of the Rio del Norte and crossed Poncha Pass to South Park and the headwaters of the Arkansas and South Platte. They had taken the ancient Ute pass known as Cochetopa to reach the upper Colorado. The Spanish trail up the Rio Chama, across the seven rivers of the Sierra de las Grullas to the Rio Tízon led explorers first, then traders, deep into the treacherous geography of the Colorado Plateau. That much is certain from documents and maps. Yet the great question will always remain: How deeply did Spaniards penetrate the central Colorado mountains

north of South Park? Did they take today's Hoosier Pass to the
Blue River valley? Did they take present-day Tennessee Pass at
the head of the Arkansas to reach the upper Colorado? Did they
reach Middle and North Parks?

Beyond the well-documented expeditions on that vast northern
frontier, however, lie documentary clues to an astounding reach by
anonymous traders and their material influences. In Louisiana in
April 1706 Le Sieur de Bienville wrote to a compatriot: "Among
the Canadians who have arrived [here] are two who went for two
years on the Missouri from village to village ... near the mines of
the Spaniards. They stopped at a village of savages to whom the
Spaniards only come to trade for buffalo hides." Frenchman Nicholas La Salle, writing in October 1708, said of the upper Missouri:
"Spaniards come very frequently with mules to this country "[50]
British traders to the Blackfeet in present-day Montana in the
1760s noted the natives had Spanish horses and gear. Historian
Marc Simmons has written that "ironware from New Mexico ...
was bartered from tribe to tribe, so that ring bits, arrow and lance
points, tomahawks, knives, scissors, and awls eventually reached
wandering tribes on the plains of Canada."[51] In the 1790s Jacques
D'Eglise reached Mandan and Hidatsa villages on the upper Missouri in present-day North Dakota and learned that those Indians
traded with New Mexico. Zenon Trudeau, lieutenant governor of
Spanish Illinois, wrote in 1792: "It seems that these Mandans ...
have communication with the Spaniards, or with nations that
know them, because they have saddles and bridles in Mexican style
for their horses, as well as other articles which this same de la Iglesia saw."[52] In 1805 French trader François-Antoine Larocque
wrote: "While we were here [on the Bighorn River of present-day
Montana] a Snake Indian arrived, he had been absent since the
spring and had seen part of his nation who trade with the Spaniards; he brought a Spanish B[r]idle and Battle ax, a large thick

blanket, striped white and black and a few other articles, such as
Beads &c." Larocque later concluded: "The more southern tribes
have dealings with the white[s] of New Mexico from whom they
get thick striped Blankets, Bridles & Battle axes in exchange for
Buffaloe robes and Deer skins, but it is probably that this Trade of
the Snakes is carried on at a second or thir[d] hand and that they
themselves have no direct trade with the Spaniard[s]."⁵³ Lewis and
Clark met Shoshone Indians in August 1805 on the Lemhi River in
present-day Idaho who told them they traded with Spanish New
Mexico for "horses mules cloth metal beads and the shells which
they woar as orniment being those of a species of perl oister."
"They informed me," Lewis noted in his journal, "that they could
pass to the Spaniards by way of the yellowstone river in 10 days. ...
These people are by no means friendly to the Spaniard[,] their
complaint is, that the Spaniards will not let them have fire arms and
amunition [*sic*]." Lewis also noted, "I saw several [horses] with
spanish brands on them, and some mules which they informed
me that they had also obtained from the Spaniards. I also saw a bridle bit of spanish manufactary, and sundry other articles which I
have no doubt were obtained from the same source."⁵⁴

With Mexican independence Hispanic traders were free to travel
east over Vial's old routes to reach St. Louis, as American traders
journeyed to New Mexico over the route later dubbed the Santa Fe
Trail. And within a decade New Mexico's traders also finally linked
Santa Fe with Los Angeles on the Pacific Coast over what came to
be known as the Spanish Trail, completing an effort begun by
Spanish explorers in the previous century. These traders' influence
extended from the Mississippi to Canada to the Pacific, encom-
passing half of what would become the United States.

Over the course of three centuries Spanish conquistadors, civil
governors, clergy, soldiers, and traders had fought distance, blistering sun, infinite prairie, imposing mountains, storms, Comanches,

Apaches, grizzlies, and rattlers. Their cultural arrogance, courage, tactics, and technology had won them a wilderness empire in North America at great cost to the region's native inhabitants. Bloodlines and beliefs of both European and native had crossed, and over centuries the two peoples reached accommodation on the upper Rio del Norte as the American westward movement gathered momentum. An age of discovery and conflict drew to a close.

Legacy

IN THE SUMMER of 1974 a construction worker digging a
foundation for a new house in Pueblo West, Colorado, felt his
backhoe strike metal about two feet below the surface. This man
recovered a slim metal object about eighteen inches long, thickly
coated with clay and dirt. He assumed it was a section of rebar
and threw it into the back of his pickup truck, where it remained
for some time. The construction site, as with the 1970s development of Pueblo West as a whole, sits on high, gently rolling prairie
above the north bank of the Arkansas River, once known as the
Rio Napestle. Fountain Creek, formerly known as the Rio Sacramento, meets the Arkansas eight miles downstream.

At one point this construction worker had occasion to clean off
the metal object he had found. It appeared to be some sort of spear
point. This man and his wife subsequently divorced, and in divid-
ing their property sold the point to a Pueblo West resident named
Ken Stanelle for less than a couple hundred dollars. Stanelle, who
passed away in 1995, was by nature a collector of intriguing historical objects. No one could tell him much about the point he had acquired on a hunch, until he visited the Museum of New Mexico
and saw a similar artifact. As it turned out, he had acquired a Spanish colonial lance point with fine silver inlay, made sometime during the two decades that followed Governor Anza's peace with
the Comanches. Curators at the Museum of New Mexico believed,
partly based on the fine workmanship of this lance point, that it
once belonged to a Spanish colonial officer. The point probably
was manufactured somewhere on New Spain's frontier, though

not in Santa Fe. Its eighteen-inch blade is still sharp, and the floral pattern with silver inlay is still largely intact. Wear and tear on the blade hint at conflict. It is not difficult, with this hefty point in one's hands, to imagine it attached to the end of an eight-foot wooden shaft. Spanish colonial soldiers wielded lances as a terribly effective weapon that could spear buffalo, bear, or human foe.[1] Little is known of this lance point's provenience, in part because the backhoe operator destroyed its archaeological context during its unearthing. Whether it belonged to an officer who traveled that wind-scoured prairie on patrol against Americans in the early 1800s, or whether it was acquired as a spoil of war, lost during a buffalo hunt, or came to be buried on the prairie in some completely unpredictable scenario, no one can know.

Such is the case with dozens of Spanish colonial artifacts found scattered across the old frontier, spread through trade or perhaps lost through accident, carelessness, or war. As a number of these items have turned up (sometimes literally, by a plow) over the past century or so, they serve primarily as tangible reminders of a not-so-distant past. Unfortunately they cannot tell us much. Even carefully excavated Spanish artifacts whose period of manufacture is known have yet to be definitively linked to any documented expedition, for several reasons. One is that pieces of armor—chain mail, spurs, and bits—usually cannot be precisely dated. The item may have belonged to any number of expeditions active within a given period. Because few if any expeditions actually stayed in one spot long enough to create an archaeological site, Spanish artifacts quite often show up in a native habitation site, once removed from Spanish ownership.[2] The location of an artifact's recovery, and its archaeological context, may therefore bear no connection with the route traced by a Spanish frontier expedition.

In modern terms these artifacts have been recovered in New Mexico, Texas, Kansas, Nebraska, Utah, and Colorado. In Colorado only a few well-documented finds have been made that can be verified today, despite a rich and infectious lore. Sometime in the 1950s a rancher found a Spanish ring bit in his field near Rye (he hung it on the side of his barn for decades). Another colonial-era bit has been recovered in Saguache County at the north end of the San Luis Valley. A Spanish spur has been found on Poncha Pass. Unverified though plausible stories trickle in, of another lance point, discovered near Rye, or of a breast plate and morion, found near Gardner. Then there are those stories for which the evidence is only a vociferous claim. This category includes the famous skeleton in Spanish armor, variously said to have been discovered in a cave near La Junta, or in the Sangre de Cristo Mountains.[3]

At the far end of the spectrum of credibility, tales of buried Spanish treasure, all told with great specificity and fervor, merely attest to the vibrant power of folklore. No one has ever established a connection between the Spaniards of colonial New Mexico and any substantial accumulation of precious metals or coins, local in origin or otherwise. (True believers point out that the Spaniards themselves would have kept such treasures and caches cloaked in secrecy, while modern discoverers naturally would have followed suit. Legend has its own logic.) The existence, in several Colorado locations, of *arrastras*—round stone platforms used to crush ore—have been confirmed, but not precisely dated. These arrastras may have been built by Mexican Americans during the gold rush of 1858–1859.[4] An accomplished archaeologist who has specialized in southeastern Colorado has reliably reported the existence of large pits, perhaps defensive trenches, on the north side of several passes in the Sangre de Cristo Mountains. He emphasizes that diagnostic work must someday be performed to understand if they are man-made, and if so, from what era. But their locations suggest they could be defensive works built at the end of the colonial period, perhaps during Governor Melgares tenure as reports of encroaching Americans alarmed the Spaniards.[5]

The old frontier's best-documented archaeological finds have occurred in Kansas and Nebraska. At the Scott County, Kansas, site now associated with El Cuartelejo, archaeologists have found bits of Tewa pottery dating to 1700–1725, and iron tools, including an axe head. (These artifacts may simply reflect the traditional trading relationship between the Apaches and certain Pueblo peoples in New Mexico.) At Liberal, Kansas, in the southwestern corner of the state, a sixteenth-century bridle has surfaced. Also in western Kansas, in Finney County, a twenty-six inch-long, sixteenth-century Spanish sword was found in 1886. It bore the inscription, NO ME SAQUES SIN RAZÓN, NO ME ENBAINES SIN HONOR—"Draw me not without reason, Sheath me not without honor." The imprinted name, "Gallegos," led nineteenth-century enthusiasts to immediately assign the sword to one of Coronado's men named Gallegos. Subsequent research established that Gallegos was a sword maker in sixteenth-century Spain. Numerous bits of chain mail have been discovered in McPherson and Rice counties in central Kansas, between the 1880s and the 1970s. Clusters of these finds near Lyons, in Rice County, have led archaeologists to suggest that the area corresponds to Coronado's Quivira. Some samples have been tentatively linked to chain mail made in Spain in the first half of the sixteenth century. (That would suggest, but certainly not establish, a connection with Coronado.) At least one archaeologist's judgment is that the lack of chain mail discoveries in the Rio Grande valley, or elsewhere along the route from Pecos to Quivira, may imply that chain mail found in Kansas derived from a plundered source. (The Leyva-Guttierrez debacle leaps to mind as a possible source.) Chain mail, as with all armor, was too precious to trade, and unlikely to simply be lost during an expedition.

In eastern Nebraska a perpetual calendar of Spanish manufacture, and Spanish coins dating from 1767 to 1804, have been recovered at the site of Fort Atkinson, just west of the Missouri River. Bits of armor have also been found on the Loup River, just west of its confluence with the Platte. A Spanish "peace medal" dated 1797—one of those ceremonial links between Spanish officials and "chiefs" of frontier tribes—has been found at a site on the Republican River, on the Nebraska state line with Kansas. In 1874 a retired civil war soldier homesteading in this area recovered a pair of sixteenth-century Spanish stirrups from one of his fields.[6]

Officially, at least, no Spanish colonial artifacts are known to have surfaced in Utah. But it seems likely, given the frequency and longevity of Spanish expeditions in that quarter that many must repose in private collections, unbeknownst to archaeologists and historians. Several inscriptions of Spanish origin have been reported from Utah to Oklahoma, including locations in Colorado. But most of these reports cannot be traced to their source, and common sense dictates that known sites not be identified, so as not to hasten their destruction. The material remains of three centuries of vigorous exploration and trade beyond the northern frontier of colonial New Mexico, when plotted on a map of the American West, in effect scatters only question marks across the land.

The more tangible legacy of Spanish colonial exploration in this region may be found in the eventual Hispanic settlement on New Mexico's northern frontier, today the southern part of Colorado. Though that subject is properly the focus of another study, by another hand, its outline should be sketched here as the logical outcome of centuries of northward exploration and Hispano cultural expansion.

In the wake of three centuries of settlement in Spanish New Mexico and exploration on its frontier, political change came rapidly to the region. Mexican independence in 1821 broke Spain's

grip on the upper Rio Grande. Trade between New Mexico and
Missouri sent traffic back and forth along the Santa Fe Trail. The
Bent brothers built their adobe fortress on the north side of the
Arkansas River on Colorado's plains for the regional Indian trade.
Frontiersmen finally connected New Mexico and California by the
Spanish Trail. Finally, in a move that has governed the political de-
finition of this region down to the present day, Americans arrived
in force in 1846 to raise their flag above Santa Fe's plaza during the
United States's war with Mexico. Three hundred years had passed
since Coronado flew a Spanish standard on the upper Rio Grande.

In the decades after Mexican independence, restless New Mexico families hungry for fresh opportunity packed their belong-
ings in *carretas*, gathered their modest flocks, and rode, walked,
and herded east, west, south, and north beyond the previous limits of settlement. Relative peace with the region's natives provided the environment for expansion. The markets of Chihuahua,
to the south, provided incentive. Settlers populated the plains east
of the Sangre de Cristos, on the Pecos, Mora, and Canadian rivers,
where La Jicarilla and other Apache groups once lived. West of
Santa Fe and Albuquerque, settlers pushed west of the Rio Puerco
into areas once held by the Navajos. On the south settlers simply
followed the great river for a hundred miles. And to the north, the
old trails served once again.

Frontier settlers were often simple countrymen known as *los
paisanos*. Frequently they were stockraisers who populated land
grants made either to individuals or to groups of settlers. Sometimes rough class distinctions distinguished wealthy *patrones*,
who perhaps owned land, from peons, or common laborers, who
worked the fields and herded stock. Many families moved north
to dare the frontier's own natural laws to try for better lives, without securing land ownership. This was particularly true of those
who moved north after the Mexican War of 1846–1848. Later,

American courts were filled with the conflicting claims of Hispanic settlers and Anglo newcomers who had secured deeds to the
same land.

Throughout the fur-trapping heyday of the 1820s in the southern Rockies, Taos served as the fur trade's base, and as the region's
oasis. When in the 1830s and 1840s Anglo-American traders built
posts on the rivers and streams east of the mountains, they sometimes took Indian wives, but often they traveled to Taos or Santa
Fe for brides. These women brought Hispanic influences with
them when they returned to the Arkansas with their husbands.
Some American traders took up residence in Taos and married into
prominent Hispanic families.

By the 1840s and 1850s, *los primeros pobladores*—"the first
settlers"—reached the spacious San Luis Valley by using the traditional trails once trod by Governor Vargas and others. These
humble settlers brought their heritage of language, faith, folklore,
and agriculture with them. They also brought something they had
earned on the frontier: a certain dignity in the face of adversity.
Slowly, in increments measured in sweat and blood, these settlers
expanded the Hispanic frontier northward to found plazas north
of Taos and Ojo Caliente. Initially they built homes of *jacale*, up-
right posts set in the ground close enough to allow plastering with
adobe. As peace with the region's natives allowed, these settlements spread out in the form of ranchos, Hispanic farmsteads
positioned along the region's streams. At first, these humble frontier settlements were periodically abandoned after attacks by Utes
who were making a doomed effort to hold their homeland. But
enough settlers returned to establish themselves permanently. As
one writer has phrased it, "the true settlers of the northern frontier
were not missionaries, soldiers, aristocrats, great landowners, European immigrants, or even government officials. ... The *paisanos*
... were overwhelmingly the backbone of Spanish settlement."[7]

Taos sent forth a steady stream of settlers, who leapfrogged from valley to valley toward the north, using the same basic trail Vargas had used one and a half centuries earlier during the Spaniards' reconquest of New Mexico. Though at first these settlements were periodically abandoned after Ute attacks, permanent towns eventually took root. The village of San Luis, Colorado's earliest, was founded in 1851. In similar fashion, San Pedro, San Pablo, San Acacio, Chama, and San Francisco all took root at the western base of the Culebra Mountains in the years that followed. The establishment of Fort Massachusetts on Sangre de Cristo Creek in this period aided the settlers by ensuring assistance against angry Utes and Apaches.

On the west side of the Rio Grande Valley, Abiquiu and Ojo Caliente sent forth families to settle the northern frontier. The plaza known as Guadalupe, on the Rio Conejos, was founded in 1854. Within two years, the nearby plazas of San Jose and San Rafael took root. Rincones was established in 1857, and in the ensuing decade, the *plazas* of San Juan, La Loma, Los Sauces, and a settlement on Saguache Creek at the north end of the San Luis Valley were founded.

Families moved north from New Mexico's plains over rocky Raton Pass to reach the upper Purgatoire River. La Plaza de los Leones became established near the site of present-day Walsenburg about 1859. Within a few years, plazas also appeared on the upper reaches of the Purgatoire and Apishipa rivers. These settlements are known to have included Madrid, San Miguel, Apodaca, Martinez, Vigil, La Junta, Cordova, Los Baros, Tijeras, San Lorenzo, San Francisco, and Trinchera.

On the northwestern frontier, settlers pushed north up the Rio Chama in the footsteps of their brethren who a century earlier had named the La Plata Mountains. By the turn of the century, Abiquiu had grown to include more than a handful of distinct

plazas, and they provided many of the settlers who moved northwest to occupy the Tierra Amarilla land grant, made in 1832. Two
decades passed before Hispanic settlers could sustain their frontier plazas. Settlements first crept cautiously along the upper
Chama, then by 1860s spread west along the tributaries of the San
Juan River. Knowledge of early settlement in this area is dim, however, and few names survive. By the 1870s plazas named Blanco,
Largo, Los Pinos, Rosa, and Coraque, and a decade later Juanita,
Trujillo, and La Fraqua all cropped up along the San Juan, most
south of the state line. As plazas were founded they produced off-
shoots, like sparks from a campfire.[8] By the Colorado gold rush of
1858–1859, which instigated the subsequent, large-scale settlement of the state by Anglo-Americans, Hispanic settlers already
had set down roots that ran centuries deep. The simple paisanos in
many cases had earned the respectful, collective term, *le gente*, "the
people." Only the steady influx of Anglo-American ranchers, and
their competition for grazing land and town sites, dampened the
northward expansion of the region's Hispanic inhabitants. The attitude of the newcomers, ironically, was akin to that of Spanish
conquistadors and settlers toward the region's natives three centuries earlier. Anglo-American political rule meant that its pur-
veyors assumed cultural superiority over the Hispanics and Native
Americans of the region, much as Coronado, Oñate, Vargas, and
others had assumed Spanish cultural superiority over the region's
native world in preceding centuries. Anglo ignorance of the region's historic fabric, woven from centuries of tradition, conflict,
and geographic knowledge sometimes wrought prejudice and suspicion of those who had preceded them.

The arrival of Anglo-Americans in force meant that the native
Utes, to name one group, would be pushed onto smaller and
smaller reservations of marginal land. Once they had ruled the
plains, mountains, and canyons of New Mexico's sprawling north-

ern frontier. By the time the Hispanic frontier reached its north-ernmost extent, the Utes of this region had been confined to a twenty-mile-wide strip of land in Colorado's southwesternmost corner, present home of the Ute Mountain Ute and the Southern Ute tribes. (The old trail taken by Rivera and Domínguez and Escalante passes through the reservation.) Comanches had obliterated the El Cuartelejo Apaches, clashed with the Spaniards, and moved to the southeast, into Oklahoma and Texas. La Jicarilla Apaches moved in the 1880s to reservation lands in northern New Mexico, also on the Spanish Trail. The Navajos, after a forced and demoralizing move to New Mexico's eastern plains in the early 1860s, eventually moved west of their old homeland to occupy northwestern New Mexico and northeastern Arizona. The score of Pueblos on the upper Rio Grande that survived four centuries of Spanish occupation have largely survived to this day, having absorbed many Spanish practices, yet remained true to native customs as well.

The Hispanic settlers of the old frontier form a living link between the days of the explorers and the present. These peoples and their descendants kept alive the traditional Spanish names for the region's rivers, valleys, mountains, mesas, and plains, and added a few of their own. Though some Hispanic names have been superseded by Anglo ones, many remain, reminiscent of the colonial period. Some names appear to have been assigned so early they defy efforts to trace their origins. The name Sangre de Cristo (blood of Christ) for the mountains east of the Rio Grande, from Poncha Pass on the north to the Pecos River on the south, is one example. The Rio del Norte was transformed to the Rio Grande, but the name Del Norte later was applied to a town on the upper river, established in the 1870s. The origin of the name San Luis Valley, for Colorado's largest mountain park, remains elusive. The name of the Sierra de las Grullas eventually changed to the San

Juan Mountains, but the Sierra de La Plata was merely translated into La Plata Mountains. The seven rivers draining the San Juan Mountains, all tributaries to the San Juan River, retain the names assigned in Spanish colonial times. The San Juan, Piedra, Los Pinos, Florida, Animas, La Plata, and Mancos all flow today with the names they had in Rivera's day; only "Rio" has changed to "River." The Sierra Mojada, east of the Sangre de Cristos, has been directly translated to the "Wet Mountains." The name Sierra del Almagre, for the Pikes Peak massif, was displaced after American explorers like John C. Fremont assigned Zebulon M. Pike's name to its highest summit. Today a lesser mountain to the southeast of Pikes Peak, with two summits over twelve thousand feet, is named Almagre Mountain. But across the southern half of Colorado, particularly along the Arkansas River and points south, within the San Luis Valley, or south of the Dolores River in the western part of the state, the land is spiced by a heartening profusion of Spanish names.

The vibrant Hispanic culture of this region is the most enduring of all the legacies left by the Spanish empire. In the first three decades of this century, researcher Aurelio M. Espinosa traced back to Iberian traditions much of the folk literature, dances, stories, and songs that survived in northern New Mexico and southern Colorado.[9] Espinosa's own family traced its lineage back to Captain Marcelo Espinosa, who arrived in New Mexico with Governor Juan de Oñate. Espinosa's birth in 1880 and upbringing at La Carnero, just northeast of present-day Del Norte, Colorado, drew Espinosa to study the region's folklore. He graduated from the University of Colorado and performed graduate work at the University of Chicago around the turn of the century, the culmination of his antecedents' dreams. In 1905 Espinosa married Maria Margarita Garcia of Santa Fe, herself a descendant of Lieutenant General Roque Madrid. Stories of academic, business, or political achievement arising from the region's deep Hispanic bloodlines is hardly unusual. Carlos Lucero, descendant of a family who arrived on the upper Rio Grande with Oñate, is a successful attorney in Alamosa and a former candidate for the U.S. Senate.

Espinosa, the folklorist, documented that Iberian traditions had not only survived on this long-isolated frontier but that they had evolved as well. This gradual cultural change also is reflected in the region's variation of the Spanish language. Beginning in the 1940s, Rubén Cobos spent decades in northern New Mexico and southern Colorado recording local stories, songs, games, and proverbs. Originally Mexican himself, Cobos took notice of the unique variation of Spanish spoken by locals in the region. Cobos eventually wrote a book, *A Dictionary of New Mexico and Southern Colorado Spanish* (1983), that documents the unique language he found. It contained archaic words and phrases from the sixteenth and seventeenth centuries, Mexican Indian words from Nahuatl (the language of the Aztecs), some Pueblo Indian words, nouns spawned by locality, even English nouns that have undergone Hispanicization. Spanish nouns here sometimes possess semantic variations, and accents can vary from Castilian and Mexican Spanish.[10] This pocket of variations changed again at the turn of the nineteenth century as Mexican laborers traveled north to work in Colorado and New Mexico's factories and fields.

Naturally, Hispanic culture in the region influenced Anglo newcomers in many ways. This region became the Southwest of the United States of America, and its language, art, architecture, cuisine, and very people have had an indelible influence on newcomers who have reached the region over the past century or so. One fundamental Spanish influence on the earliest Anglo-American arrivals was the former's development of ranching in the vast, open land of the West. As one writer has remarked, "It was the Spaniards who introduced the first animals, developed the techniques for working vast herds, and established the basis for widespread and profitable pastoral industries in the New World."[11] Before coming to the New World, Spaniards had become accustomed to herding cattle from horseback. On the high plains and in the mountain parks of the West, they perfected their techniques, and transferred them to newcomers. The Spaniards' vaquero provided the Anglo-American cowboy with his memorable nickname of "buckeroo." The buckeroo borrowed Spanish saddle and stirrup designs, and made good use of the *reata*, or lariat, during two other Spanish traditions, the roundup and the drive. (*Rodeo* is Spanish for "roundup.") The radical geography of the West, combining as it does high plains and even higher mountains, created summer and winter range, and cattle and sheep had to be moved to reach them. On the open range of the West, brands became necessary. These had been a feature in Spanish ranching on the Iberian Peninsula since the tenth century.

In like fashion, Spanish and Mexican mining techniques inspired the Anglo-American sourdough to utilize the *arrastra* for crushing ore for transport to a smelter. These devices used a round base stone of some ten or twelve feet in diameter, and a central pole, about which mules might turn to drag a large stone over the ore for crushing. This method had for centuries been used on the northern frontier of New Spain, and today the remains of arrastras in the mountains of central Colorado still inspire the belief that colonial Spaniards had exploited Colorado's gold-laced ores.

The most lasting and compelling influences of the Spanish colonial era, however, are the living, breathing descendants of New Mexico's earliest families, and of the explorers themselves. Phone books in northern New Mexico and southern Colorado are packed with names like Archuleta, Espinosa, Flores, Garcia, Hernandez, Lucero, Montoya, Vargas, Ulibarrí, and Ruybalid. Even the names of the earliest French traders to reach New Mexico crop up, such as Gurulé and Archibeque. These names evoke an earlier day, when European and native met on the high plains and in this region's mountains and canyons. Spanish explorers who dared

traverse the fabulous geography of colonial New Mexico's northern frontier confirmed the usefulness of native trails during their
dramatic *entradas*. So useful were these native byways used by
Spanish explorers that they often became highways in the modern
age. The success of Spanish colonial explorations directly contributed to the long-term survival of colonial New Mexico and
thus to the Hispanic flavor of this region. The explorers' journals
recorded this region's earliest history and portrayed the nature of
native tribes before they disappeared forever. As with explorers in
other times and other places, Spanish explorers here often led the
way for subsequent settlements. They bequeathed to us a vibrant,
living legacy of place names, lore, and cultural practices that con-
tinues to grow. Rather than being a historical relic of a bygone
age, use of the Spanish language and the vibrancy of Spanish cultural influences in the United States's Southwest expands today.
Chicano and Latino political movements continue to seek equity,
justice, and peace for descendants of the Spanish empire who form
a bright thread within this region's rich tapestry of cultures. The
sons and daughters of the conquistadors live among us.

Glossary

A number of Spanish terms have made their way into the English lexicon. Those that appear throughout this book are listed below in roman type. Others, which derive from the Spanish colonial period, are given in italics below and the first time they are mentioned in a chapter.

alcalde: a civil official in colonial New Mexico much like a mayor, with the powers of a judge

auto: a government edict

bando: a government proclamation

carreta: a two-wheeled cart

cavallada: a horse train

cibolero: a Spanish buffalo hunter

comanchero: a Spanish trader to the Comanches and other Plains tribes

cosas de España: "a Spanish matter," a phrase referring to the inevitable sluggishness of Spanish bureaucracies

Dinetah: literally, "among the people," the Navajo's homeland northwest of colonial New Mexico

El Camino Real: "The Royal Road," specifically a route that linked Mexico City to New Mexico

El Cuartelejo: "The Far Quarter," an Apache settlement north of the Arkansas River near the Colorado-Kansas border

encomienda: a parcel of land and the labor of its native inhabitants, granted to a leading settler

encomendero: the holder of an *encomienda*

entrada: a journey of exploration into unknown lands

escopetas: primitive muskets wielded by 16th and 17th century Spaniards in the New World *genízaro:* a Christianized Indian of colonial New Mexico who has lost tribal affiliation

Gran Teguayo: a mythical realm once thought to lie northwest of colonial New Mexico

indios barbaros: nomadic Indians on New Mexico's frontier

jornada: a waterless journey, typically of a day's duration

La Jicarilla: the tablelands of Raton Mesa, occupied by Jicarilla Apache

Laguna de Copala: Lake of Copala, a mythical realm once thought to lie north of colonial New Mexico

más allá: "further on," a phrase that captures the Spanish drive to find conquest

mestizo: a person of mixed blood, common to New Spain's frontier

milpas: cornfields

mulada: a mule train

plaza: a rectangular arrangement of houses with common walls, a gate, and a courtyard

rancheria: a native settlement on the plains

rancho: an individual, rural Spanish settlement that included a house, outbuildings, cultivated fields, and pastures

requerimiento: the "requisition," an address read by invading Spaniards to New World natives demanding allegiance to Spanish law, customs, and religion

Rio del Norte: today's Rio Grande, site of ancient Pueblo Indian settlements and subsequent Spanish settlement, named for its source north of colonial New Mexico, in Colorado's San Juan mountains

Rio Napestle: a Spanish adaptation of an Indian name for the Arkansas River

Rio Tízon: the "River of Firebrands," today's Colorado River

Sierra Azul: a mythical mountain range said to contain gold and mercury west of colonial New Mexico

Sierra de las Grullas: "Mountains of the Cranes," a colonial Spanish name for today's San Juan Mountains of southwestern Colorado

soldados de cueras: leather-jacketed soldiers common on New Spain's frontier

vecino, vecina: a Spanish settler, or taxpayer, in colonial New Mexico

villa: a Spanish town

Yutas, Yuttas: the early Spanish reference to the Ute Indians on colonial New Mexico's northern frontier

Chronology

(Spanish Expeditions Across New Mexico's Northern Frontier and Related Events)

1492   Ferdinand of Aragon and Isabella of Castile consolidate their monarchies and complete the Spanish reconquest of Iberia by expelling Moors from Granada.

Christopher Columbus sails for the Indies under a Spanish flag but reaches the Caribbean instead, sparking European invasion of the New World and conquests by Spaniards. Natives are referred to as "Indians."

1519–21   Hernán Cortés conquers the Aztecs of Mexico.

1528   Pánfilo de Narváez disembarks at Tampa Bay on an ill-fated expedition to conquer "Florida."

1528–36   Following the demise of Narváez's expedition, survivor Cabeza de Vaca and three companions trek west to Mexico across the interior of North America. They are the first Europeans to see the interior and learn of its peoples.

1532–33   Francisco Pizarro conquers the Incas of Peru.

1539   Esteban, a slave of one of Cabeza de Vaca's companions, and Fray Marcos de Niza travel north to find rich native civilizations. Zunis kill Esteban, but Fray Marcos returns with reports of the Seven Cities of Cíbola.

1540–42   Francisco Vásquez de Coronado leads an expedition north to investigate Fray Marcos's stories, attacks Zuni and Hopi pueblos, and camps on the upper Rio Grande in New Mexico, where he attacks Pueblo tribes. Coronado explores east to central Kansas; López de Cárdenas explores west as far as the Grand Canyon.

1573   Spain's King Philip II issues the Comprehensive Orders, which sought to curb abuses by conquistadors. The orders limit subsequent explorations in the Indies to those introducing Christianity to the Indians.

1581   Fray Agustín Rodríguez, Hernan Gallegos, and Francisco Sánchez Chamuscado travel north to the upper Rio Grande to investigate stories of natives who live in houses and to convert native souls to Christianity. Fray Agustín is martyred by Pueblo Indians.

1582   Antonio Espejo seeks word of Fray Agustín and explores in Coronado's footsteps with the same results. Espejo makes the first documentary mention of the Rio del Norte.

1585   King Philip II of Spain authorizes the colonization of "the Kingdom and Province of New Mexico."

1590   Gaspar Castaño de Sosa leads an unauthorized expedition north to colonize the upper Rio Grande but is stopped by Spanish officials.

1593   Francisco Levya de Bonilla leads another unauthorized journey north to the upper Rio Grande, which ends in tragedy on the high plains.

1598   Governor Don Juan de Oñate founds the Kingdom and Province of New Mexico and establishes its capital at San Gabriel. Oñate searches in vain for another El Dorado and is stripped of his governorship after abuses.

1607   English colonists settle Jamestown on North America's eastern seaboard.

       Oñate is replaced by Don Pedro de Peralta. New Mexico shifts from a royal fiefdom to a missionary outpost.

1610   Peralta establishes his new capital at a fledgling settlement on the Rio Santa Fe. Civil and religious authorities begin to clash over authority in New Mexico.

1617   A Spanish mission is established at Taos.

1620   Pilgrims land at Plymouth Rock on the eastern seaboard of North America.

1625   Fray Alonso de Benavides travels northwest from Santa Fe to the Navajos, probably up the Rio Chama.

1629   Governor Francisco de Sylva, Fray Bartolomé Romero, and Fray Francisco Muñoz travel to the Navajos.

1640   Taos Indians revolt at Spanish abuses and flee to an Apache settlement far to the northeast dubbed El Cuartelejo, "The Far Quarter," north of the Arkansas River on the Colorado-Kansas border.

1642	Captain Juan de Archuleta travels to El Cuartelejo to retrieve the Taos Indians, possibly crossing southeastern Colorado.
1640–70s	Captain Juan Domínguez de Mendoza leads expeditions against the Navajos and other native groups on the northern frontier.
1661	Taos Indians rebel again and flee to El Cuartelejo. A Spanish expedition may have been sent across New Mexico's northeastern frontier to retrieve them.
1680	Nearly all Pueblo groups unite in a successful revolt against the Spanish, who are driven south to El Paso del Norte on the lower Rio Grande.
1681	Exiled governor Antonio de Otermín tries and fails to retake New Mexico.
1682	Robert Cavelier, sieur de La Salle, locates the mouth of the Mississippi River for France.
1692–96	Governor Diego de Vargas leads the reconquest of New Mexico, as Pueblo unity dissolves into factionalism.
1694	Governor Vargas obtains grain for starving settlers from Taos Pueblo, then loops north to avoid ambush. He crosses the Rio Grande in Colorado's San Luis Valley and encounters friendly Utes.
1696	In a last gasp of revolt, Taos and Picurís Indians flee to El Cuartelejo.
1705	Captain Roque Madrid rides north and west against the Navajos, possibly reaching today's Colorado state line.
	Comanches, brought by Utes, first appear at a Taos trade fair.
1706	Captain Juan de Ulibarrí crosses southeastern Colorado en route to retrieve the runaway Taos and Picurís Indians at El Cuartelejo.
1716	Captain Crístobal de la Serna rides north from Santa Fe, possibly as far as the Colorado state line, in pursuit of Comanches.
1719	In pursuit of Comanches, Governor Antonio Valverde y Cosio crosses the Sangre de Cristo Mountains east of Taos and rides north up Colorado's Front Range as far as today's Black Forest Divide.
1720	Lieutenant Governor Pedro de Villasur scours the frontier for Frenchmen, stopping at El Cuartelejo before reaching the Platte-Loup confluence in present-day Nebraska, where his expedition is decimated by Pawnee and Oto Indians.

1730s   Spanish officials repeatedly forbid New Mexicans from trading with frontier tribes, a practice that flourished during this period.

1739   The Mallet brothers are the first French traders to reach New Mexico from the Missouri River valley.

1740s   Spanish expeditions in search of silver and the Ute trade—both authorized and illicit—ascend the Rio Chama northwest of Santa Fe, possibly reaching as far as Colorado's La Plata Mountains.

1748–52   Several parties of French traders reach New Mexico by traveling up the Arkansas River and over the high plains.

1752   Hispanic frontiersmen and *genízaros* establish Abiquiu on the Rio Chama.

1763   Spain acquires Louisiana from France.

1765   Governor Tomás Velez Cachupín sends Juan Maria Antonio de Rivera northwest up the Rio Chama to the Colorado River to seek tribes said to live beyond the Utes and also to prospect for silver in the mountains. Traders follow in Rivera's footsteps, just as they preceded him.

1768   Spaniards kill a Comanche leader, Cuerno Verde (senior), at Ojo Caliente, an outlying settlement on New Mexico's northwestern frontier.

1776–77   Two Franciscan priests, Atanasio Domínguez and Silvestre Vélez de Escalante, travel northwest up the Rio Chama across western Colorado and deep into Utah in search of a path to the Pacific Ocean. Facing a winter crossing of the Great Basin, the party returns to Santa Fe. Afterward, traders continue to use this route to reach the Utes to obtain furs and slaves.

1776   Thirteen British colonies on the continent's eastern seaboard declare their independence from the British Crown.

1779   Governor Juan Bautista de Anza travels north through Colorado's San Luis Valley and crosses South Park to traverse Ute Pass on Pikes Peak's northern flank to make a decisive attack on a Comanche chief, Cuerno Verde (junior), near present-day Rye, Colorado.

1787   Spaniards and Comanches sign a comprehensive treaty at Pecos Pueblo. About this time, Spanish *comancheros* and *ciboleros* engage in annual trade with plains tribes between the upper Rio Grande and Colorado's Front Range.

1792	Pedro Vial blazes a route from Santa Fe to St. Louis by heading east from settled New Mexico and crossing the plains by an unknown route.
1802	Spain relinquishes its claim to Louisiana, which reverts to French ownership with the stipulation that it not pass into American hands.
1803	U.S. President Thomas Jefferson purchases Louisiana from Napoleon, thrusting the United States's disputed southwestern border up against the northeastern border of New Spain (and New Mexico).
1804–06	Meriwether Lewis and William Clark travel from St. Louis to the Pacific Ocean via the upper Missouri River and return alive.
	Pedro Vial is sent northeast to the Pawnees on the Platte River of present-day Nebraska to learn the whereabouts of Lewis and Clark and stop them, if possible. By the time Vial reaches the Pawnees, Lewis and Clark have already passed by.
1805	James Purcell, a frontiersman from Kentucky, becomes the first American to reach Santa Fe.
1806	Spanish lieutenant Facundo Melgares is sent on a wide reconnaissance of the high plains in a vain search for Lewis and Clark.
1806–07	An American, Lieutenant Zebulon Montgomery Pike, ascends the Arkansas River to the Rockies and is arrested by Spanish lieutenant Ignacio Sotelo on the Rio Grande on New Mexico's northern frontier, today's San Luis Valley of Colorado.
1807	Lieutenant Sotelo rides north to cross Sangre de Cristo Pass and reaches Fountain Creek in search of American interlopers, one among many similar Spanish expeditions during this period.
1810	Father Hidalgo's movement toward Mexican independence from Spain is squelched by loyalist forces.
	American traders Joseph McLanahan and Reuben Smith reach New Mexico, believing that Father Hidalgo has succeeded. The Americans are arrested and jailed, among the first of a string of Americans to reach New Mexico for trade.
1812	Americans Robert McNight, James Baird, and Samuel Chambers reach Santa Fe from St. Louis seeking trade, but are arrested and jailed.

1815–17   Americans Auguste Chouteau and Jules DeMun trap the upper Arkansas and Platte rivers in Colorado's mountains. Though they seek permission from Spanish authorities, Chouteau, DeMun, and their men are ultimately arrested and expelled from New Mexico.

1818   Lieutenant José Maria de Arze leads an expedition in search of Americans to locations in the San Luis Valley and on the upper Arkansas River.

Josef Charvet leads a Spanish party north from Santa Fe to the Yellowstone River in present-day Montana.

1819   Spanish soldiers and laborers build a fort on the north side of Sangre de Cristo Pass within the present-day boundaries of Colorado. The fort's Spanish garrison is later decimated by Indians, perhaps Pawnees.

American secretary of state John Quincy Adams and Spanish minister Luis de Onis sign a treaty setting the Arkansas River as the international boundary between the United States and New Spain.

1820   Major Stephen Long leads a geographic and scientific reconnaissance up the Platte River from Missouri, then south along Colorado's Front Range.

Long's botanist, Edwin James, climbs Pikes Peak. Then the expedition splits into two groups and descends the Arkansas and Canadian rivers. These Americans encounter no Spaniards.

1821   Mexico becomes independent from Spain and opens its doors to foreign trade. Captain Pedro Ignacio Gallego rides northeast from Santa Fe to deter Comanches but instead encounters an American trader, William Becknell, who reaches New Mexico for profit, sparking trade over the Santa Fe Trail.

Notes

Introduction

1. David J. Weber, *The Spanish Frontier in North America* (New Haven, Conn.: Yale University Press, 1992), 198.

The Northern Lure: 1492–1598

1. Henri Folmer, *Franco-Spanish Rivalry in North America, 1524–1763* (Glendale, Calif.: Arthur H. Clark, 1953), 24.

2. David J. Weber, *The Spanish Frontier in North America* (New Haven, Conn.: Yale University Press, 1992), 15.

3. J. H. Elliott, *Imperial Spain, 1469–1716* (1963; reprint, New York: Penguin Books, 1990), 64.

4. Cyclone Covey, *Cabeza de Vaca's Adventures in the Unknown Interior of America* (Albuquerque: University of New Mexico Press, 1986), 119. This version of Cabeza de Vaca's testimony on his ordeal is a gripping exploration narrative and the earliest known European account of the American Southwest.

5. Spanish surnames typically combine the names of one's father (first) and mother (second). When addressing someone by only one name, most often the father's name is used. Thus Francisco Vásquez de Coronado is properly referred to on second reference as Vásquez. However, through ignorance, Anglo historians have made many Spanish explorers like Coronado familiar by erroneously using only their "last," maternal names. However, the rule is not steadfast. In Alvar Nuñez Cabeza de Vaca's case, he preferred to use his more illustrious maternal name, Cabeza de Vaca. To avoid confusion in this text, well-known explorers often are referred to by their familiar names.

6. Herbert E. Bolton, *Coronado, Knight of Pueblos and Plains* (Albuquerque: University of New Mexico Press, 1949), 245.

7. National Park Service, "Coronado Expedition National Trail Study," Department of the Interior, Denver, Colo., 1992, passim.

8. George P. Hammond and Agapito Rey, *The Rediscovery of New Mexico, 1580–1594* (Albuquerque: University of New Mexico, 1966), 50. See pp. 323–326 for Jusepe's testimony.

9. Ibid., 325–326.

10. Marc Simmons, *The Last Conquistador: Juan de Oñate and the Settling of the Far Southwest* (Norman: University of Oklahoma Press, 1991), passim.

11. F. S. Curtis, Jr., "The Influence of Weapons on New Mexico History," *New Mexico Historical Review* 1 (July 1926): 325.

New Mexico in Disarray: 1598–1680

1. Marc Simmons, *The Last Conquistador: Juan de Oñate and the Settling of the Far Southwest* (Norman: University of Oklahoma Press, 1991).

2. For Oñate's explorations, including his retracing Leyva's footsteps, see George P. Hammond and Agapito Rey, *The Rediscovery of New Mexico, 1580–1594* (Albuquerque: University of New Mexico, 1966), 50, 323–326; George P. Hammond and Agapito Rey, *Juan de Oñate, Colonizer of New Mexico, 1595–1628*, 2 vols. (Albuquerque: University of New Mexico Press, 1953); Simmons, *The Last Conquistador*. In this last volume, see especially pp. 199–200 for further sources.

3. Both quotes in this paragraph are found in Alfred B. Thomas, *After Coronado: Spanish Explorations Northeast of New Mexico, 1696–1727* (Norman: University of Oklahoma Press, 1935), 9.

4. Spaniards first heard of the elusive Lake of Copala in 1545, and in the 1560s Francisco de Ibarra founded Nueva Vizcaya while searching in vain for Copala along the northern frontier of Zacatecas. Espejo also heard of Copala in 1583. See S. Lyman Tyler, "The Myth of the Lake of Copala and Land of Teguayo," *Utah Historical Quarterly* 20 (October 1952): 313–329, and David J. Weber, *New Spain's Far Northern Frontier: Essays on Spain in the American West, 1540–1821* (1979; reprint, Albuquerque: University of New Mexico Press, 1984), 29–30.

5. For a description of this inscription-laden formation, see John M. Slater's *El Morro: Inscription Rock, New Mexico* (Los Angeles: The Plantin Press, 1961). The site is well worth visiting.

6. Charles R. Cutter, *The Protector de Indios in Colonial New Mexico, 1659–1821* (Albuquerque: University of New Mexico Press, 1986), 23–24.

7. Oakah L. Jones, Jr., *Pueblo Warriors and Spanish Conquest* (Norman: University of Oklahoma Press, 1966), 3–4.

8. For tribal trading relations, see Jack D. Forbes, *Apache, Navaho, and Spaniard* (1960; reprint, Norman: University of Oklahoma Press, 1982), 282.

9. France V. Scholes, "Civil Government and Society in New Mexico in the Seventeenth Century," *New Mexico Historical Review* 10 (April 1935): 71–72.

10. David J. Weber, telephone conversation, June 1993. Quoted in Phil Carson, "The Early Explorers of Colorado," *The Pueblo Chieftain* newspaper, June 13, 1993, D-1.

11. Frank D. Reeve, "Seventeenth-Century Navaho-Spanish Relations," *New Mexico Historical Review* 32 (January 1957): 43.

12. See Cutter, *Protector de Indios,* passim.

13. A good deal has been written about the church-state rivalry of seventeenth-century New Mexico, based on documents containing charges and countercharges between factions that reached Mexico City and Spain before the 1680 Pueblo revolt destroyed local archives in New Mexico. In chronological order of publication, those sources include: Scholes, "Civil Government and Society in New Mexico," 71–111; France V. Scholes, "Church and State in New Mexico, 1610–1650," *New Mexico Historical Review* 11 (1936): 9–76; France V. Scholes, "Troublous Times in New Mexico, 1659–1670," *New Mexico Historical Review* 12 (April 1937): 134–173; Forbes, *Apache, Navaho, and Spaniard,* 113–176; Frank McNitt, *Navajo Wars: Military Campaigns, Slave Raids, and Reprisals* (Albuquerque: University of New Mexico, 1972), 13–17; and Cutter, *Protector de Indios,* 9–19, 37–39.

14. Thomas, *After Coronado,* 10.

15. Weber, *New Spain's Far Northern Frontier,* 30.

16. Lansing Bloom, "Fray Estevan de Perea's *Relacion,*" *New Mexico Historical Review* 8 (1933): 226; and Thomas, *After Coronado,* 9. Note that Thomas is incorrect as to dates and the primacy of this expedition, and unaware that the group referred to are Navajo-Apache. Fray Perea served in New Mexico from 1609 until his death in 1638, and Governor Francisco Manuel de Silva Nieto held office 1629–1632. So the expedition Fray Perea refers to took place sometime in Silva's tenure. For further clarification of this expedition, see Reeve, "Seventeenth-Century Navaho-Spanish Relations," 36–52, especially pp. 40–41.

17. Ruth Marie Colville, author of *La Vereda: A Trail Through Time* (Alamosa, Colo.: San Luis Valley Historical Society, 1996), believes this attack took place near San Antonio Mountain.

18. Discussions on El Cuartelejo and its location have produced a voluminous literature. Significant publications include: James H. Gunnerson, "Protohistoric Apaches in Northeastern New Mexico," in *Guidebook to the Ethnohistory and Selected Protohistoric Sites of the Southern Plains* (Lubbock: Museum of Texas Tech University, 1992), 91–102; and Thomas, *After Coronado,* passim; Waldo R. Wedel, *An Introduction to Kansas Archaeology* (Washington, D.C.: Government Printing Office, 1959),19–27, 68–75, 88–91, 460–469; Thomas A. Witty, "An Archaeological Review of the Scott County Pueblo," *Oklahoma Anthropological Society Bulletin* 32 (1983): 99–106.

19. Direct evidence is limited to a letter that traces early New Mexico history and was written by Fray Silvestre Vélez de Escalante to Fray Agustín de Morphi on April 2, 1778; see Ralph E. Twitchell, *The Spanish Archives of New Mexico,* vol. 2 (Cedar Rapids, Iowa: Torch Press, 1914), 268–280.

20. See Bloom, "Fray Estevan de Perea's *Relacion,*" 212.

21. Forbes, *Apache, Navaho, and Spaniard,* 139.

22. Ibid., 143.

23. Ibid., 139.

24. Reeve, "Navaho-Spanish Relations," 47.

25. McNitt, *Navajo Wars*, 17–18.

26. Scholes, "Troublous Times," 316.

27. Frank Roe, in his book *The Indian and the Horse* (1955; reprint, Norman: University of Oklahoma Press, 1979), 75, states that the first *mounted* Apache attack on New Mexico on record took place in 1659.

28. Myra Ellen Jenkins, "Taos Pueblo and its Neighbors, 1540–1847," *New Mexico Historical Review* 41 (April 1966): 85–111; quote on p. 89. Jenkins cites Charles W. Hackett, *Historical Documents Relating to New Mexico, Nueva Vizcaya, and Approaches thereto, to 1773*, vol. 3 (Washington, D.C.: Carnegie Institution, 1937), 263–264. Alfred B. Thomas states that Taos rebelled after 1664, when Juan de Archuleta and twenty soldiers retrieved them; but here he may be misinterpreting the Escalante letter to Fray Agustín de Morphi. Jack Forbes writes that Penalosa led a punitive foray to El Cuartelejo and doesn't mention a second Archuleta; he quotes Hackett also. See also, Forbes's *Apache, Navaho, and Spaniard*, 157; he quotes Hackett, *Historical Documents*, 3: 263–264. Weber, in *Spanish Frontier*, 149, doubts that Penalosa's claimed 1662 journey to El Cuartelejo ever took place.

29. Forbes, *Apache, Navaho, and Spaniard*, 157; quotes Hackett, *Historical Documents*, 3: 263–264.

30. Weber, *New Spain*, 31.

31. Tyler, "Myth," 322–323.

32. Forbes, *Apache, Navajo, and Spaniard*, 175.

33. Twitchell, *The Spanish Archives of New Mexico*, 2: 43–44.

34. Ibid., 50.

35. Forbes, *Apache, Navajo, and Spaniard*, 179; see also, Charles W. Hackett, ed., *The Revolt of the Pueblo Indians of New Mexico and Otermín's Attempted Reconquest, 1680–1682*, vol. 1 (Albuquerque: University of New Mexico Press, 1942), 13–99.

Respite and Reconquest: 1680–1706

1. Ralph E. Twitchell, *The Spanish Archives of New Mexico*, vol. 2 (Cedar Rapids, Iowa: Torch Press, 1914), 63.

2. For Spanish attempts at reconquest, I've followed writings by Fray Silvestre Vélez de Escalante a century later, found in Twitchell, 2: 268–280, especially pp. 272–273, 276.

3. Jack Forbes, *Apache, Navajo, and Spaniard* (Norman: University of Oklahoma Press, 1960), 282.

4. F. S. Curtis, Jr., "The Influence of Weapons on New Mexico History," *New Mexico Historical Review* 1 (July 1926): 328–329.

5. Don Diego's portrait was painted at age twenty-nine, just before he left for the New World. As of 1985, that painting hung in a chapel in the residence of Vargas's great-great-great-great-great-grandson and granddaughter in Madrid. See John Kessell, ed., *Remote Beyond Compare: Letters of Don Diego de Vargas to His Family from New Spain and New Mexico, 1675–1706* (Albuquerque: University of New Mexico Press, 1989). Kessell's work in Spain in 1982 and 1983 brought to light reams of letters and documents in Vargas's hand that have formed the basis for the University of New Mexico's Vargas Project.

6. The Crown retained a monopoly over quicksilver, a vital smeltering agent. Doing so aided measurement of gold production, which in turn ensured payment of the king's royal "fifth"—the traditional one-fifth cut designated for the Crown.

7. Charles R. Cutter, *The Protector de Indios in Colonial New Mexico, 1659–1821* (Albuquerque: University of New Mexico Press, 1986), 43.

8. Forbes, *Apache, Navajo, and Spaniard*, 252.

9. Ruth Marie Colville, "Introduction to the 1694 de Vargas Expedition to the San Luis Valley," *San Luis Valley Historian* 26 (1994): 34–54.

10. F. S. Curtis, Jr. "Spanish Arms and Armor in the Southwest," *New Mexico Historical Review* 2 (April 1927): 120.

11. J. Manuel Espinosa, "Journal of the Vargas Expedition into Colorado," *Colorado Magazine* 16 (May 1939): 82. Tonnage estimated by John Kessell and Ruth Marie Colville in July 1993: 80 mules × 200 to 300 pounds each = 16,000 to 24,000 pounds, or 10 tons.

12. Ibid., 82–84. Mathías Luxán, or Lujan, served as alcalde mayor of Tanos Indians at San Lazaro and San Cristóbal. In 1695 he joined the founding of Santa Cruz de la Canada. Alfonso Rael de Aguilar also served as *protector de indios* during the reconquest.

13. Ibid., 86.

14. Ruth Marie Colville, conversations, July 10, 1993, and July 10, 1994, at the site of Vargas's ford on the Rio Grande. Colville is the author of *La Vereda: A Trail Through Time* (Alamosa, Colo.: San Luis Valley Historical Society, 1996), a thirty-year study of Vargas's entrada in 1694.

15. Espinosa, "Journal," 86.

16. Ruth Marie Colville says of Vargas's successful ford: "We know about Washington crossing the Delaware, but we don't talk about Vargas crossing the Rio Grande." And, of the Tewa guide: "It isn't always governors and kings who make history. Ordinary people make it, too." The remnants of a nineteenth-century ferry at the site reveal that settlers in the San Luis Valley of Colorado also found the spot useful for crossing, long after Vargas had passed by. Colville led a party to Vargas's ford site on July 10, 1994, three hundred years to the day after Vargas himself had passed.

17. Espinosa, "Journal," 86.

18. Eleanor Richie, "General Mano Mocha and the Utes," *Colorado Magazine* 9 (July 1932): 150.

19. Foregoing quotes, terms, and account of Vargas's ford, buffalo hunt, Ute battle, and route out and back are from Colville's *La Vereda*, 183–224. Colville became interested in Vargas's journey through her adopted homeland in the San Luis Valley in the early 1960s, and spent the next thirty years retracing his steps. She believes the Spaniards lit their signal fire atop South Piñon Hill (which I climbed with John Kessell in 1993 for a view of the scene), and that Vargas's assailants were Moache Utes.

Manuel J. Espinosa of St. Louis University published the first treatment of this *entrada* in "Governor Vargas in Colorado," *New Mexico Historical Review* 11 (1936): 178–187, and in "Journal," 81–90. He implies that Herbert Bolton made copies of the original campaign journal of 1694, found in the National Archives at Mexico City, and deposited those copies in the Bancroft Library at the University of California at Berkeley. Later, Espinosa used copies from the Archives of the Indies at Seville, Spain, the Library of Congress, and the Coronado Library in Albuquerque, New Mexico.

20. Kessell, *Remote Beyond Compare*, 168.

21. Accusers in the *residencia* often abused the situation to cripple many governors, fairly or not, in early New Mexico.

22. In a talk he gives on the subject, John Kessell asks the rhetorical question: "Who was Don Diego de Vargas?" And, as a good professor, he answers it: "He was the personification of the age of Don Quixote. He was a proud, tenacious aristocrat who celebrated the tradition of Spain's greatness, while coping with the realities of Spain's decline."

23. Rick Hendricks and John P. Wilson, *The Navajo in 1705: Roque Madrid's Campaign Journal* (Albuquerque: University of New Mexico Press, 1996) 13, 16. About 1990 the New Mexico Records Center obtained the Sender Collection, which contained Madrid's original journal. That original was said to have been salvaged by Jose Segura of Santa Fe when, in 1870, Governor William A. Pile ordered many archives to be dumped onto Santa Fe's streets.

24. Ibid., 18.

25. Ibid., 19.

26. Frank D. Reeve, "Navajo-Spanish Wars," *New Mexico Historical Review* 33 (July 1958): 221–222.

27. S. Lyman Tyler, "The Myth of the Lake Copala and Land of Teguayo," *Utah Historical Quarterly* 20 (October 1952): 325.

28. Borderlands scholar Herbert Bolton located Ulibarrí's original journal in Mexico's national archives in the early 1930s, and student Alfred. B. Thomas translated the document for his 1935 book, *After Coronado: Spanish Explo-*

rations in Northeast New Mexico, 1696–1727 (Norman: University of Oklahoma Press, 1935). Route discussed in n.34.

29. Biographical details from Fray Angelico Chavez, *Origins of New Mexico Families: A Genealogy of the Spanish Colonial Period* (Santa Fe: Museum of New Mexico Press, 1992), 299–300, and various listings in Twitchell's *The Spanish Archives of New Mexico.* Twitchell's source reflects that Ulibarrí later asked for a land grant near Albuquerque in 1709, registered mines of unknown type in 1709 and 1710, and became an alcalde in Santa Fe in 1710. By 1711 he attained the rank of general and served Antonio Valverde y Cosio. Soon after he was summoned to Mexico City to answer charges lodged by certain Tafoya brothers, and spent some time in prison. He passed away in Mexico City in 1716. For a few more details, see the biographical sketch in Hendricks and Wilson's *The Navajos in 1705*, 126–128.

30. Thomas, *After Coronado*, 59–60.

31. Ibid., 62.

32. Naranjo is one of the more interesting characters to emerge in this period. He later made several frontier journeys on the Spaniards' behalf; see Thomas, *After Coronado*, 101, 112, 156, 275 n.118. For Naranjo's background, see James Hanson, "Spain on the Plains," *Nebraska History*, 74 (Spring 1993): 7.

33. Thomas, *After Coronado*, 262, n.6.

34. Thomas apparently worked from maps, not "on the ground," and postulated that Ulibarrí crossed the Sangre de Cristos at Taos, passed north over Raton Pass, and ascended the front range to the Arkansas at present-day Pueblo. Thomas, relying on the directions and mileage given in Ulibarrí's journal, placed El Cuartelejo on Horse Creek in Crowley County, Colorado. The location of El Cuartelejo is the key to unraveling Ulibarrí's itinerary, and I side with Waldo Wedel, Arnold Withers, Albert Schroeder, and James and Dee Gunnerson in placing El Cuartelejo in the region of an archaeological site in Scott County, Kansas, that has yielded an adobe structure and Pueblo-related artifacts. Withers/Schroeder in 1959 and Dee Gunnerson shortly thereafter offered significant revisions of Thomas's route for Ulibarrí, sending him across northeastern New Mexico, over the eastern end of Raton Mesa. James Gunnerson has suggested that the Spaniards were unaware of compass declination, and that in 1706 it would have been twelve degrees east of magnetic north; thus, the directions in Ulibarrí's diary should be adjusted. The most well-documented reconstruction of Ulibarrí's route appears in James Gunnerson's 1992 publication, "Protohistoric Apaches in Northeastern New Mexico," in *Guidebook to the Ethnohistory and Selected Protohistoric Sites of the Southern Plains* (Lubbock: Museum of Texas Tech University, 1992), 91–96. That route is followed here.

35. All foregoing quotes in this paragraph from Ulibarrí's journal are in Thomas, *After Coronado*, 62–66.

36. This brief reference to the source of the Arkansas River is documented reflection of Spanish knowledge of land north of Poncha Pass, perhaps gleaned in pre-revolt days.

37. Ibid., 66. Contrast Ulibarrí's glowing descriptions with Major Stephen Long and Edwin James's assessment of the region in 1820 as a "Great American Desert." This may well have been a climatic difference.

38. Ibid, 66.

39. This establishes the diffuse nature of El Cuartelejo, and that Ulibarrí's Santo Domingo was but one of many principal settlements within that Apache region. Former Kansas state archaeologist Thomas Witte cautions that it remains uncertain whether Ulibarrí's Santo Domingo is equivalent to today's site of adobe ruins in Scott County State Park, though Jim Gunnerson believes so. In *After Coronado*, p. 264, n.23, Thomas writes: "One of the Spaniards with Ulibarrí at this time testified thirteen years later that he had seen at El Cuartelejo 'some ruins which according to the reports were made a long time ago by the Taos tribe.'" Further, on p. 262, n.6, Thomas quotes an eighteenth-century abstract of Ulibarrí's expedition that at El Cuartelejo, "where had been restored the houses which the fugitive Taos built in the past century," adobe ruins had been seen—a possible reference to the Taos' flight in 1696, but conceivably a reference to the Taos' flight in 1640.

40. After the reconquest Spaniards often presented silver-headed canes, uniforms, medals, and flags to native leaders, both in local pueblos and on the frontier. The practice encouraged a hierarchical structure in native society which facilitated peace and trade. It also provided symbolic rewards to native groups allied with the Spanish of New Mexico. Perhaps these crosses and medals played the same role before the revolt.

41. All foregoing quotes in this paragraph from Thomas, *After Coronado*, 69, 72–75.

French and Comanche Threats: 1682–1752

1. Henri Folmer, *Franco-Spanish Rivalry in North America, 1524–1763* (Glendale, Calif.: Arthur H. Clark, 1953), 71.

2. Ibid., 132.

3. David J. Weber, *The Spanish Frontier in North America* (New Haven, Conn.: Yale University Press, 1992),159.

4. Ralph E. Twitchell, *The Spanish Archives of New Mexico*, vol. 2 (Cedar Rapids, Iowa: Torch Press, 1914), 169, doc. 185; also David J. Weber, *The Taos Trappers* (Norman: University of Oklahoma Press, 1968), 23.

5. Alfred B. Thomas, *After Coronado* (Norman: University of Oklahoma, 1935), 231.

6. Ibid., 138, 139.

7. Elizabeth John, *Storms Brewed in Other Men's Worlds: The Confrontation of Indians, Spanish, and French in the Southwest, 1540–1795* (Lincoln: University of Nebraska Press, 1975), 307.

8. Frank Roe, *The Indian and the Horse* (Norman: University of Oklahoma, 1955), 60.

9. Thomas, *After Coronado*, 27. Thomas cites Amado Chaves, *The Defeat of the Comanches in 1716* (Santa Fe: New Mexico Historical Society, 1906), pub. #8, and Twitchell, *Spanish Archives*, 2: 184, doc. 279.

10. Thomas, *After Colorado*, 110.

11. Ibid., 111.

12. Ibid., 122.

13. Weber, *Spanish Frontier*, 327–332.

14. Thomas, *After Coronado*, 111.

15. Ibid., 116.

16. Ibid.

17. Ibid. The passage on crossing Raton Pass both informs and vexes. Why did Naranjo choose to lead Valverde's enormous army over rocky Raton Pass, when easier routes lay at the mesa's eastern end? The mesa's rough terrain might have left the expedition vulnerable to ambush. Perhaps this was an early attempt at catching the Comanches off guard, by descending from a pass rather than crossing the plains, where a large army would be visible at a distance.

18. Ibid., 118.

19. Ibid., 121.

20. Ibid., 122. This road would be the Taos Trail of latter times, which led from the Arkansas-Fountain confluence southwest across the Huerfano River, threaded Sangre de Cristo Pass, and kept to the east margin of the San Luis Valley en route to Taos.

21. Ibid., 122. The scribe's comment about the wine: perhaps a small advertisement for the governor's vineyards, woven into his campaign journal? It appears that Valverde seized every chance for toasting the saints.

22. Ibid., 123. The "range of mountains" would be later dubbed the Sierra Almagre, or "Mountains of Red Ochre"—today's Garden of the Gods and the Pikes Peak massif.

23. Ibid., 124.

24. Ibid., 126.

25. Ibid., 127–128.

26. Ibid., 129.

27. Ibid., 132.

28. Ibid., 133. Thomas suggested that the expedition used the trail over Sangre de Cristo Pass.

29. Ibid., 144–145.

30. Although that plan never materialized due to a shortage of resources, it is interesting to speculate where a fort might have been built. The summits or passes of Raton Mesa were familiar to the Spaniards and might have served.

31. Thomas, *After Coronado*, 37.

32. Ibid., 134.

33. Ibid., 137.

34. Ibid., 227–228.

35. Ibid., 229–230. Tamariz testified that at Santa Fe he created another account from memory. This has not been found, and would be most enlightening. See Thomas, *After Coronado*, 174–175.

36. It has been assumed Fray Mínguez died at the scene, as he didn't return to New Mexico with the survivors. But there's a scrap of evidence that suggests he may have been taken by the Indians to a French post on the Missouri River. See Twitchell, *Spanish Archives*, 2: 170–174.

37. Doug Scott, archaeologist with the National Park Service, thinks the battlefield site may yet yield evidence of the massacre. The exact spot has never been identified in modern terms, probably due to the meandering of both streams and a lack of interest.

38. Phil Carson, "Artists Capture Chilling Details of 18th-Century Massacre," *The Pueblo Chieftain*, August 8, 1993, D1.

39. Thomas E. Chávez, "The Segesser Hide Paintings: History, Discovery, Art," *Great Plains Quarterly* 10 (Spring 1990): 96–109. A symposium on the Segesser hide paintings, sponsored by the Museum of New Mexico, was tape-recorded and filed at the museum library.

40. Twitchell, *Spanish Archives*, 2: 229, doc. 518.

41. Historians such as Janet Lecompte have conjectured that the Mallets crossed Colorado's Sangre de Cristo Pass en route to the Spanish settlements, but Donald Blakeslee's work on the Pawnee Trail suggests otherwise. See Donald J. Blakeslee, *Along Ancient Trails: The Mallet Expedition of 1739* (Niwot: University Press of Colorado, 1995), passim.

42. Henri Folmer, "Contraband Trade Between Louisiana and New Mexico in the Eighteenth Century," *New Mexico Historical Review* 16 (July 1941): 264.

43. Ibid., 272.

44. For the 1748 letter, see Twitchell, *Spanish Archives*, 1: 148–151, item 499.

45. Folmer, "Contraband Trade," 267–268.

46. See Alfred B. Thomas, *The Plains Indians and New Mexico, 1751–1778* (Albuquerque: University of New Mexico Press, 1940), 21–24, for a list of trade items.

La Plata and Rio del Tizon: 1720–1776

1. One suspects that Spanish traders crossed the Sierra de las Grullas's western mountains in the 1600s. So far, however, the record is silent until the 1740s.

2. John Kessell, *Remote Beyond Compare* (Albuquerque: University of New Mexico Press, 1989), 168.

3. Ralph E. Twitchell, *The Spanish Archives of New Mexico,* vol. 2 (Cedar Rapids, Iowa: Torch Press, 1914), 234, doc. 530.

4. All prior quotes in this paragraph from the depositions taken by Governor Codallos are translated by Leon Bright from a microfilm copy of manuscripts known as the "New Mexico Originals" in the Bancroft Library, University of California at Berkeley.

5. Frank D. Reeve, "The Navajo-Spanish Peace, 1720s–1770s," *New Mexico Historical Review* 34 (January 1959): 11. The expedition sought silver, thought to originate in the mountains beyond the Navajo's Rio Grande. But questions arise: Who led the expedition? What route did it take? Who had gone before, and guided it? What has become of the requisite expedition journal?

6. Later, Spanish settlement moved west from the Rio del Norte, uncomfortably close to Navajo homelands near Cebolleta. By the 1770s the Navajos grew hostile and cast them out. The two sides remained hostile for nearly a century, until the 1860s.

7. Alfred B. Thomas, *The Plains Indians and New Mexico, 1751–1778* (Albuquerque: University of New Mexico Press, 1940), 17, 30.

8. Prior quotes in this paragraph and information on the numbers of New Mexico's defenders from Robert R. Miller, "New Mexico in Mid-Eighteenth Century: A Report Based on Governor Velez Cachupín's Inspection," *Southwest Historical Quarterly* 79 (October 1975): 166–181. The adjective *remote* crops up regularly in Spanish colonial descriptions of New Mexico. Today it's hard to appreciate how such a great distance from Mexico City, or even El Paso del Norte, flavored New Mexican life in the sixteenth, seventeenth, and eighteenth centuries.

9. Thomas, *Plains Indians,* 146.

10. Miller, "New Mexico," 172.

11. Twitchell, *Spanish Archives,* 2: 234, doc. 530, and 2: 258, doc. 697.

12. G. Clell Jacobs, "The Phantom Pathfinder: Juan Maria Antonio de Rivera and his Expedition," *Utah Historical Quarterly* 60 (Summer 1992): 202, 222–223.

13. David J. Weber, *The Spanish Frontier in North America* (New Haven, Conn.: Yale University Press, 1992): 205.

14. Austin N. Leiby, *Borderland Pathfinders: The 1765 Diaries of Juan Maria Antonio de Rivera* (Ann Arbor, Mich.: University Microfilms, 1985), 111. The

little we know of Rivera has been recently uncovered, due to the discovery, translation, and publication of his diaries from 1765. The story of Rivera's diaries and the scholars who have vied to bring them to publication is in itself a small chapter in the historiography of the Southwest. I believe, along with trail hound Clell Jacobs and the discoverer of Rivera's diaries, Austin N. Leiby, that Rivera made it to the ford on the Rio Tízon. Archaeologist Steve Baker, working for historian Donald Cutter, believes instead that he reached the confluence of the Uncompahgre and Gunnison rivers. The late Gregory Crampton and Steve Madsen, who retraced twelve hundred miles of the Spanish Trail, believe that Rivera headed northwest, but fell short of the Rio Tízon.

15. Leiby, *Borderland Pathfinders*, 133–137.

16. Ibid., 172.

17. This is where Clell Jacobs and Steve Baker (see n.14 this chapter) part company. It is a reflection upon the difficulty and pitfalls of route reconstruction from exploration journals that both men are equally convinced of their different interpretations. Jacobs sends his man from the Dolores northwest down north-west-southeast-trending canyons to the northeast-southwest flowing Colorado/Tízon. Baker sends him northeast across northwest-southeast-trending valleys and plateaus to the Gunnison/Tomichi. Yet both assured me that there could be no doubt about the correctness of their interpretation. Despite some apparently contrary evidence, I side with Jacobs, though the precision of his interpretation calls it into question. It appears the savvy Utes did attempt to steer the Spaniards astray, and Rivera does seem to have found the Utes' traditional ford on the Colorado.

18. Leiby, *Borderland Pathfinders*, 200–206.

19. Ibid., 208–214. Leiby suggests this could be a reference to Spaniards on the Pacific Coast, but it seems more likely, though just as difficult to establish, that the reference might be to French traders on the Bear River northeast of Salt Lake. Then again, it might simply have been a tall tale to deter the Spaniards.

20. Does this reference describe a fatal encounter somewhere along the Ute slave trail? Had Spanish traders reached the Tízon years before Rivera? The questions raised by this reference cry out for answers, and they underscore that undocumented traders almost always preceded official expeditions.

21. In 1776 these Timpanogos, or Laguna Utes, were sought by Domínguez and Escalante by an incredibly roundabout route. The Ute trail to the lower river later became the Spanish Trail. Yet this was four years before the founding of San Diego, so the Spaniards as yet had no use for it.

22. Leiby, *Borderland Pathfinders*, 220, and n.34.

23. Elizabeth John, *Storms Brewed in Other Men's Worlds: The Confrontation of English, Spanish, and French in the Southwest, 1540–1795* (Lincoln: University of Nebraska Press, 1975), 432–433.

24. Escalante's appearance is presumably based on physical traits found in that region. See Eleanor B. Adams, "Fray Francisco Atanasio Domínguez and Fray Silvestre Vélez de Escalante," *Utah Historical Quarterly* 44 (Winter 1976): 43. On his kidney ailment, see Ted J. Warner, "The Significance of the Domínguez-Vélez de Escalante Expedition," *Essays on the American West, 1973–74* (Provo: Brigham Young University Press, 1975): 69.

25. Ibid., 66.

26. Adams, "Fray Francisco," 48.

27. Ibid., 52.

28. Ibid., 53.

29. See Herbert E. Bolton, *Pageant in the Wilderness* (Salt Lake: Utah State Historical Society, 1950), and Joseph Cerquone, *In Behalf of the Light: The Domínguez and Escalante Expedition of 1776* (Denver: Paragon Press, 1975). The best work is that which merely provides the expedition journal and its translation, with annotations: Ted J. Warner, ed., *The Domínguez-Escalante Journal,* trans. Angelico Chavez (Provo, Utah: Brigham Young University Press, 1976).

30. Warner, *Domínguez-Escalante Journal,* 12. More than two centuries ago, the name La Plata was already ancient.

31. Ibid., 14. The ruins noted by Escalante may or may not be those so named at the Anasazi Heritage Center in Dolores, Colorado.

32. Ibid., 15. The best route undoubtedly changed year to year, and these guides, like most, relied on memory rather than maps. Perhaps Escalante's comment reflects a little self-righteousness here. But it does illustrate the schism that existed from the start between the high-minded, somewhat naive but principled friars and their rough-hewn guides.

33. Ibid., 18.

34. In "Phantom Pathfinder," 222, Jacobs writes: "The Domínguez-Escalante expedition failed to find the Ute Crossing of the Colorado that was shown to Rivera. Though Escalante tried to follow Rivera's trail, as he had either a copy of the journal or else intimate knowledge about it, he did not have a Payuchi Ute guide and therefore missed Rivera's campground of the first day out of the Dolores River stopping place. … That cost him the total success of his undertaking in proceeding on to Monterey, California, as he lost many precious weeks in his detour through the Colorado mountains."

The fathers knew Rivera traveled east, six miles from a campsite named el Puerto de San Francisco, then north through a steep canyon. Not knowing where el Puerto was, they guesstimated and turned north. They were "one mile too far east," Jacobs asserts. Upon descending present Summit Canyon to the Dolores, they lost their way. The fathers' ultimate determination to cross the Great Basin is open to question.

35. Warner, *The Domínguez-Escalante Journal*, 22.

36. Ibid., 22–25. Although by this time Spaniards were familiar with the Sierra de las Grullas and La Plata, the familiar names for the La Sal and Abajo mountains—gateway to the Colorado River crossing—seem to indicate prior Spanish expeditions to Rivera's and Domínguez-Escalante's treks.

37. All quotes in this paragraph and the next five paragraphs, ibid., 28–33.

38. The Muñiz brothers might be forgiven for not embracing almost certain martyrdom with the same zeal as the two padres. One senses in Escalante's tone that he and Father Domínguez may well have possessed an air of self-righteousness their companions (understandably) might have found irritating.

39. Ibid., 34–37. The crossing was made somewhere between the towns of Grand Valley and Debeque. Note that this description of the Colorado River's source is misleading. It rises in today's Rocky Mountain National Park, far to the north of the San Juan Mountains.

40. Ibid., 40. Other pictographs, though perhaps not these, remain visible on the walls of Douglas Creek's canyon to this day. They were made by the so-called Fremont Indians, who had contact with the Anasazi of the Four Corners region in the period A.D. 900–1300. Thus, these paintings were already ancient when Domínguez and Escalante saw them two centuries ago.

41. The waters of Lake Powell buried this site. It was known as The Crossing of the Fathers, and was photographed by the late C. Gregory Crampton, archaeologist, historian, author, and pathfinder.

42. Correctly retracing Rivera's tracks to the ford, and taking the Sabuagana trail southwest across the northern tributaries to the Colorado might have opened what later became known as the Spanish Trail in the colonial era, a half-century before Mexican and American merchants and fur trappers made the connection. A monumental opportunity for the Spaniards had been missed. Yet the trail to California might also have sent them to their deaths.

43. Adams, "Fray Francisco," 57.

44. Quotes in this paragraph and the previous one from Carl I. Wheat, *Mapping the Trans-Mississippi West*, vol. 1. (San Francisco: Institute of Historical Cartography, 1957), 108–111. Three versions of Miera's map have survived, all with significant differences. The one described here, "Type C," was signed at Chihuahua in 1778.

Provincias Internas: 1776–1803

1. David J. Weber, *The Spanish Frontier in North America* (New Haven, Conn.: Yale University Press, 1992), 209.

2. J. J. Hill, "Spanish and Mexican Exploration and Trade Northwest from New Mexico into the Great Basin, 1765–1853," *Utah Historical Quarterly* 3 (January 1930): 262.

3. Weber, *Spanish Frontier,* 212.

4. The Comanches' nomadic lifestyle or their opportunistic temperament may have stymied attempts at propagating their own herds.

5. Carl I. Wheat, *Mapping the Trans-Mississippi West,* vol. 1 (San Francisco: Institute of Historical Cartography, 1957), 109.

6. Alfred B. Thomas, *The Plains Indians and New Mexico, 1751–1778* (Albuquerque: University of New Mexico Press, 1940), 165, for both quotes in this paragraph. Such meager details make it impossible to place Mendinueta in modern geographical terms.

7. Ibid., 166–167.

8. Elizabeth John, *Storms Brewed in Other Men's Worlds: The Confrontation of Indians, Spanish, and French in the Southwest, 1540–1795* (Lincoln: University of Nebraska Press, 1975), 310.

9. Comanche authority Tom Kavanaugh points out that another "Cuerno Verde" turned up in this region in 1803. Kavanaugh is an anthropologist and curator of the American Indian Studies Research Institute at Indiana University, Bloomington. A 1993 computerized search of Spanish archives in the Southwest for the name Cuerno Verde (conducted by Fritz Jandry of the Arizona State Museum), turned up yet another individual of the same name. The latter two, however, have no direct bearing on the individuals in this narrative.

10. "The standard ethnography will only say that a chief led by example, by argument, by forming consensus," comments anthropologist Tom Kavanaugh. "But there are numerous examples of leaders who used coercive force. We've had this idealistic view of Indian societies. These leaders were politicians, and as motivated by their own psychological need for glory as they were looking out for the good of the people." Tom Kavanaugh, telephone conversation, September 1993.

11. Alfred B. Thomas, *The Plains Indians and New Mexico, 1751–1778* (Albuquerque, University of New Mexico Press, 1940), 169. The tenacious Comanches did not always use well-trod passes, but might cross the Sangre de Cristo Mountains at any point.

12. Ibid., 172. Apparently a Spanish soldier captured by the Comanches about 1762 had assimilated into his captors' culture and advised them on the habits of his former countrymen.

13. Tom Kavanaugh believes this lopsided battle may have provided the historical event on which the folk play known in New Mexico as "*Los Cumanches*" is based.

14. Thomas, *Plains Indians,* 184.

15. Alfred B. Thomas, *Teodoro de Croix and the Northern Frontier of New Spain, 1776–1783* (Norman: University of Oklahoma Press, 1941), 141.

16. Don Garate, telephone conversation, November 25, 1997. Garate is lead interpreter at Tumacacori National Historic Park, south of Tucson, Arizona.

17. Alfred B. Thomas, *Forgotten Frontiers: A Study of the Spanish-Indian Policy of Don Juan Bautista de Anza, Governor of New Mexico, 1777–1787* (Norman: University of Oklahoma Press, 1932), 123.

18. Ibid., 124.

19. J. H. Elliott, *Imperial Spain, 1469–1716* (1963; reprint, New York: Penguin Books, 1990), 67.

20. Thomas, *Forgotten Frontiers,* 125.

21. Ibid., 126. Ron Kessler has assiduously retraced most of Anza's 1779 route. In 1994 he showed me a possible ford site east of Del Norte, Colorado.

22. Ibid., 126.

23. Ibid., 127. Camping at night without a fire along the eight-thousand-foot-high margin of the San Luis Valley, even in summer, must have been quite chilly. During this stretch of the campaign, Anza makes no mention of any trail heading off to Cochetopa Pass on the west, though a traditional trail did so.

24. Ibid., 128.

25. The 1778 *bando* referenced here is listed in Twitchell, *Spanish Archives,* 2: 263, doc. 740.

26. Thomas, *Forgotten Frontiers,* 128, 129.

27. When this name became established is unknown. Note, however, that Governor Valverde, on his reconnaissance along the front range in 1719, did not use the term.

28. Thomas, *Forgotten Frontiers,* 129, 130, 132. Later the Cuerno Verde route was used by Anglo trappers and named the Taos Trail for its ultimate destination.

29. Ibid., 132.

30. John, *Storms Brewed,* 588.

31. Thomas, *Forgotten Frontiers,* 134.

32. Ibid., 135–136.

33. Ibid., 137.

34. To ascertain the truth, I reviewed all published documents from the period, thought by John Kessell and Marc Simmons to contain a reference to the headdress's travels beyond Arispe. I interviewed a dozen leading Southwestern historians, anthropologists, and authors, and attempted, through various avenues and offices, to contact the Vatican—without success. The headdress may just as easily exist at Arispe or Mexico City, or long since have returned to dust. What a grisly find it would be at this late date!

35. Don Bernardo Miera y Pacheco, birth date unknown, was an officer of the Engineering Corps of the Spanish army. He emigrated to the frontier province of New Mexico in 1744 from Chihuahua and lived at Zuni Pueblo in 1747. Miera mapped Escalante's trek to the Moquis/Hopis in 1775. Three years later he created a map of the Domínguez-Escalante expedition across the northern frontier, which he had accompanied. In 1779 he not only turned out the map of Anza's

expedition against Cuerno Verde, but executed a finely detailed map of the province of New Mexico as far north as Taos, west to the Zunis, and east to the Sangre de Cristos. It is not known whether he accompanied Anza, but mistakes on his map hint that he had not. He may have been near sixty—very advanced years for those days—when he completed his maps in 1779. Biographical information found in Thomas, *Forgotten Frontiers*, 378, n.48.

36. Anglo explorers like John C. Fremont and his guide, the trapper Bill Williams, as late as 1849 considered Carnero Creek to be the source. See Patricia Joy Richmond's book, *Trail to Disaster* (1990; reprint, Niwot: University Press of Colorado, 1996), passim.

37. The preceding statements on New Mexico's draft on settlers and illicit trade are based on Twitchell, *Spanish Archives*, 2: 282–297, docs. 790, 796, 828, 855, 871, 902, 912, 913, 1138.

38. Tom Kavanaugh suggests that the Casa de Palo might be the cottonwood grove on the Arkansas River traditionally known by the 1830s as "Big Timbers," where in 1853 William Bent built "Bent's New Fort."

39. Forrest D. Monahan, "The Kiowas and New Mexico, 1800–1845," *Journal of the West* 8 (January 1969): 69.

40. Alfred B. Thomas, "San Carlos: A Comanche Pueblo on the Arkansas River, 1787," *Colorado Magazine* 6 (May 1929): 79–91, quote on page 86.

41. Ibid., 90.

42. Anza subsequently had to omit from his service record his California achievements and his defeat of Cuerno Verde.

43. Although it has been widely reported, even celebrated, that Anza's grave lay under the main chapel floor, it appears that he actually may lie under the floor of a side chapel.

44. See S. Lyman Tyler, "The Spaniard and the Ute," *Utah Historical Quarterly* 22 (October 1954): 343–361, quote on page 355: "There seems to have been an almost continuous contact maintained between the Yutas Timpanogos (near) Utah Lake from Domínguez and Escalante to the Mormons." See also Alfred B. Thomas, "The Yellowstone River, James Long, and Spanish Reaction to American Intrusion into Spanish Domains, 1818–1819," *New Mexico Historical Review* 4 (April 1929): 164–177.

45. Vial's biography found in Noel M. Loomis and A. P. Nasatir's *Pedro Vial and the Roads to Santa Fe* (Norman: University of Oklahoma Press, 1967).

46. Wichita State University's Don Blakeslee believes Vial's sketch combined personal experience with secondhand knowledge. Few men could have drawn such a map that year.

47. Donald Blakeslee, telephone conversation, October 1993.

48. Note that Vial's journeys between St. Louis and Santa Fe predated the Santa Fe Trail by three decades. Don Blakeslee says, however, that Pierre and

Paul Mallet in 1739 get his vote for the sobriquet, "Father(s) of the Santa Fe Trail."

49. Loomis and Nasatir, *Pedro Vial,* 426.

Interlopers: 1803–1821

1. Since Juan de Oñate's time, a number of New Mexico's Spanish-speaking population came from Spain or were a few generations removed. On the frontier, Spaniards (never a homogenous group) mixed with their own, and Spaniards bred with Indians of various nations. Over time, ethnic distinctions became more complicated. Frontier expeditions drew on all elements of New Mexico's inhabitants, who were nominally Spanish. It may therefore be fair in describing the events of the nineteenth century to use the term *New Mexican,* rather than *Spanish,* for the majority of expeditions, which drew on a variegated populace shaped as much by the local environment and cultural mixes as by allegiances to a distant monarch.

2. Marc Simmons and Frank Turley write: "The governors of New Mexico throughout colonial times maintained a vested interest in the Indian trade, usually in violation of strict laws prohibiting officials from participating in such commerce" (*Southwestern Colonial Ironwork* [Santa Fe: Museum of New Mexico Press, 1989], 36). Some details on the period's slave trade in Charles W. Hackett, *Historical Documents Relating to New Mexico, Nueva Vizcaya, and Approaches thereto, 1773,* vol. 3 (Washington, D.C.: Carnegie Institution, 1937), 130, 486, 494.

3. Englishman Robert Gray reached the mouth of the Columbia River in 1792.

4. Marshall Sprague, *So Vast, So Beautiful Land: Louisiana and the Purchase* (Boston: Little, Brown, 1974), 293–295.

5. Noel M. Loomis and A. P. Nasatir, *Pedro Vial and the Roads to Santa Fe* (Norman: University of Oklahoma Press, 1967), 186–187.

6. Ibid., 189.

7. Vial's 1804 diary was discovered about 1970 in the Archives of the Indies at Seville, Spain. Tom Kavanaugh has located Vial's 1785 diary.

8. A. P. Nasatir, "More On Pedro Vial in Upper Louisiana," in John Francis McDermott's *The Spanish in the Mississippi Valley, 1762–1804* (Urbana: University of Illinois Press, 1974), 115.

9. Ibid., 115. Chacuaco Creek gathers waters off Raton Mesa and Mesa de Maya and heads north to join the Animas, (Purgatoire) River, which joins the Napestle (Arkansas), near the present-day town of Las Animas, Colorado. Anthropologist James Gunnerson has worked out a tentative route reconstruction that places Vial in Smith Canyon, east of Chacuaco Creek. But I disagree, as place names, rather than distance and direction traveled, places Vial in Chacuaco Creek's canyon.

10. Ibid., 117. We know Vial visited the Pawnees in 1795, and it appears that his fellow interpreter, Joseph Charvet, did as well in 1803. There may have been other Spanish visits, which supplied the various frontier chiefs with flags, uniforms, and silver-headed canes representative of a Pawnee-Spanish allegiance. Patents were written statements of allegiance, akin to a contract.

11. Ibid., 119.

12. James H. Gunnerson and Dolores A. Gunnerson, *Ethnohistory of the High Plains,* Cultural Resource Series, no. 26 (Denver: Bureau of Land Management, 1988), 13.

13. Other French Americans arrived in Santa Fe in 1805, including Lalande's companions, Jeanot Meteyer, Laurent Durocher, and Jacques D'Eglise.

14. Loomis and Nasatir, Pedro Vial, 424. Noel M. Loomis and A. P. Nasatir believe that the Cuampe are actually Arapahos (*Pedro Vial,* 424); James and Dolores Gunnerson believe the Cuampes were a band of Kiowas and that the Aas were Skidi Pawnees; see Gunnerson and Gunnerson, *Ethnohistory of the High Plains,* 13. I follow the Gunnersons.

15. Joseph Charvet, jn an echo of Vial, had been found in 1795, a man of twenty-eight years, living among Taovayas and Tawakonis in present-day Texas. Spanish officials found him repairing guns, and hunting buffalo and mustangs. Reportedly he had left Philadelphia six years earlier. His nationality remains unclear. After being sent to Coahuila, west of San Antonio, he reached New Mexico and sought work as an interpreter in the spring of 1805. Somehow he had acquired a measure of familiarity with the Pawnees, thus his value to officials at Santa Fe. His name is variously spelled Gervais, Chalvert, Jarvet, Tarvet, etc. See both Loomis and Nasatir, *Pedro Vial,* 412, and Ralph E. Twitchell's *The Spanish Archives of Santa Fe,* vol. 2 (Cedar Rapids, Iowa: Torch Press, 1914), 470, doc. 1796.

16. Loomis and Nasatir, *Pedro Vial,* 428–429.

17. Led by local ranchers Lonnie Jackson and Willard Louden, I visited a section of Chacuaco Canyon in November 1993. In its red rock meanders, we located an underhang of considerable size. We concluded that Vial camped in such a "cave."

18. Loomis and Nasatir, *Pedro Vial,* 435–436.

19. Ibid., 434–436. Speculation about Vial's attackers focuses on an undocumented group of American trappers and hunters working on the Arkansas River. Some of Vial's details are questionable. If he was attacked at night, how could he see the color of his attackers' garb? Did his claim that they were "white, red, and blue" imply that they were Americans, in a bit of propaganda akin to the Segesser hide paintings?

20. Ibid., 438.

21. It's likely that among the crowd that gathered for Lewis and Clark's arrival on September 23, 1806, were Silas Bent, recently appointed surveyor of Louisiana

Territory, and his eldest son, Charles, age seven. The Bents had just arrived in St. Louis.

22. A. P. Nasatir, *Borderland in Retreat: From Spanish Louisiana to the Far Southwest* (Albuquerque: University of New Mexico Press, 1976), 139.

23. Why that information was important to Wilkinson is not known with certainty, but clearly it would assist either his own grand designs or those of the United States—whichever suited him.

24. Pike's initial, uncertain view of the Rockies would be experienced by many westering American parties, and they would use similar language to describe the shimmering horizon.

25. Donald Jackson, ed., *The Journals of Zebulon Montgomery Pike*, vol. 1 (Norman: University of Oklahoma Press, 1966), 349. As with many Americans to follow, Pike was baffled by the clarity of the high plains' atmosphere, which made objects appear closer than they actually were.

26. Ibid., 350–351. Twenty-two-year-old botanist Edwin James made the first recorded ascent, with two companions, on July 13–15, 1820, while on Major Stephen H. Long's expedition to the Rockies. An interesting contrast between the predilections of Americans and Spaniards regarding the mountains: Pike, the first "official" American visitor to the region spotted the "blue mountain" and immediately tried to climb it; over three centuries, only Anza's diary hints that the men with him in 1779 had been to the summit of the Sierra de las Grullas.

27. Twitchell, in his 1914 volume, *The Spanish Archives of New Mexico*, 509, writes: "The archives recounting the arrest of Lieutenant Zebulon Montgomery Pike with his command, and the experiences of Dr. Robinson, have disappeared from the archives, carried away by some person fully cognizant of their value." Conceivably, this record may surface in the future.

28. Jackson, *The Journals of Zebulon Montgomery Pike*, 2: 197.

29. Ibid.

30. Herbert E. Bolton, "New Light on Manuel Lisa and the Spanish Fur Trade," *Texas State Historical Association Quarterly* (*Southwestern Historical Quarterly*) 17, no. 1 (July 1913): 63–64.

31. H. Bailey Carroll and J. Villasana Haggard, eds. and trans., *Three New Mexico Chronicles* (Albuquerque, Quivira Society, 1942), 134.

32. Quotes from Carroll and Haggard, *Three New Mexico Chronicles*, 134. These simplified geographic descriptions don't allow route reconstruction. However, one might speculate that three-months' travel at an average of ten miles per day is nine hundred miles. That could have taken Sarracino to the Snake, or even Columbia River. That sounds far-fetched at first blush. But the Spaniards' record over three centuries establishes that nothing can be ruled out. However, Don Pedro might well have meant that the group traveled a total of three months. Still, four hundred fifty miles one way might have taken the Spaniards to the

Snake or perhaps the Green. Don Pedro Bautista Pino's written description of Sarracino's activities stemmed from the fact that New Mexico had on February 14, 1810, been accorded representation in the Spanish Cortes. Don Pedro, an influential, native New Mexican, was selected as a delegate and traveled to Spain in 1812. He used the Sarracino case to illustrate to the Crown the need for more royal support for the isolated province.

33. J. J. Hill, "Spanish and Mexican Exploration and Trade Northwest from New Mexico into the Great Basin, 1765–1853," *Utah Historical Quarterly* 3 (1930): 18. Although one tends to think of these poorly documented journeys as "out and back," it's tempting to speculate on how well the Spaniards really knew their northwest frontier. Did they merely retrace the outward journey? Or could Arze and Garcia have taken a southern route back through southern Utah, northern Arizona, and western New Mexico, as Domínguez and Escalante had?

34. Thomas Marshall, ed., "The Journals of Jules DeMun," *Missouri Historical Society Collections*, 5, nos. 2, 3 (February, June 1928): 200, 201, 207.

35. David J. Weber, *The Taos Trappers* (Norman: University of Oklahoma Press, 1968), 46.

36. Marshall, "Journals of Jules DeMun," 177. It's interesting that Spanish officials believed that a fort was being erected where the Bent brothers eventually built their adobe fortress in 1832–1834.

37. Ibid., 181. DeMun in 1817 was thinking big, despite his troubles with Spanish officials. DeMun wrote that his ultimate plans were foiled by Spanish interference:

Much delay having taken place by the coming of the Spaniards, it was now impossible for us to proceed to the headwaters of the Columbia by the route we had at first intended to go, which was by following the foot of the mountains, up the Rio del Almagre, and then turn west. [Ute Pass!] Though we knew the road to be good, we could not undertake it for want of time, therefore we resolved to enter the mountains on the north side of the Arkansas River. We passed the first chain with great ease, but we were no sooner on the other side than we foresaw all the difficulties we had to encounter. We had before us a chain of snow-capped mountains much higher than the one we left behind. The cold was intense, and the recital of hardships would renew the sufferings we underwent. After three days of steady labor through the snow, in order to cut a route, we had the mortification to retrace our way back.

38. Alfred B. Thomas, "An Anonymous Description of New Mexico, 1818" *Southwestern Historical Quarterly* 33 (July 1929): 62–66. For the author of the "Notes," see Nasatir, *Borderland in Retreat*, 153. The third pass is Medano Pass over the Sangre de Cristos.

39. The translated text of Melgares's report is found in Thomas, "Anonymous," 68–72.

40. Archaeologist William Buckles, formerly of the University of Southern Colorado, Pueblo, has found what may be the remains of defensive trenches from this period on several passes in the Sangre de Cristos.

41. In retrospect, if Hernandez had been trading illegally, he might have had a motive for lying. He might have voluntarily joined the Pawnees and exaggerated or fabricated an American threat to win leniency upon his return to the province. In fact, Lieutenant José Maria de Arze met Hernandez August 31 and remarked, "I saw through his conversation that the report was not of the validity that I considered before." Alfred B. Thomas, "Documents Bearing Upon the Northern Frontier of New Mexico, 1818–19," *New Mexico Historical Review* 9 (April 1929): 146–164.

42. Ibid., 159. Here Arze asked Don José to take Poncha Pass from the San Luis Valley to reach the Arkansas River, probably cross South Park to Ute Pass on the "Sierra Almagre," and check Manitou Springs ("where the waters boil"). Rendezvous was set for the confluence of Fountain Creek and the Arkansas at present-day Pueblo, Colorado, an ancient crossroads. This is the earliest reference by name to the San Luis Valley I have seen.

43. In 1929 author Alfred B. Thomas received a tracing from a Mr. William E. Baker of Boise City, Oklahoma, of Spanish names and dates etched into rock on the Cimarron River in the western panhandle of Oklahoma. Thomas could positively make out only a date, May 1818. Traders or soldiers? The area was crawling with both that year.

44. Loomis and Nasatir, *Pedro Vial*, 455–456; James Hanson, "Spain on Plains," *Nebraska History*, 74 (Spring 1993): 17; Eleanor Richie, "The Disputed International Boundary in Colorado," *Colorado Magazine* 13 (September 1936): 171–180; Thomas, "Anonymous," 51.

45. Edwin James, on the Long expedition in 1820, mentioned an abandoned Pawnee camp on the South Platte with a striking arrangement of buffalo bones that guide Joséph Bijeau said commemorated a great victory. Some have supposed that that victory was a Pawnee assault on the Spanish fort sometime in late 1819, early 1820. The site of the fort was verified by state historian Leroy Hafen in 1934 but has since been lost (Alfred B. Thomas, "The Spanish Fort in Colorado," *Colorado Magazine* 14 [May 1937]: 81–85). The site was between two branches of Oak Creek, southwest of Badito, Colorado, five miles below the north side of Sangre de Cristo Pass. Jacob Fowler, passing by on February 22, 1822, actually camped there: "Set out Early about South along the foot of the mountains for about ten miles to a Crick about five miles to whar there the Remains of a Spanish fort to apperence ocepied about one year back—Hear We Camped for the night which Was Cold and Windey—" (Elliot Coues, ed., *The Journal of Jacob Fowler* [Minneapolis: Ross and Haines, 1965], 98).

46. These negotiations referred to in the paragraph used a map of North America drawn by Scotsman John Melish at Philadelphia in 1816 and updated in 1818. Melish relied on the maps of Lewis and Clark and Pike to compose his own.

47. Richard G. Wood, *Stephen Harriman Long, 1794–1864: Army Engineer, Explorer, Inventor* (Glendale, Calif.: Arthur H. Clark, 1966), 92.

48. *Missouri Intelligencer*, June 10, 1821.

49. See Mike L. Olsen and Harry C. Myers, "The Diary of Pedro Ignacio Gallego," *Wagon Tracks*, 7, no. 1 (November 1992): 15–20.

50. Addison E. Sheldon, "Discovery and Exploration: The Missouri River Region as Seen by the First White Explorers," *Nebraska History Magazine* 8 (January–March 1925): 7.

51. Simmons and Turley, *Southwestern Colonial Ironwork*, 37.

52. A. P. Nasatir, *Before Lewis and Clark: Documents Illustrating the History of the Missouri, 1785–1804* (1990; reprint, St. Louis: St. Louis Documents Foundation, 1952), 161.

53. W. Raymond Wood and Thomas D. Thiessen, *Early Fur Trade on the Northern Plains: Canadian Traders Among the Mandan and Hidatsa Indians, 1738–1818* (Norman: University of Oklahoma, 1985), 189, 202.

54. Gary Moulton, ed. *The Journals of the Lewis and Clark Expedition* (Lincoln: University of Nebraska Press, 1988), 89, 91, 92.

Legacy

1. Ken Stanelle, interview by author, Pueblo West, Colorado, August 2, 1993. Also, see "Stanelle has 'priceless' Spanish lance head," *The Pueblo Chieftain*, August 8, 1977, 2B. Before passing away, Stanelle loaned the lance point to El Pueblo Museum in Pueblo, Colorado, for public display.

2. It is a tantalizing possibility that a Spanish expedition of hundreds of men might have created a site after one night's stay in a location. Also, local historians dream that the site of Villasur's massacre, or Anza's victory over Cuerno Verde, may someday be located. Why can't artifacts be linked to specific expeditions? I find Waldo Wedel's arguments persuasive. See Wedel's books and articles: *An Introduction to Kansas Archaeology* (Washington, D.C.: Government Printing Office, 1959); "Chain Mail in Plains Archeology," *Plains Anthropologist* (1975): 187–196; and "Coronado, Quivira, and Kansas: An Archeologist's View," *Great Plains Quarterly* 10 (Summer 1990): 139–151.

3. Between 1993 and 1996, I attempted to track down every Spanish colonial artifact alleged to have been recovered within the confines of Colorado. Of dozens of leads, less than a handful could be traced to an actual artifact. Less than a handful have been definitively linked to the Spanish, as opposed to Mexican, period.

4. Arthur L. Campa's book of folktales, *Treasure of the Sangre de Cristos: Tales and Traditions of the Spanish Southwest* (1963; reprint, Norman: University of Oklahoma Press, 1984) gives the flavor of the endless supply of legend and lore associated with the Spanish colonial period in this region. However, in coffee shops from the Arkansas River south, the mere mention of the phrase "Spanish gold" will invoke a stream of sworn testimonials to the existence of fabulous caches in caves, mounds, and tree trunks. Often the treasure was allegedly retrieved by a close relative, who has since passed away, leaving the treasure's location in question.

5. Talk by archaeologist Bill Buckles to the Pueblo County Archaeological Society, Pueblo, Colorado, 1993. Kansas's former state archaeologist, Thomas A. Witty, Jr., provided slides, articles, and commentary on Spanish artifacts found in Kansas. Letters to the author, January 4, 1993, and December 16, 1993. See W. E. Richie, "Early Spanish Explorations and Indian Implements in Kansas," *Transactions of the Kansas State Historical Society, 1903–1904*, vol. 8 (Topeka, Kans.: Geo. A. Clark, 1904), 158–160; Thomas A. Witty, Jr., "An Archeological Review of the Scott County Pueblo," *Oklahoma Anthropological Society* 32 (1983): 99–106.

6. James A. Hanson provided leads on Spanish artifacts uncovered in Nebraska. See James A. Hanson, "Spain on the Plains," *Nebraska History* 74 (Spring 1993): 2–21. See also "Spanish Chain Armor on the Loup," 7 (July–September 1924): 95–96; "The Famous Spanish Stirrups," *Nebraska History* 7 (October–December 1924): 97–101; cover illustration of peace medal in *Nebraska History* 47 (December 1966).

7. Oakah L. Jones, Jr., *Los Paisanos: Spanish Settlers on the Northern Frontier of New Spain* (Norman: University of Oklahoma Press, 1979), 255. For the process and details of settlement on the Hispanic frontier north and northeast of the upper Rio Grande, the single best source, which supersedes earlier articles in *Colorado Magazine*, is Richard L. Nostrand's "The Century of Hispano Expansion," *New Mexico Historical Review* 62 (October 1987) 361–386.

8. Settlement beyond Abiquiu on New Mexico's northwestern frontier is detailed in Frances L. Swadesh, *Los Primeros Pobladores: Hispanic Americans of the Ute Frontier* (Notre Dame: University of Notre Dame Press, 1974), passim.

9. See Aurelio M. Espinosa and J. Manuel Espinosa, *The Folklore of Spain in the American Southwest: Traditional Spanish Folk Literature in Northern New Mexico and Southern Colorado* (Norman: University of Oklahoma Press, 1985).

10. Ruben Cobos, *A Dictionary of New Mexico and Southern Colorado Spanish* (Santa Fe: Museum of New Mexico Press, 1983).

11. Sandra Myres, "Spanish Institutional Backgrounds of the Plains Cattle Industry," *Essays on the American West* (Austin: University of Texas, 1969), 21.

Bibliography

The main sources of unpublished material for this work are the Spanish archives of New Mexico at the New Mexico Records and Archives Center in Santa Fe. Microfilm copies are available at the Denver Public Library's Western History Collection. Also useful are the New Mexico Originals at the Bancroft Library at the University of California at Berkeley. Most of the remaining primary sources used here have been published and are cited below.

Primary Sources

Bloom, Lansing. "Fray Estevan de Perea's *Relacion*." *New Mexico Historical Review* 8 (1933).

Carroll, H. Bailey, and J. Villasan Haggard, eds. and trans. *Three New Mexico Chronicles.* Albuquerque: Quivira Society, 1942.

Castaneda, Pedro de, et al. *The Journey of Coronado.* 1933. Reprint, San Francisco: Grabhorn Press, 1990.

Chavez, Angelico. *Origins of New Mexico Families: A Genealogy of the Spanish Colonial Period* Santa Fe: Museum of New Mexico Press, 1992.

Colville, Ruth Marie. *La Vereda: A Trail Through Time.* Alamosa: San Luis Valley Historical Society, 1996.

Coues, Elliot, ed. *The Journal of Jacob Fowler.* Minneapolis: Ross and Haines, 1965.

Covey, Cyclone. *Cabeza de Vaca's Adventures in the Unknown Interior of America.* Albuquerque: University of New Mexico Press, 1986.

Espinosa, J. Manuel. "Journal of the Vargas Expedition into Colorado." *Colorado Magazine* 16 (May 1939).

Hackett, Charles W. *Historical Documents Relating to New Mexico, Nueva Vizcaya, and Approaches thereto, to 1773.* Vol. 3. Washington, D.C.: Carnegie Institution, 1937.

Hendricks, Rick, and John P. Wilson. *The Navajo in 1705: Roque Madrid's Campaign Journal.* Albuquerque: University of New Mexico Press, 1996.

Jackson, Donald, ed. *The Journals of Zebulon Montgomery Pike.* 2 vols. Norman: University of Oklahoma Press, 1966.

Jacobs, G. Clell. "The Phantom Pathfinder: Juan Maria Antonio de Rivera and His Expedition." *Utah Historical Quarterly* 60 (Summer 1992).

James, Edwin. *Account of an Expedition from Pittsburgh to the Rocky Mountains.* 1823. Reprint, Philadelphia: Carey and Lea, 1966.

———. James Letters, Western Americana, Beinecke Library, Yale University, New Haven, Conn.

———. "Notes of a part of the Exp.n of Discovery Commanded by S.H. Long, Maj., U.S. Esq., 1820." Manuscript journal, Special Collections, Butler Library, Columbia University, New York.

Kessell, John, ed. *Remote Beyond Compare: Letters of Don Diego de Vargas to His Family from New Spain and New Mexico, 1675–1706.* Albuquerque: University of New Mexico Press, 1989.

Leiby, Austin N. *Borderland Pathfinders: The 1765 Diaries of Juan Maria Antonio de Rivera.* Ann Arbor: University Microfilms, 1985.

Loomis, Noel M., and A. P. Nasatir. *Pedro Vial and the Roads to Santa Fe.* Norman: University of Oklahoma Press, 1967.

Marshall, Thomas, ed. "The Journals of Jules DeMun." *Missouri Historical Society Collections* 5, nos. 2, 3 (February, June 1928).

Miller, Robert R. "New Mexico in Mid-Eighteenth Century: A Report Based on Governor Velez Cachupin's Inspection." *Southwest Historical Quarterly* 79 (October 1975).

Moulton, Gary, ed. *The Journals of the Lewis and Clark Expedition.* Lincoln: University of Nebraska Press, 1988.

Nasatir, A. P. *Before Lewis and Clark: Documents Illustrating the History of the Missouri, 1785–1804.* St. Louis: St. Louis Documents Foundation, 1952.

———."More On Pedro Vial in Upper Louisiana." In *The Spanish in the Mississippi Valley, 1762–1804.* Urbana: University of Illinois Press, 1974.

Olsen, Mike L., and Harry C. Myers. "The Diary of Pedro Ignacio Gallego." *Wagon Tracks* 7, no. 1 (November 1992).

Thomas, Alfred B. *After Coronado: Spanish Explorations Northeast of New Mexico, 1696–1727.* Norman: University of Oklahoma Press, 1935.

———. "An Anonymous Description of New Mexico, 1818." *Southwestern Historical Quarterly* 83 (July 1929).

———. *Forgotten Frontiers: A Study of the Spanish-Indian Policy of Don Juan Bautista de Anza, Governor of New Mexico, 1777–1787*. Norman: University of Oklahoma Press, 1932.

Twitchell, Ralph E. *The Spanish Archives of New Mexico*. 2 vols. Cedar Rapids, Iowa: Torch Press, 1914.

Warner, Ted J., ed. *The Dominguez-Escalante Journal*. Translated by Angelico Chavez. Provo, Utah: Brigham Young University Press, 1976.

Wheat, Carl I. *Mapping the Trans-Mississippi West*. Vol. 1. San Francisco: Institute of Historical Cartography, 1957.

Secondary Sources

Adams, Eleanor, B. "Fray Francisco Atanasio Domínguez and Fray Silvestre Velez de Escalante." *Utah Historical Quarterly* 44 (Winter 1976).

Blakeslee, Donald J. *Along Ancient Trails: The Mallet Expedition of 1739*. Niwot: University Press of Colorado, 1995.

Bolton, Herbert E. *Coronado, Knight of Pueblos and Plains*. Albuquerque: University of New Mexico Press, 1949.

———. "New Light on Manuel Lisa and the Spanish Fur Trade." *Texas Historical Association Quarterly (Southwestern Historical Quarterly)* 17, no.1 (July 1913).

Campa, Arthur L. *Treasure of the Sangre de Cristos: Tales and Traditions of the Spanish Southwest*. 1963. Reprint, Norman: University of Oklahoma Press, 1984.

Carter, Clarence E. "Burr-Wilkinson Intrigues in St. Louis." *Missouri Historical Society Bulletin* 10 (July 1954).

Carson, Phil. "The Early Explorers of Colorado." *The Pueblo Chieftain* newspaper, June 13, 1993, D-1.

Cassells, E. Steve. *The Archaeology of Colorado*. Boulder, Colo.: Johnson Books, 1983.

Cobos, Ruben. *A Dictionary of New Mexico and Southern Colorado Spanish*. Santa Fe: Museum of New Mexico Press, 1983.

Colville, Ruth Marie. "Introduction to the 1964 de Vargas Expedition to the San Luis Valley." *San Luis Valley Historian* 26 (1994).

Curtis, F. S., Jr. "The Influence of Weapons on New Mexico History." *New Mexico Historical Review* 1 (July 1926).

Cutter, Charles R. *The Protector de Indios in Colonial New Mexico, 1659–1821*. Albuquerque: University of New Mexico Press, 1986.

Douglas, Walter. "Ezekiel Williams' Adventures in Colorado." *Missouri Historical Society Collections* (1913).

Dutton, Bertha P. *American Indians of the Southwest.* Albuquerque: University of New Mexico Press, 1983.

Elliott, J. H. *Imperial Spain, 1469–1716.* 1963. Reprint, New York: Penguin Books, 1990.

Espinosa, Aurelio M., and J. Manuel Espinosa. *The Folklore of Spain in the American Southwest: Traditional Spanish Folk Literature in Northern New Mexico and Southern Colorado.* Norman: University of Oklahoma Press, 1985.

Espinosa, J. Manuel, "Governor Vargas in Colorado." *New Mexico Historical Review* 11 (1936).

Folmer, Henri. "Contraband Trade Between Louisiana and New Mexico in the Eighteenth Century." *New Mexico Historical Review* 16 (July 1941).

———. *Franco-Spanish Rivalry in North America, 1524–1763.* Glendale, Calif.: Arthur H. Clark Co., 1953.

Forbes, Jack D. *Apache, Navajo, and Spaniard.* 1960. Reprint, Norman: University of Oklahoma Press, 1960.

Gunnerson, James H. "Documentary Clues and Northeastern New Mexico Archaeology." In *New Mexico Archaeological Council Proceedings* 6, no. 1. Lincoln: University of Nebraska State Museum, 1984.

——— "Protohistoric Apaches in Northeastern New Mexico." In *Guidebook to the Ethnohistory and Selected Protohistoric Sites of the Southern Plains.* Lubbock Lake Landmark Quaternary Research Center Series, no. 3. Lubbock: Museum of Texas Tech University, 1992.

Gunnerson, James H., and Dolores A. Gunnerson. *Ethnohistory of the High Plains.* Denver: Bureau of Land Management Cultural Resource Series, no. 26, 1988.

Hackett, Charles Wilson, ed. *Revolt of the Pueblo Indians and Otermín's Attempted Reconquest, 1680–1682.* 2 vols. Albuquerque: University of New Mexico Press, 1941.

Hammond, George P., and Agapito Rey. *Juan de Oñate, Colonizer of New Mexico, 1595–1628.* 2 vols. Albuquerque: University of New Mexico Press, 1953.

Hammond, George P., and Agapito Rey. *The Rediscovery of New Mexico, 1580–1594.* Albuquerque: University of New Mexico, 1966.

Hanson, James. "Spain on the Plains." *Nebraska History* 74 (Spring 1993).

Hill, J. J. "Spanish and Mexican Exploration and Trade Northwest from New Mexico into the Great Basin, 1765–1853." *Utah Historical Quarterly* 3 (1930).

Hughes, J. Donald. *American Indians in Colorado.* Boulder, Colo.: Pruett Publishing, 1977.

Hurtado, Albert L., and Peter Iverson, eds. *Major Problems in American Indian History.* Lexington, Ky.: D.C. Heath, 1994.

Jenkins, Myra Ellen. "Taos Pueblo and its Neighbors, 1540–1847." *New Mexico Historical Review* 41 (April 1966).

John, Elizabeth. *Storms Brewed in Other Men's Worlds: The Confrontation of Indians, Spanish, and French in the Southwest, 1540–1795.* Lincoln: University of Nebraska Press, 1975.

Jones, Oakah L., Jr. *Los Paisanos: Spanish Settlers on the Northern Frontier of New Spain.* Norman: University of Oklahoma Press, 1979.

———. *Pueblo Warriors and Spanish Conquest.* Norman: University of Oklahoma Press, 1966.

McNitt, Frank. *Navajo Wars: Military Campaigns, Slave Raids, and Reprisals.* Albuquerque: University of New Mexico Press, 1972.

Monahan, Forrest D. "The Kiowas and New Mexico, 1800–1845." *Journal of the West* 8 (January 1969).

Morison, Samuel. *The Great Explorers: The European Discovery of America.* New York: Oxford University Press, 1978.

Myres, Sandra. "Spanish Institutional Backgrounds of the Plains Cattle Industry." In *Essays on the American West.* Austin: University of Texas, 1969.

Nasatir, A. P. *Borderland in Retreat: From Spanish Louisiana to the Far Southwest.* Albuquerque: University of New Mexico Press, 1976.

National Park Service. "Coronado Expedition National Trail Study." Denver: Department of the Interior, 1992.

Nostrand, Richard L. "The Century of Hispano Expansion." *New Mexico Historical Review* 62 (October 1987).

Oglesby, Richard. *Manuel Lisa and the Opening of the Missouri Fur Trade.* Norman: University of Oklahoma Press, 1963.

Reeve, Frank K. "Seventeenth Century Navaho-Spanish Relations," *New Mexico Historical Review* 32 (January 1957).

———. "The Navajo-Spanish Peace, 1720s–1770s." *New Mexico Historical Review* 34 (January 1959).

————. "The Navajo-Spanish Wars." *New Mexico Historical Review* 33 (July 1958).

Richie, Eleanor. "General Mano Mocha and the Utes." *Colorado Magazine* 9 (July 1932).

————. "The Disputed International Boundary in Colorado." *Colorado Magazine* 13 (September 1936).

Richie, W. E. "Early Spanish Explorations and Indian Implements in Kansas." *Transactions of the Kansas State Historical Society 1903–1904*. vol. 8. Topeka, Kans.: Geo. A. Clark, 1904.

Roe, Frank. *The Indian and the Horse*. 1955. Reprint, Norman: University of Oklahoma Press, 1979.

Scholes, France V. "Church and State in New Mexico, 1610–1650." *New Mexico Historical Review* 11 (1936).

————. "Civil Government and Society in New Mexico in the Seventeenth Century." *New Mexico Historical Review* 10 (April 1935).

————. "Troublous Times in New Mexico, 1659–1670." *New Mexico Historical Review* 12 (April 1937).

Simmons, Marc, and Frank Turley. *Southwestern Colonial Ironwork*. Santa Fe: Museum of New Mexico Press, 1980.

Simmons, Marc. *The Last Conquistador: Juan de Oñate and the Settling of the Far Southwest*. Norman: University of Oklahoma Press, 1991.

Slater, John M. *El Morro: Inscription Rock, New Mexico*. Los Angeles: The Plantin Press, 1961.

Sprague, Marshall. *So Vast, So Beautiful a Land: Louisiana and the Purchase*. Boston: Little, Brown, 1974.

Swadesh, Frances L. *Los Primeros Pobladores: Hispanic Americans of the Ute Frontier*. Notre Dame, Ind.: University of Notre Dame Press, 1974.

Thomas, Alfred B. *The Plains Indians and New Mexico, 1751–1778*. Albuquerque: University of New Mexico Press, 1940.

————. "San Carlos: A Comanche Pueblo on the Arkansas River, 1787." *Colorado Magazine* 6 (May 1929).

————. "The Spanish Fort in Colorado." *Colorado Magazine* 14 (May 1937).

————. *Teodoro de Croix and the Northern Frontier of New Spain, 1776–1783*. Norman: University of Oklahoma Press, 1941.

Tucker, John. "Major Long's Route from the Arkansas to the Canadian River, 1820." *New Mexico Historical Review* 38 (July 1963).

Tyler, S. Lyman. "The Myth of the Lake of Copala and the Land of Teguayo." *Utah Historical Quarterly* 20 (October 1952).

———. "The Spaniard and the Ute." *Utah Historical Quarterly* 22 (October 1954).

Ulibarri, George. "The Chouteau-DeMun Expedition of 1815–1817." *New Mexico Historical Review* 36 (October 1961).

Warner, Ted J. "The Significance of the Domínguez-Velez de Escalante Expedition." *Essays on the American West, 1973–74.* Provo: Brigham Young University Press, 1975.

Weber, David J. *New Spain's Far Northern Frontier: Essays on Spain in the American West, 1540–1821.* 1979. Reprint, Albuquerque: University of New Mexico Press, 1984.

———. *The Spanish Frontier in North America.* New Haven, Conn.: Yale University Press, 1992.

———. *The Taos Trappers.* Norman: University of Oklahoma Press, 1968.

Wedel, Waldo R. *An Introduction to Kansas Archaeology.* Washington, D.C.: Government Printing Office, 1959.

———. "Chain Mail in Plains Archaeology." *Plains Anthropologist* (1975).

———. "Coronado, Quivira, and Kansas: An Archaeologists's View." *Great Plains Quarterly* 10 (Summer 1990).

Witty, Thomas A. "An Archaeological Review of the Scott County Pueblo." *Oklahoma Anthropological Society Bulletin* 32 (1983).

Wood, Richard G. *Stephen Harriman Long, 1794–1864: Army Engineer, Explorer, Inventor.* Glendale, Calif.: Arthur H. Clark, 1966.

Wood, W. Raymond, and Thomas D. Thiessen. *Early Fur Trade on the Northern Plains: Canadian Traders Among the Mandan and Hidatsa Indians, 1738–1818.* Norman: University of Oklahoma Press, 1985.

Index